D1276622

QuickC™
Programming for the IBM®

fff

HOWARD W. SAMS & COMPANY/HAYDEN BOOKS

Related Titles

**The Waite Group's
Advanced C Primer ++**
Stephen Prata

**The Waite Group's
C Primer Plus,
Revised Edition**
*Mitchell Waite, Stephen Prata, and
Donald Martin*

**The Waite Group's
Microsoft® C Programming
for the IBM®**
Robert Lafore

**The Waite Group's
Turbo C Programming for the
IBM®**
Robert Lafore

**C Programmer's Guide to
Serial Communications**
Joe Campbell

**C with Excellence:
Programming Proverbs**
Henry Ledgard with John Tauer

Kochan & Wood's
Hayden Books C Library

**Programming in C, Revised
Edition**
Stephen G. Kochan

Programming in ANSI C
Stephen G. Kochan (forthcoming)

**Advanced C: Tips and
Techniques**
*Paul Anderson and Gail Anderson
(forthcoming)*

Kochan & Wood's
**Hayden Books UNIX®
System Library**

Topics in C Programming
Stephen G. Kochan and Patrick H. Wood

*For the retailer nearest you, or to order directly from the publisher,
call 800-428-SAMS. In Indiana, Alaska, and Hawaii call 317-298-5699.*

QuickC™
Programming for the IBM®

Carl Townsend

HOWARD W. SAMS & COMPANY

A Division of Macmillan, Inc.
4300 West 62nd Street
Indianapolis, Indiana 46268 USA

©1988 by Carl Townsend

FIRST EDITION

FIRST PRINTING—1988

All rights reserved. No part of this book shall be reproduced,
stored in a retrieval system, or transmitted by any means,
electronic, mechanical, photocopying, recording, or otherwise,
without written permission from the publisher. No patent liability is
assumed with respect to the use of the information contained
herein. While every precaution has been taken in the preparation of
this book, the publisher and author assume no responsibility for
errors or omissions. Neither is any liability assumed for damages
resulting from the use of the information contained herein.

International standard book Number: 0-672-22622-7
Library of Congress Catalog Card Number: 88-60063

Acquisitions Editor: *James S. Hill*
Technical Review: *Mike Maurice*
Editor: *C. Herbert Feltner*
Illustrator: *Wm. D. Basham*
Indexer: *Northwind Editorial Services*
Cover Graphic: *Keni Hill, Meridian Design Studio Inc.*
Compositor: *Shepard Poorman Communications Corp.,
Indianapolis*

Trademark Acknowledgements

All terms mentioned in this book that are known to be trademarks or service marks are listed below. In
addition, terms suspected of being trademarks or service marks have been appropriately capitalized. Howard
W. Sams & Company cannot attest to the accuracy of this information. Use of a term in this book should
not be regarded as affecting the validity of any trademark or service mark.

Ashton-Tate and dBASE III are registered trademarks of Ashton-
     Tate
DEC is a registered trademark of Digital Equipment Corporation
Hotshot is a trademark of SYMSOFT
IBM PC, XT, and AT are registered trademarks of International
     Business Machines Corporation
Lotus 1-2-3 is a registered trademark of Lotus Development
     Corporation
Microsoft is a registered trademark of Microsoft Corporation
PageMaker is a registered trademark of Aldus Corporation
Paradox is a registered trademark of ANSA Software
QuickC is a trademark of Microsoft Corporation
Turbo C is a registered trademark of Borland International
UNIX is a registered trademark of AT&T Bell Laboratories

Printed in the United States of America

Contents

Part III Developing Programs with QuickC

Appendices

Preface

C is a simple yet sophisticated programming language that is the choice of many professional programmers. QuickC is an implementation of this language that permits rapid prototyping with an integrated editor, debugger, and in-memory MAKE utility.

This book is designed as a tutorial introduction to the design of systems using the QuickC language. It places special emphasis on the new features of QuickC that have never been a part of any C language before.

The book contains three parts:

- Introduction
- The Language
- Developing Programs with QuickC

The first part is a basic introduction to the language with a simple example to show you the power of QuickC. The second part is a language tutorial, guiding you through the basics of the language with exercises and examples. The third part is a tutorial in structured programming, with a mailing list program in QuickC as an example.

Don't just read the chapters. Use your QuickC to execute the examples, trying you own hand at seeing what will happen if you experiment with them. The examples are purposely kept simple to illustrate basic principles. Many of the examples are components of the mailing list program in the last section. Most will work with other C compilers, but don't expect too much portability. In particular, some of the graphic routines of Chapter 14 will work only with QuickC or Microsoft's Version 5.0 C compiler or later.

I wish you exciting adventures on your quest in learning the C language.

CARL TOWNSEND

Acknowledgments

I would like to express my appreciation to the many people who helped make this book possible.

A special thanks to Mike Maurice, who helped with much of the technical review and has been my mentor in learning the C language.

Thanks to Microsoft for supplying QuickC and providing technical support during the authoring of the book.

The screen dumps were created with Hotshot™, a product of SYMSOFT. A special thanks to my wife, Sandy, who helped with proofing, printing, and other related tasks.

At Howard W. Sams & Company, thanks to Jim Hill and Jim Rounds for their support and encouragement as well as keeping the project on track.

I

Overview of QuickC

1

Introduction to QuickC

Almost all today's major application products for the personal computer are developed using the C language. Ashton-Tate®, Microsoft®, and Lotus® Corporation have all chosen this language as the primary vehicle for their product development. Why has this been true? What is it about C that has caused it to become the language of choice among almost every serious product developer? This chapter will describe some of the basic features of C that have made it popular and introduce Microsoft's QuickC.

A Short History of C

The C language is a modern language. It was developed by Dennis Ritchie of Bell Laboratories in 1972 as a tool for developing the UNIX® operating system. It evolved from an earlier B language developed by Ken Thompson, who also helped develop this same operating system. Unlike other languages of the time, C was developed for professional programmers and designed to support their specific needs.

The original language was simple, but elegant. Serious programmers quickly recognized the extensive capabilities of the language and C eventually migrated to the early microcomputers. Application products developed in C were almost always faster than competing products. Moreover, products could be developed on larger machines in C and then "ported," or converted, to the personal computer.

The introduction of low-cost compilers such as QuickC and Borland International's Turbo C® has introduced a new dimension in the development of new application software. For the first time, developers have an integrated compiler and editor that can produce executable code in seconds.

Why C?

Why are most applications written today developed in C? The answer is very simple. The C language offers a versatility, power, and efficiency that is unsurpassed by any other language.

FORTRAN and COBOL, two of the original languages, were developed for mainframe systems and are the Model T Ford's of the computer languages. Later, BASIC was developed to resemble the English language and to simplify the use of computers. You could compare BASIC to a second-hand Volvo with a rebuilt engine and patched upholstery. Pascal was designed to teach good programming techniques. It's like a little Civic Honda—small but sturdy, getting the job done sometimes. LISP is like an expensive electric car, a little slow without a lot of pickup, but excellent for certain applications. C, in contrast, is a red Pontiac Firebird. It's the car with optional quadraphonic radio (with equalizer and compact disk), dual carburetors, fuzzbuster, and widetrack tires. It was created as a serious tool for developers. The language is like a true sports car—you are close to the road with plenty of control of the engine and the car's performance, but you also have the full risks and dangers of that kind of driving.

Features of C

Now let's look at C's specific advantages (all are also true of QuickC):

- C is one of the most efficient languages available for procedural applications. Programs developed in C will often run faster than those developed in any other language except assembler. Developers generally develop their original program in C, then identify the portions of the program that still cause bottlenecks (loss of speed). These portions are then converted to assembler language, leaving the primary portion in C.

- C has already become significant by producing the fastest executable code of any language compiler (except assembly). QuickC has taken this another step forward. Both QuickC and Microsoft's Version 5 Compiler offer significant speed advantages over the earlier Microsoft C compilers.

- C is standard. Most compiler writers adhere closely to the ANSI standard, which means source programs can be compiled with any version of C. The difference is primarily in the extended features, such as the graphic support.

- C is portable. Programs developed in C can generally be moved to other systems easily with a minimum of change. Personal computer programs can be moved up to minicomputers and mainframes, and those on the larger systems converted to run on the personal computer. Programs can even be moved to other operating systems with a minimum of change, such as from MS-DOS® to UNIX. Portability has suffered over the years; however, extensions to the language have developed with the various compilers.

- C provides access to every feature of the computer available to software. You can use it to write operating systems, other language compilers, modem programs, or artificial intelligence tools.

- C is a modern language and supports the new programming techniques that have become popular today: structured programming, top-down planning, recursion, and modular design.

- C is low in cost with a large number of optional support tools available (at additional cost) for menu design, database management, communications, windowing, and graphics. The market for C tools and libraries is large, competition is keen—thus prices are low and the variety is large.

- C supports a wide variety of data structures, permitting extensive flexibility in representing information.

Limitations of C

It would not be fair, however, to praise the language without also mentioning its limitations:

- C is a medium-level language (see later section in this chapter), requiring many lines of code for a typical application. For most applications, the user will need to purchase additional libraries to use with the language to support the specific application. Purchasing commercial libraries reduces development time and the amount of code the developer has to write, but adds to the cost of the original language tool.

- C is a procedural language. Before you can use it, you need to know the procedure to solve the problem. It is difficult to apply C to artificial intelligence applications in which the procedure is not known. Prolog and LISP are often more efficient in these areas. (You can, however, write a Prolog or LISP compiler in C.)

- C is not as readable as other languages, and its extensive features make it more difficult to master in comparison with many other languages.

Basic Programming Ideas

Before looking specifically at C, let's review some basic programming ideas.

What Is a Programming Language?

First, exactly what is a programming language? Computers are notorious for using a specialized language of bits and bytes that none but a true professional programmer can understand. To be useful, there must be some way of translating your specific problem into the language of the machine.

To solve a problem with a computer, the first step is to find a specific procedure, or algorithm, that can solve the problem (Figure 1.1). For example, suppose you are purchasing a car. You know the price (PV), interest (RATE), and the payment schedule (NPER, or number of payments). What would be the procedure for calculating the payments?

This could be reduced to a simple equation as:

$$\text{Payment} = ((1+RATE)^{NPER})*PV*RATE/(1+RATE)^{NPER-1})$$

The second step is to translate this procedure into a computer language that can be understood by a machine. This listing of the procedure in the computer language is called the *source code*. Computer languages, then, are the bridge for communicating with computers (Figure 1.2). Any language will work as long as it can be understood by both the computer and the human. Some languages are more human-like than others (such as BASIC). Others, such as assembly language, are more like the computer's internal language. An example of the source code for solving the previous problem in C is shown in Listing 1.1.

The source code has a special structure that depends upon the language used. In this example there is a comment section, some directives for the compiler, some declarations, and the main body (Figure 1.3). Don't worry too much about the details of how the program works just now, but do examine this basic structure. In the next chapter you will type it in and execute it. Here is an overview of each program section:

Comments: These are statements that describe the purpose of the program, the author's name, an audit trail for changes to the program, and other details. Comments always begin with a slash-asterisk and end with an asterisk-slash.

Compiler Directives: These are directions to the compiler about other files that will be needed during compiling or definitions that are assumed. Directives have no terminating semicolon.

Declarations: These associate identifiers in your program with C objects, such as variables, functions, or types. Each declaration is terminated by a semicolon. Declarations will be discussed more in Chapter 4.

The Body: These are the statements that implement the desired procedure and produce the desired action or output. Each statement is terminated with a semicolon. Statements control the order and flow of the program execution.

Figure 1.1
Steps for Solving a Problem

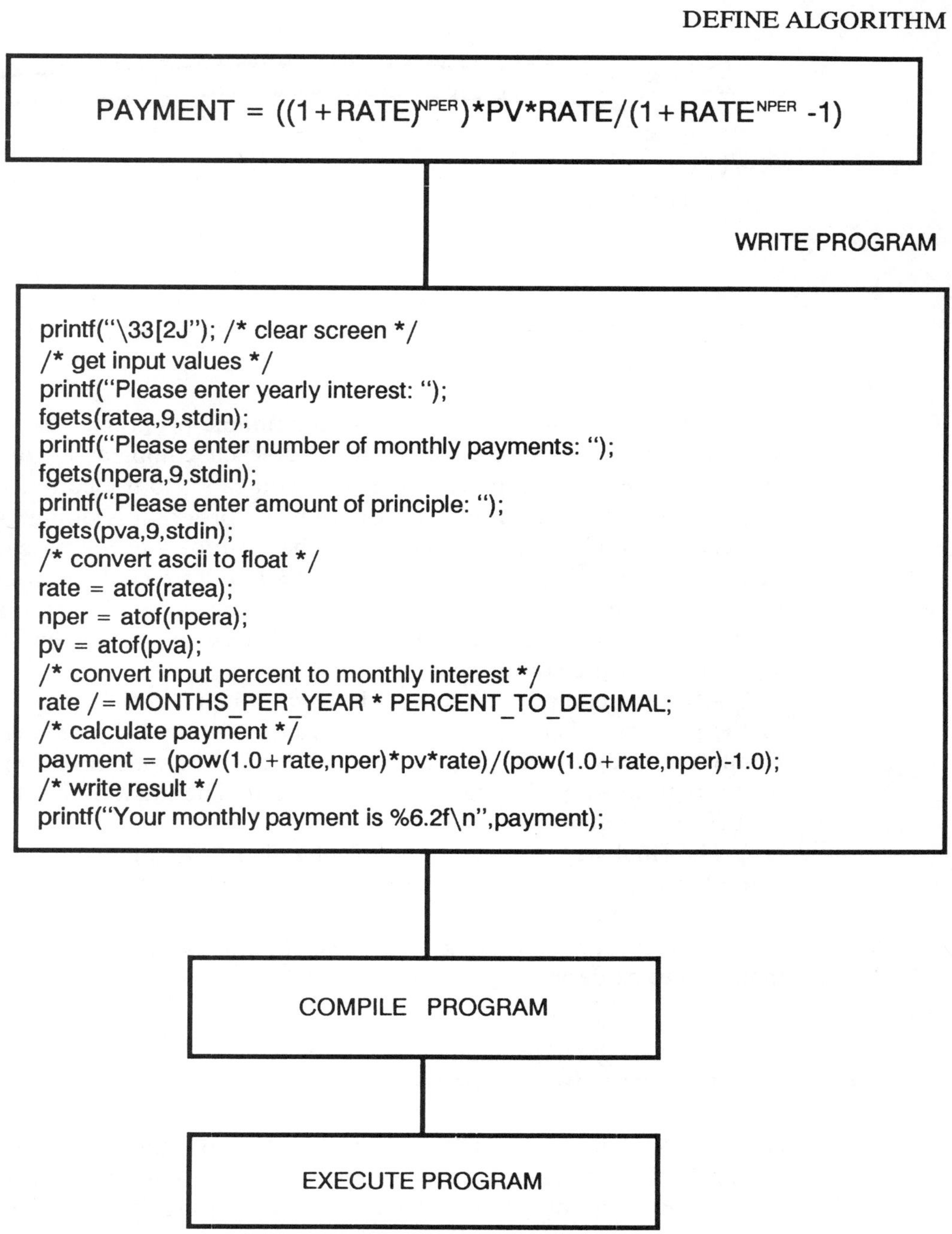

DEFINE ALGORITHM

$$PAYMENT = ((1+RATE)^{NPER})*PV*RATE/(1+RATE^{NPER} -1)$$

WRITE PROGRAM

```
printf("\33[2J"); /* clear screen */
/* get input values */
printf("Please enter yearly interest: ");
fgets(ratea,9,stdin);
printf("Please enter number of monthly payments: ");
fgets(npera,9,stdin);
printf("Please enter amount of principle: ");
fgets(pva,9,stdin);
/* convert ascii to float */
rate = atof(ratea);
nper = atof(npera);
pv = atof(pva);
/* convert input percent to monthly interest */
rate /= MONTHS_PER_YEAR * PERCENT_TO_DECIMAL;
/* calculate payment */
payment = (pow(1.0+rate,nper)*pv*rate)/(pow(1.0+rate,nper)-1.0);
/* write result */
printf("Your monthly payment is %6.2f\n",payment);
```

COMPILE PROGRAM

EXECUTE PROGRAM

Figure 1.2
Computer Languages Are Bridges

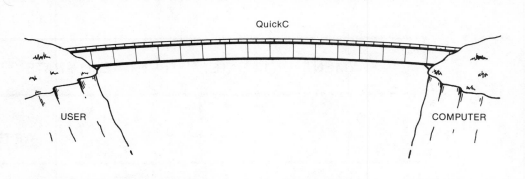

Note the various components in this sample program. The program begins with a comment. As noted in Figure 1.3, each comment begins with a slash-asterisk and ends with an asterisk-slash. You can also use comments in the body to provide a narrative discussion of what the program is doing. After the comments are several compiler directives in the form of *#define* statements. This will be explained in Chapter 8, but here the *#define* statement specifies replacements the compiler should use in compiling. You might also add some *#include* directives here that instruct the compiler to pull in some definitions located in files separate from the source code file.

After the compiler directives the *main( )* name defines the actual beginning of the program. The name of the program is followed by the declarations, and finally the body of the program. All QuickC programs begin with this *main( )* name, regardless of the name of the program. The main body of the program is set off with braces.

The final step in solving the problem is to use a compiler or interpreter to compile the program (see next section), after which the program is executed to get the desired answer.

Once the programming is completed, the same program can be used as many times as desired with different input data.

Compilers Versus Interpreters

A computer language can be designed and used either as a compiler or interpreter. If the language is an *interpreter*, it remains in memory with the source code as the program executes. Each time you execute the program the interpreter reads each line, interprets it, and then executes it. For this reason, interpreters are slower than compilers. The second disadvantage is that they always remain in

Figure 1.3
Components of a QuickC Program

```
/* Program to calculate monthly payment */        COMMENTS

#include <math.h>
#include <stdio.h>                                  DIRECTIVES
#define MONTHS_PER_YEAR 12
#define PERCENT_TO_DECIMAL 100

main()
{
                                                              BODY
    float pv,rate,nper,payment;          DECLARATIONS
    char ratea[10], npera[10], pva[10];

    printf("\33[2J"); /* clear screen */
    /* get input values */
    printf("Please enter yearly interest: ");
    fgets(ratea,9,stdin);
    printf("Please enter number of monthly payments: ");
    fgets(npera,9,stdin);
    printf("Please enter amount of principle: ");
    fgets(pva,9,stdin);
    /* convert ascii to float */
    rate = atof(ratea);
    nper = atof(npera);
    pv = atof(pva);
    /* convert input percent to monthly interest */
    rate /= MONTHS_PER_YEAR * PERCENT_TO_DECIMAL;
    /* calculate payment */
    payment = (pow(1.0+rate,nper)*pv*rate)/(pow(1.0+rate,nper)-1.0);
    /* write result */
    printf("Your monthly payment is %6.2f\n",payment);
}
```

memory, occupying critical memory space. Third, the user must have a copy of the interpreter to run the application program. Finally, the source code is difficult to protect. The user must have the source code to execute the program. Anyone who can read the source code can easily see how you solved the problem, and you may wish to keep that proprietary.

Interpreters do have a distinct advantage, however. The interpreter is always in control of the program execution. The execution can be stopped at any point, variables examined or altered, and the execution resumed at the same point in the program, or another point. For this reason, interpreters are popular with developers. BASICA is an example of a computer language interpreter.

A *compiler*, in contrast, is used as part of a process that converts the source code to a machine language program that can then be run without any additional language support. The source code is created with an editor or any word processor in a nondocument mode. A compiler is then used to convert the program to an OBJ file. A *linker* is then used to convert the OBJ file to an EXE file (Figure 1.4).

The EXE file, then, can be executed as many times as desired. It runs quickly, since it is already in the computer's language and no interpreting is necessary. Moreover, it is very difficult to work backwards to discover the original source code.

The compiler alternative also offers another advantage—frequently used code can be compiled and kept in a library. This library can be used with many source programs. Finally, large programs can be broken down to several smaller programs and each compiled separately, even by different programmers. The linker can then combine all the compiled OBJ files with any necessary library files, producing a final large EXE file.

Figure 1.4
The QuickC Process

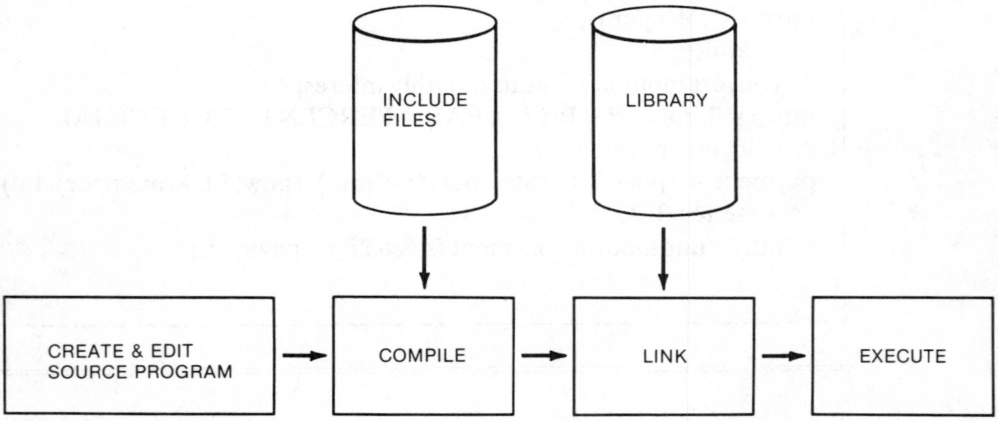

QuickC is a true compiler, yet also provides almost all the best features of an interpreter with those of a compiler (Table 1.1).

Table 1.1
The Compiler, Interpreter, and QuickC

Compiler	Interpreter	QuickC
Fast	Slow	Fast
Minimum use of memory	Extensive use of memory	Extensive use of memory
Source code protected	Source code not protected	Source code protected
Program execution unmanaged	Execution managed under interpreter	Execution unmanaged
Difficult to debug	Easy to debug	Easy to debug

Low-Level, Medium-Level, and High-Level Languages

The C language is considered a medium-level language. A medium-level language is one in which a single line of source code converts to a single (or very few) lines of machine code instructions. With a high-level language, a single line of source code converts to many lines of machine code instructions.

The dBASE III® language is an example of a very high-level interpreted language. A single line of source code converts to many, many lines of machine-code instructions. dBASE III is always in memory with the source program. Assembly languages, in contrast, are examples of low-level languages. A line of code in assembly language converts to a single line of machine-code instruction. BASIC and FORTRAN are both high-level languages.

With a high-level language, you can get a lot done with a few programming lines. A programmer can generally write a fixed number of lines of code a day, regardless of the language used. A complex program can be written much, much faster in a high-level language. For example, a typical program in dBASE III can be written about ten times faster than one using BASIC, which is a lower-level language than dBASE III.

The high-level language, however, does have some disadvantages. You are limited to the specific commands of the language. Almost any high-level language is oriented for a specific type of application and is not efficient with other types of applications. Very high-level languages (such as dBASE III) are very application-specific. Low-level languages, in contrast, can be used for any type of application.

C is a medium-level language. Source code listings are lengthy and development times can be long. You can make C work, however, as a high-level language. The trick is to build a library of C functions and code that can be a part of any program you create. In effect, you create your own command language. QuickC already contains an extensive library of functions that are ready to use. You can add to these with the purchase of menu programs, database management functions, and other tools as you work with the language. What is more, the tools can be application specific. If you are doing artificial intelligence work, for example, the functions you use will be quite different from what you would use to write a spreadsheet program.

Looking at QuickC

QuickC is a complete version of the C language that is fully compatible with its parent, Microsoft C version 4.0, with many additional features and functions. QuickC is also fully compatible with Microsoft's new Version 5 Compiler.

Advantages of QuickC

Here are a few of the advantages of QuickC over other C compilers that have been on the market:

- QuickC contains its own internal editor that permits the user to enter, edit, compile, and execute programs without leaving the QuickC environment. With a few keystrokes, you can initiate a compile at an incredible speed of up to 10,000 lines a minute. If there are any errors, the error count is indicated and the cursor is placed on the first error for editing. You can then correct and step through each error (to a maximum of 26 errors). If there are no errors, the program is ready for immediate execution.
- The Microsoft QuickC supports a source code debugger. You can define variables you wish to watch, then single-step your program or use breakpoints to watch the variables change.
- Full-featured help screens (see next chapter) give you instant information from ASCII codes to how to set up a function call.
- QuickC includes a graphic library.
- QuickC includes the full library functions that are available with Microsoft C Version 5.0. QuickC supports over 350 routines, including UNIX System V, Microsoft specific, and proposed ANSI standard routines.
- QuickC supports small, medium, compact, and large model programs and includes the same libraries as the Microsoft C Version 5.0.

Compare these features with any other integrated C compiler.

Disadvantages of QuickC

QuickC also has a few disadvantages concerning Microsoft's Version 5.0 C Compiler:

- QuickC is not an optimizing compiler, which means it compiles to slower code than competing optimizing compilers, such as Turbo C. QuickC code is, however, faster than the Microsoft's Version 4.0 compiler.

- The first release of QuickC does not support the Microsoft Windows interface. Such interfacing requires special compile switches, which are not yet available in QuickC.

- Microsoft's Codeview debugger is not included with QuickC. QuickC does, however, include a debugger which is a subset of the full Codeview®-line features (and even outdoes Codeview in some respects). If you are mixing object code from several languages or need more debugging power (such as watching registers), you will need to purchase Microsoft's C Version 5.0 with its Codeview debugger. The later versions of Codeview will work with QuickC.

What You Will Need

To use Microsoft's QuickC, you will need the following:

- IBM Compatible computer.
- 448K of memory (a 640K computer can compile almost 200K of source code in the QuickC environment).
- Two floppy-disk drives or a floppy-disk drive and one hard disk.

Although the use of a mouse is optional, it is highly advisable. Only the Microsoft mouse and compatibles are supported. Editing is faster with a mouse.

QuickC and Microsoft C Compilers

If you have been using Microsoft C Version 4.0, you will find QuickC is an enhanced version of this earlier product. The QuickC language is completely compatible with Microsoft's Version 5 of C.

Here is a summary of the enhancements of QuickC and Version 5 over Version 4.0:

- New functions have been added to support graphics, additional BIOS primitives, and other procedures.
- The compile and execution speed has been radically improved.
- The language has been changed slightly to bring it in alignment with the ANSI C standard.

All of the examples in this book can be used with both QuickC and Microsoft C Version 5.0. The main example of Part III of this book, the mailing list program, specifically takes advantage of the new graphic functions and cannot be used with Microsoft C Version 4.0.

Listing 1.1.
A Sample Source Code in QuickC for Solving the PMT Problem

```
include <stdio.h>
include <math.h>
define MONTHS_PER_YEAR 12
define PERCENT_TO_DECIMAL 100

main()
{

    float pv,rate,nper,payment;
    char ratea[10], npera[10], pva[10];

    printf("\33[2J"); /* clear screen */
    /* get input values */
    printf("Please enter yearly interest: ");
    fgets(ratea,9,stdin);
    printf("Please enter number of monthly payments: ");
    fgets(npera,9,stdin);
    printf("Please enter amount of principle: ");
    fgets(pva,9,stdin);
    /* convert ascii to float */
    rate = atof(ratea);
    nper = atof(npera);
    pv = atof(pva);
    /* convert input percent to monthly interest */
    rate /= MONTHS_PER_YEAR * PERCENT_TO_DECIMAL;
    /* calculate payment */
    payment = (pow(1.0+rate,nper)*pv*rate)/(pow(1.0+rate,nper)-1.0);
    /* write result */
    printf("Your monthly payment is %6.2f\n",payment);
}
```

Exercises

1. Define and give an example of each

    Low-level language

    High-level language

Interpreter

Compiler

Linker

Library

Directive

2. Define these:

Source language

Procedural language

ANSI C standard

3. Compare QuickC with BASIC. What are the advantages and disadvantages of each?

4. Compare QuickC with an assembler language. What are the advantages and disadvantages of each?

5. Give an example of an application that could probably be done in another language better than in C.

Answers

1. **Low-level language:** a computer language in which one line of source code converts to very few lines of machine code. Example: assembly.

   High-level language: a computer language in which one line of source code converts to many lines of machine code. Examples: BASIC and dBASE III.

   Interpreter: a computer language program that resides in memory with the source code and executes the code by compiling, or interpreting, one instruction at a time.

   Compiler: a computer language tool that converts a source program into a pseudocode that can be converted, with a linker, to an executable form.

   Linker: a computer language tool that converts the pseudocode output from a compiler to an executable form. Specifically, it converts the relative references of the pseudocode to absolute memory references and resolves unresolved references using library routines. Example: the LINK program.

   Compiler directive: data in the source code that is used to give directions to the compiler. In the C compiler, directives begin with the pound sign (#). Examples: *#include* and *#define.*

2. **Source language:** the language used by a programmer in writing a computer program.

   Procedural language: a language that supports the execution of a defined procedure, or algorithm, for the solution of problems.

ANSI standard: A C language standard defined by the American National Standards Institute.

3. **QuickC**

QuickC	BASICA
Fast in execution	Slow in execution
Compiler	Interpreter
Source code protected	Source code not protected
Program execution unmanaged	Controlled environment
Very easy to debug	Easy to debug
Well-defined standard	No standard
Library support	No library support
Structured programming support	No structured programming support
Extensive memory use	Extensive memory use
Medium-level	High-level

4. **QuickC**

QuickC	Assembler
Fast	Very fast
Source code protected	Source code protected
Program execution unmanaged	Program execution very unmanaged
Easy to debug	Easy to debug (with Codeview)
Extensive use of memory	Minimum use of memory
Stack management	Programmer manages stack
Extensive libraries available	Few libraries available
Structured programming support	No structured support
Higher level than assembler	Very low level
Well-defined standard for any processor or operating system	No standard and language varies with processor

5. Data-driven application problems are generally best solved in languages closer to this type of application. Typical applications include AI programs such as expert systems, mapping problems, and natural language processing.

2

Getting Started

This chapter takes you on a quick tour of the features of QuickC, guiding you through the creation and execution of a simple C program.

Installing QuickC

Installing QuickC includes the following steps:

1. Organizing the hard disk.
2. Backing up the program disks.
3. Reading README.DOC files on the disks.
4. Running the QuickC SETUP program to install the software to the proper directories. This step also creates five directories for the QuickC product: Include, LIB, TMP, BIN (or QC or C5), and a working directory (C or SRC).
5. Modifying the CONFIG.SYS file to expand the environment to include the new SET commands.
6. Modifying the AUTOEXEC.BAT file to define the new system variables and include the new path.

If you have not installed QuickC, install it using the directions of Appendix A.

A Quick Tour

Change to the directory where you keep your source files (extension .C) on your disk. Then enter the QC command as

```
C:\C>QC /lqclib        <Enter>
```

Note

qclib is not provided with QuickC. See Appendix A for specifics.

QuickC should load (be sure to use a lowercase l after the slash). Figure 2.1 shows the screen that should be displayed.

Figure 2.1
The QuickC Screen

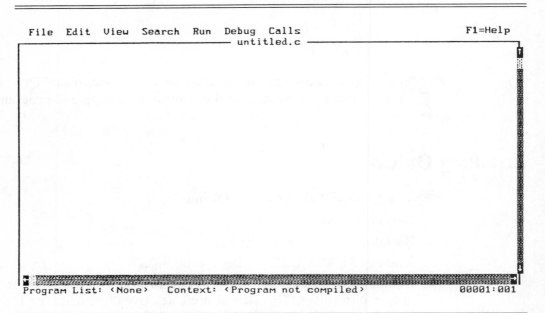

```
 File  Edit  View  Search  Run  Debug  Calls                    F1=Help
                          untitled.c
Program List: <None>    Context: <Program not compiled>        00001:001
```

Note

If the program fails to load and displays a message "Bad Command or File Name," you probably do not have the path command set up properly. Refer to Appendix A to check your installation.

The Initial Screen

After QuickC has loaded, examine the displayed screen. The major portion of the screen is the view window for your source program. At the present time the view window will be empty because you have entered no source program.

The cursor will appear as an underline at the upper left of the view window (the underline cursor). This is the point at which text will be entered, if you begin typing from the keyboard.

You will also see a mouse cursor as a small rectangle at the upper left of the screen. As you move the mouse, this rectangle should move.

At the top line of the screen is a menu bar with seven options. Here is a brief overview of each:

File: Used to load, save or print a file.

Edit: Permits you to change the source program that is displayed in the view window.

View: Controls the QuickC programming environment.

Search: Permits searching on the source file. This is useful for editing or debugging.

Run: Initiates, compiles, and controls compiling and run-time options.

Debug: Controls the debugging features of the program.

Calls: Useful for debugging.

At the very top of the view window, a title indicates "untitled.c". This indicates the title of the current source program. Since you have not created or saved a source file, this title defaults to "untitled.c".

At the bottom of the screen is a status line. A scroll bar is at the right and bottom of the view window. These will be explained in the next section.

Program Creation

Now enter the program of the previous chapter (Figure 1.1) that calculates the PMT (see Figure 2.2). For the moment, don't worry about how it works. Your main purpose here is to understand the mechanics of creating and compiling a QuickC program. Enter the program exactly as shown. If you make a mistake, use the Edit option of the menu to make the correction.

You can use spaces as necessary in any statement to improve readability. Spaces, line feeds, carriage returns, and form feeds in the program source are called *white space* and are ignored by the compiler.

Saving the Program

Before compiling your program, save your work in case something goes wrong during the compile or execution. Use the File Menu and select Save As to save the program. When the dialog box is displayed, enter the program name as PMT.

Figure 2.2
Entering the Program

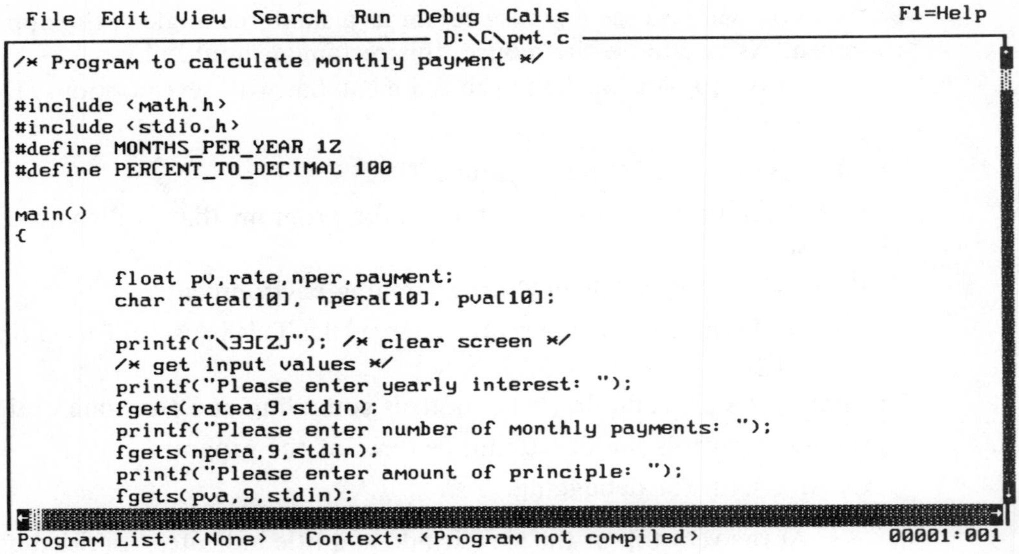

```
 File  Edit  View  Search  Run  Debug  Calls                    F1=Help
 ────────────────────────── D:\C\pmt.c ──────────────────────────
/* Program to calculate monthly payment */

#include <math.h>
#include <stdio.h>
#define MONTHS_PER_YEAR 12
#define PERCENT_TO_DECIMAL 100

main()
{
        float pv,rate,nper,payment;
        char ratea[10], npera[10], pva[10];

        printf("\33[2J"); /* clear screen */
        /* get input values */
        printf("Please enter yearly interest: ");
        fgets(ratea,9,stdin);
        printf("Please enter number of monthly payments: ");
        fgets(npera,9,stdin);
        printf("Please enter amount of principle: ");
        fgets(pva,9,stdin);

 Program List: <None>   Context: <Program not compiled>         00001:001
```

(Figure 2.3). Click OK or press ⟨Enter⟩. This will save the program as PMT.C. After saving, the program remains in the work area.

Editing the Program

Any program in the view window can be edited with the Edit menu. To use the Edit menu, first use the mouse cursor to point to the text to change. Click the left button, and the underline cursor will move to the mouse cursor. Type any text to insert at that point. You can also drag the cursor to select multiple characters, then use the Cut command of the Edit menu (or the ⟨Del⟩ key) to delete the characters.

The ⟨Del⟩ key always deletes the marked text or the text under the cursor. The ⟨Backspace⟩ key deletes the text to the left of the cursor.

In selecting the Edit menu, it is not necessary to pull down the menu. Simply clicking on the menu option of the menu bar forces the menu to appear. Clicking outside the displayed menu or on another menu causes it to disappear.

To the right of the view window and below it are the scroll bars. You can use the mouse to click the arrows to the right to scroll the window up or down, and the arrows at the bottom to scroll left or right. You can also drag the thumb (dark area) in the scroll bar to move the window over a document. The scroll bars do not drag the document, but rather move the window over the document. The

Figure 2.3
Saving the Program

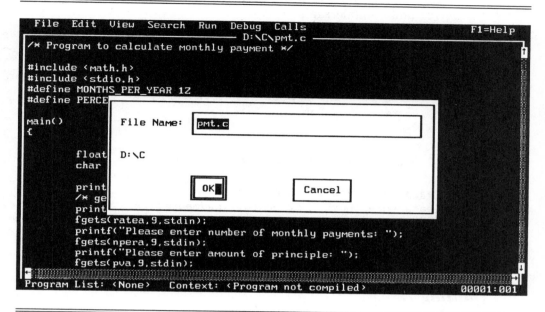

```
 File  Edit  View  Search  Run  Debug  Calls                F1=Help
────────────────────── D:\C\pmt.c ────────────────────────────
/* Program to calculate monthly payment */

#include <math.h>
#include <stdio.h>
#define MONTHS_PER_YEAR 12
#define PERCE
                  ┌─────────────────────────────────────┐
main()            │  File Name:  pmt.c                   │
{                 │                                      │
        float│    │  D:\C                                │
        char │    │                                      │
                  │        ┌──────┐       ┌──────────┐   │
        print│    │        │ OK   │       │  Cancel  │   │
        /* ge│    │        └──────┘       └──────────┘   │
        print└─────────────────────────────────────────┘
        fgets(ratea,9,stdin);
        printf("Please enter number of monthly payments: ");
        fgets(npera,9,stdin);
        printf("Please enter amount of principle: ");
        fgets(pva,9,stdin);
Program List: <None>   Context: <Program not compiled>      00001:001
```

arrows refer to the direction that you wish to move the window (not the document). You can turn the scroll bars on or off using the Options command on the View window.

The last line below the window is a status line. To the far right is an indicator that shows the line and character position within the line for the cursor. At the middle of the line is the status, which currently indicates the program is not compiled.

The Edit menu also provides for block operations such as move and copy. To move a block of text, drag the cursor over the block until all text to move is highlighted. Use the Edit Cut command to remove the text from the current position. Now move the cursor to the new location for the text and click the Edit Paste command to put the text at the new location. To copy a block, highlight the text and click the Edit Copy command. Move the cursor to the new location and use the Edit Paste command to paste the copy at the new location.

After editing the program, be sure to save it again before compiling.

Compiling

Be sure the program has been saved since the last edit. Select the Run menu option and then click Start. The program should compile within a few seconds. There should be no errors or unresolved references.

If there were any errors on compiling, the cursor will point to the first error with a message in the status area to indicate the type of error. Edit to correct the error and compile again.

Note

If there are unresolved references, check your spelling at the point of the error. If the error still persists, the QCLIB library was not created correctly. See Appendix A.

The program will then prompt for input:

```
Please enter yearly interest: 9
Please enter number of monthly payments: 24
Please enter amount of principle: 12000
Your monthly payment is 548.22
```

Quitting

Be sure the program has been saved since your last edit. Select the Edit menu and then select Exit.

Check your directory, and you will see that only PMT.C exists on the directory. For the moment, no OBJ or EXE file was created. The executable "image" of EXE was created in memory. Later you will learn how to create executable files and save them to disk.

Basic Strategy

With most C compilers, the source code is written with an editor and then saved with the extension .C. The program is then compiled with a compiler, linked with a linker, and then executed:

```
C>NE TEST.C                    (Creation and Editing)
<Program created and edited>
C>MSC TEST    <Enter>          (Compiling)
C>LINK TEST   <Enter>          (Linking)
C>TEST        <Enter>          (Execution)
```

There are four separate steps (Figure 2.4). If you find a mistake at step four, you must repeat all four steps to test the program again.

Figure 2.4
Creating an Executable Program Using C

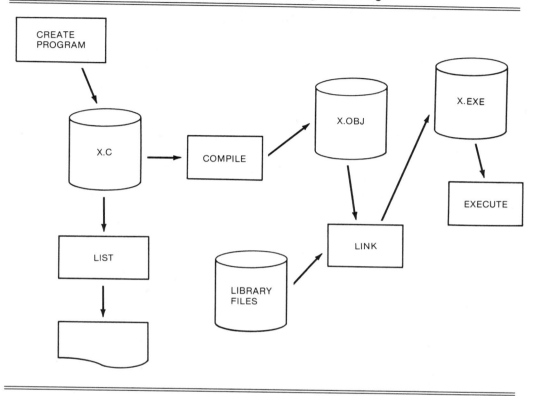

With QuickC, all four steps are integrated in a single environment. You *create* and *edit* the program with the QuickC editor. When you *compile* and *link* your program internal to QuickC using Run Start, an executable image is created and executed. In addition to integrating all four steps in a single environment, QuickC also has an additional speed advantage, as more is done in memory and there are less disk operations.

The Program

Even though this program is named PMT.C, it begins with the *main( )* function name. Every program has a primary function called *main( )*. Every program also has some initialization code that is a part of the program and hidden from the user. When the program is started, the initialization code begins executing, which in turn calls the *main( )* program.

Larger programs consist of many functions. The *main( )* function is executed on starting (Figure 2.5), and then calls functions which may, in turn, call other functions. The complete program, then, is a hierarchy of functions, with *main( )* always the name of the primary program function (regardless of the file name of the program on the disk).

Figure 2.5
A Program as a Hierarchy of Functions

```
                        ┌──────────┐
                        │   MAIN   │
                        └────┬─────┘
        ┌──────────┬─────────┼──────────┐
   ┌────┴───┐ ┌────┴───┐ ┌───┴─────┐ ┌──┴─────┐
   │  ADD   │ │  EDIT  │ │ REPORTS │ │ DELETE │
   └────────┘ └────────┘ └───┬─────┘ └────────┘
                             │    ┌──────────┐
                             ├────│  LABELS  │
                             │    └──────────┘
                             │    ┌───────────┐
                             └────│ DIRECTORY │
                                  └───────────┘
```

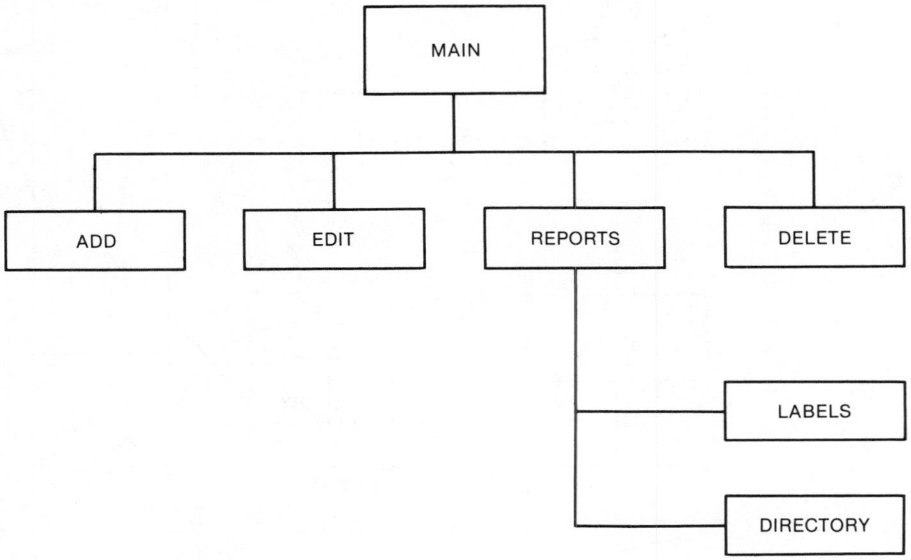

When a function is called, it executes until it reaches a *return* statement (which returns execution to the calling function) or an *exit( )* function (which terminates the program execution). Functions can have arguments that are used to pass values to functions from the calling program. Functions can also return values to the calling program (see Chapter 8).

Notice that after the function name, an opening curly brace appears. There is another closing curly brace at the end of the *main( )* function. A *block* is a sequence of declarations and statements within curly braces. Braces always occur in pairs. A program or function always consists of at least one block, but braces may be used to define other blocks within the main block.

Getting Help

QuickC provides extensive help information that is always within a few keystrokes. Help methods are accessible when you are typing or editing. Help information is provided at three levels: general, context-sensitive, and topical.

General

Several help screens are only a keystroke away. Use ⟨F1⟩ to see the first, then use ⟨Shift-F1⟩ to move to the next panel. You'll find ASCII codes, editing commands, and more at your fingertips (Figure 2.6). Press ⟨Esc⟩ to close the help screens.

Figure 2.6
The Help Screen for ASCII Codes

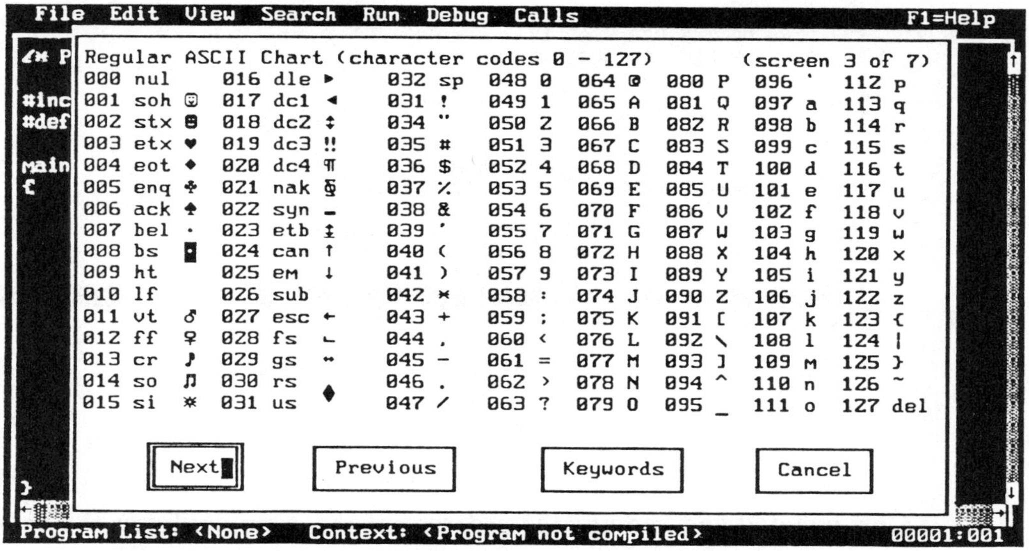

Context-Sensitive

If you are editing a function and can't remember how it's supposed to be used, put the cursor on the function name and press ⟨Shift-F1⟩. You'll see a summary of the functions on the screen (Figure 2.7). Press ⟨Esc⟩ to return from help.

Topical

If you are not on a function name and press ⟨Shift-F1⟩, you will see a dialog box with available topics. Use the direction keys to select a topic, then press ⟨Enter⟩. Press ⟨F1⟩ to return to your program.

Figure 2.7
The Help Screen for the *printf()* Function

```
  File  Edit  View  Search  Run  Debug  Calls                    F1=Help
Include:     <stdio.h>

Prototype:   int printf(const char *format[, argument]...);

Returns:     the number of characters printed.
                                    ── D:\C\pmt.c ──────────────────────
/* Program to calculate monthly payment */

#include <math.h>
#include <stdio.h>
#define MONTHS_PER_YEAR 12
#define PERCENT_TO_DECIMAL 100

main()
{

        float pv,rate,nper,payment;
        char ratea[10], npera[10], pva[10];

        printf("\33[2J"); /* clear screen */
        /* get input values */
        printf("Please enter yearly interest: ");

Program List: <None>   Context: <Program not running>      ^P    00014:013
```

Exercises

1. Load and compile the program of the example. Enter the data for borrowing $15,000 at 10% interest for three years. What is the monthly payment?
2. How many general help screens are there? List each.
3. Compile the program external to QuickC using the following:

```
C>QCL PMT.C   <Enter>
```

  a. What files does this produce?

  b. What happens if you leave the C extension off?

  c. After compiling, what happens if you type:

```
C>PMT   <Enter>
```

Answers

1. $484.01
2. There are eight screens:

Editing commands

C operator precedence

ASCII codes

Extended ASCII codes

C escape sequences

Format codes

C data ranges

Key words

3.

    a. PMT.OBJ and PMT.EXE files

    b. Assumes PMT command line argument is PMT.OBJ and tries to link

    c. The compiled program begins execution

This procedure compiles and links a C program external to QuickC. No library name needs to be added.

II

The Language

This part will introduce you to the QuickC language and is a guided tutorial with examples and tips for any C user. The functions developed in these chapters will be used as parts of application programs in Part III.

If the C language is new for you, read all these chapters in sequence. If you are familiar with C but not QuickC, read beginning from Chapter 14.

3

Representing Data

When you use a computer, information about the real world is abstracted to data. The program processes the data (Figure 3.1). Data is always an abstraction of reality, a symbol of something in the real world.

Figure 3.1
From the Real World to Data

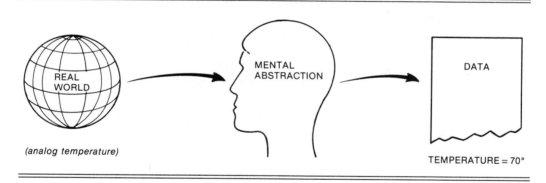

This chapter will introduce you to the fundamental aspects of data management used in a QuickC program. You'll learn what types of variables and constants can be used in QuickC, how to declare variables, and the techniques for initializing variables and constants.

Let's take a specific example. Suppose we have a need for a QuickC program to convert a temperature from Fahrenheit to Celsius. A temperature is a real-world entity. If the temperature is 70 degrees Fahrenheit, we know in the real-world it is comfortable. To the computer, however, the 70 is simply a number that represents something. It is a symbol, or data. Programs process data based on a defined algorithm. A program only gives the right answer if (1) the input data is correct, (2) the algorithm for the program is correct, and (3) the program is written properly to support the algorithm.

Variables and Constants

A computer program uses basically two types of data: constants and variables. *Variables* are data that can change. *Constants* are variables which do not change in value during the execution of the program. Variables always have names. Constants may or may not have names.

As an example, let's look at our simple Fahrenheit to Celsius conversion program. The basic equation for the conversion is:

$$\text{Celsius} = (5.0/9.0) * (\text{Fahrenheit} - 32.0)$$

In this equation the values of 5.0, 9.0, and 32.0 are constants. They do not change during the program execution. Celsius and Fahrenheit are variables. *Variable data* will change during the program execution.

Declaring Variables

In any C program, all variables and other identifiers must be *declared* before you can use them. *Declaring* a variable means associating the variable with some type of C object such as a variable, function, or type. The declaring of identifiers is generally done at the beginning of the program.

DeclaringW a variable also indirectly defines how much space the variable will use, names the storage location for the variable, and limits the type and range of values the variable can have. If a variable is declared as *float* (floating point) in QuickC, for example, the compiler will allow twice as much storage space than if you defined it as int (integer). The range of permissible storage values is also different. The amount of memory used to store different variable types and the range of values supported by that type varies with the C compiler.

As an example, look at the following program that converts Fahrenheit temperatures to Celsius:

```
/* Fahrenheit to Celsius Converter */
#include <stdio.h>
main()
{
     float fahrenheit, celsius;
     char fahrena[10];

     printf("What is the temperature in fahrenheit? ");
     fgets(fahrena,10,stdin);
     fahrenheit = atof(fahrena);
```

continued

```
celsius = (5.0/9.0) * (fahrenheit - 32.0);
printf("The temperature is %6.1f degrees Celsius\n", celsius);
}
```

The program begins by declaring *fahrenheit* and *celsius* as *float* variables. *Float* is a keyword to the QuickC compiler. It reserves a space of 32 bits for each of the two variables. This also defines the maximum and minimum values the program will accept for each of these variables. For QuickC, this would be –3.4E+38 to 3.4E+38.

This limit is in exponential notation here, but can be converted easily to decimal notation or a numeric value. For example, 3.4E+38 represents 3.4×10^{38} in decimal notation, or 34 with 37 zeros after it in standard numeric notation.

Notice the general form of the declaration. A keyword defining the data type is followed by one or more variable names, with the names separated by commas. The statement is terminated with a semicolon.

In the C language, a variable is the name of a storage location in memory. For example, suppose you enter the statement:

```
celsius = 10;
```

When the program executes, it will store the value of 10 in a location previously named as *celsius*.

When the sample program of this chapter is executed, the *printf( )* function queries for an input value. The *fgets( )* function obtains this value from the user as a character string. The character string is then converted to a float value and stored in a location called *fahrenheit*. The Celsius equivalent temperature is then calculated and stored in a location called *celsius*. The output of the *celsius* location is then displayed with the *printf( )* function.

You can also use multiple declaration statements such as:

```
float fahrenheit;
float celsius;
```

or, you could use:

```
float fahrenheit, celsius;
```

The declaring of variables gives you, as the developer, several advantages:

- Having the variables declared in one place makes it easier to see what the program is doing and to add appropriate comments.
- It is easier to add, edit, and delete variables when they are declared in a single location. You can also prevent duplications easier.
- You have better control of the environment during compiling and execution.

- Declaring variables forces the designer to think ahead and plan what the program is doing.
- Declaring variables helps you to find variable names that are misspelled in the program.

Note

You *must* declare all variables used in QuickC.

Naming Variables

With QuickC, you have a great deal of flexibility in naming your variables. The general rules are as follows:

- Variable names must start with a letter or an underscore.
- The remainder of the variable name can be letters, underscores, or digits. Any other special characters are not allowed. To use a two-word name, separate the two words with an underscore as:

```
last_name
```

- Only the first 31 characters of the variable name are significant.
- Variable names are case sensitive. The variable name *Initial* is not the same as *initial*.
- It is illegal to use keywords as identifier names. For QuickC, the keywords are

auto	else	int	static
break	enum	long	struct
case	extern	near	switch
cdel	far	pascal	typedef
char	float	register	union
const	for	return	unsigned
continue	fortran	short	void
default	goto	signed	volatile
do	huge	sizeof	while
double	if		

- Avoid beginning a variable name with an underscore. Names beginning with an underscore are reserved for system use.

> **Tip**
>
> In naming variables in your program, pick names that are meaningful in the context of the program. This will dramatically improve the readability of the program.

Data Types

There are four general variable types in QuickC: integer, floating point numbers, characters, and pointers. Each of these, in turn, can have several variations. This gives QuickC a large amount of flexibility in managing data. In addition, there are other special data types that will be introduced in later chapters. You can also define your own data types.

Integers

The most common type of data in QuickC is the integer. An integer is a whole number such as 123, 1, or –12. For numeric data processing, you should use integer data types as much as possible. Processing is much faster and more accurate than with the use of floating point data types.

You can express variable values for integers in decimal, octal, or hexadecimal numbering. The following rules apply to indicate the numbering system used:

- Prefix the number with 0x or 0X to indicate a hexadecimal value.
- Prefix the number with 0 to indicate an octal value.
- If no prefix is used, the number is assumed decimal.

The following are all equivalent:

$$012 = 0XA = 0xA = 10$$

Any input value, regardless of the way it is entered, is stored as the same binary value. You will see an example of this in the next section.

There are three basic types of integer variable keywords: *short*, *int*, and *long*. There is also another keyword, *unsigned*, that you can use to extend the positive range of any other keyword. For example, *unsigned int* permits the storage of positive values only, but you can store values as much as twice as large as with an *int* type.

Tip

Use integer values and the *int* type as much as possible in your programs. This will save storage, improve accuracy, and increase execution speed.

The *short* Integer Type

The *short* keyword can be used to declare a variable that is used to represent a signed whole number from –32768 to +32767 on an IBM PC. In QuickC a *short* requires two bytes of storage.

For example, you could declare a *counter* variable as:

```
short counter;
```

Now you can write a short program that shows how input numbers in the different number bases are all stored in an equivalent form:

```
main()
{

        short number1, number2, number3;
        number1 = 012;
        number2 = OXA;
        number3 = 10;
        printf("Number1 is %d\n",number1);
        printf("Number2 is %d\n",number2);
        printf("Number3 is %d\n",number3);
}
```

What is the output when this is executed?

Although the *short* type may seem the best alternative for the programmer, most compilers are designed to produce their most efficient code with the *int* type, which is the preferred alternative.

The *int* Integer Type

In the standard C language, the *int* keyword defines an integer type that has limited numeric range. In QuickC, for a PC, XT, AT, or PS/2 compatible computer the numeric range of an *int* variable is the same as a *short* variable. For most computers, the *int* type is the most efficient for calculations, and should be used whenever possible in your program.

With any given C version, the representation of a *short* variable is generally 16 bits and a *long* variable is 32 bits. QuickC uses the same representation. The representation of an *int* variable, however, is design dependent. With QuickC, it is 16 bits (the same as a *short* variable). The DEC PDP-11 also uses 16 bits. A DEC VAX, however, uses a 32 bit *int* variable.

The *long* Integer Type

In the standard C language, the *long* keyword defines an integer (whole number) type that has an extended numeric range. With QuickC, a variable declared as *long* requires 32 bits (4 bytes) of storage; that is, twice as much as a *short* variable. It can be used to represent any integer from –2,147,482,648 to 2,147,482,647.

As with a *short* variable, the declaration may or may not contain the *int* keyword. These are both the same type of declarations:

```
long quantity1;
long int quantity2;
```

In using constants in a program, QuickC automatically picks the proper storage type that will work for the numeric value. For example, 900,000 would be stored as a long integer. If you have a short integer constant and wish to store it as a long integer, the value must be terminated with an L to indicate it is *long*. For example: 0X1AL, 23L.

Unsigned Integers

You can use the *unsigned* keyword with *int*, *short*, or *long* to extend the positive range of a variable if negative values are excluded. For example:

```
unsigned int counter1;
unsigned counter2;
unsigned long int counter3;
unsigned long counter4;
```

Notice that if *unsigned* is used with no additional keywords, *int* is assumed. In this example *counter1* has the same positive range as *counter3*, a long integer (approximately 64,000). The variable *counter1*, however, cannot be used with negative numbers.

The *unsigned short* type has a range of 0 to 65,535. The *unsigned long* type has a range from 0 to 4,294,967,295.

Floating Point Numbers

A floating point number is a number that can contain a fractional part, such as 123.23 or –34.5. They are roughly equivalent to the real numbers used by mathematicians.

Floating point numbers in QuickC are stored as binary numbers, not as decimal numbers. The base part and exponent are stored separately. This permits you to store a far greater numeric range than with integer values and to represent decimal fractions.

Floating point variable values and floating point constants can be expressed in either of two ways: numeric values or exponential notation. For example, either of the following is acceptable, and represent the same value:

3.248E2

324.8

You cannot use octal or hexadecimal floating point numbers.

You can use decimal or *exponential* notation:

- The decimal notation contains a decimal point, such as 10.23. This is the most common notation for most people.
- The exponential notation consists of two parts separated by an e or E, such as 1023E–2. The first part is the mantissa. The second part is the exponent, and represents a power of ten. 10.23, then, is the decimal equivalent to 1023E–2.

Note

Floating point numbers are subject to round-off errors and other problems if you are not careful. Use integers whenever possible to improve accuracy. Use floating point numbers when decimal values or extended numeric ranges are necessary.

In *exponential* notation, QuickC provides two methods of declaring floating point numbers: *float* and *double*.

The *float* Type

The *float* keyword is used for the most general form of floating point declaration. For QuickC, this requires 32 bits of storage (4 bytes), which is the same amount of storage used for a *long* integer. The numeric range that can be stored, however, is much larger: –3.4E–38 to 3.4E+38 in QuickC.

Note

Be careful to distinguish between the precision of a number and its range. Try the following example to understand the difference between precision and range. You will see that the output is not the exact value of x. QuickC only uses two bytes to store the mantissa, and if a number is too precise, some digits will get lost. Try the following. Why does the output not match the value of x exactly?

```
/* FLOAT example */
main()
{
    float x;

    x =123456789.0;
    printf("%f",x);
}
```

QuickC can handle the range in this example, but not at the precision of the variable x. To declare a floating point number, use the *float* keyword with the name of one or more variables as:

```
float celsius, fahrenheit;
```

The *double* Type

Declaring a variable as *double* permits you to allocate twice as much storage space to the variable, or 64 bits (8 bytes). This gives you a higher precision and greater range for floating number types. Try the previous example again with x declared as *double*. What happens now? The full precision is maintained.

To declare a floating point number as *double*, use the *double* keyword with the name of one or more variables as:

```
double celsius, fahrenheit;
```

The range for a QuickC double type is from –1.7E–308 to 1.7E+308.

Characters

You can also declare a variable a *char* to store a single character. Variable values can be any valid character, including special and nonprintable characters. The character must be enclosed in single quotes. Only one byte of storage is used.

Characters are declared using the *char* keyword. For example:

```
main()
{
```

continued

```
        char c;

        c = 'C';
        .
        .
        .
}
```

Technically, this is simply a form of integer storage. The C program stores a character by using an integer value. The program converts the input character to an integer, stores it, and then converts it back to a character when writing.

The numeric codes used to represent characters have been standardized by the American National Standards Institute and called the ASCII code. The code consists of 94 printable characters and 34 nonprintable control characters. On the IBM PC systems, this range has been extended by a range of graphic characters. The complete list is shown in Appendix C and is also available on a QuickC help screen.

You can also declare an *unsigned char* type. The *char* type has a value of –128 to 127. The *unsigned char* type has a range from 0 to 255.

You might think a *char* type is a good way to store a small integer, as it only uses one byte of storage. In practice, however, the converse is true. The *char* type is generally a poor choice for storing even single characters. Compilers are generally designed to be most efficient with the *int* type, and in addition the *char* type may introduce unusual errors in some cases. Use the *int* type to store character constants. Use the *char* type primarily for character strings (arrays).

Pointers

You can also use a variable to store the address of where something is stored. Then, the variable is said to be a *pointer*, as it points to the address of the variable. The pointer variable is declared as an address by beginning the variable name with an asterisk. For example:

```
char *message;
```

Here, *message* is the pointer or address of the beginning of a text string. The next section will explain how this is used.

One of the reasons why C is such a powerful language is its support of pointers. As you explore arrays (Chapter 11) and create your own data structures (Chapter 12), you will gain a greater appreciation for the power of using pointers.

Overflow and Underflow

If you try a numeric calculation and the result exceeds the range permitted by QuickC, an error condition results. If the result is too small, an underflow condition is said to result. If the result is too large, an overflow condition results. In either case, QuickC will give you an error message.

For example, try the following program:

```
main()
{
    int x = 5;
    int y = 0;
    int z;

    z = x/y;
}
```

When this is executed, a division by zero is attempted and QuickC returns the message:

```
run-time error R6003
- integer division by 0
```

Storing Text Strings

Sometimes you may wish to store a string of characters instead of a single character. QuickC provides two methods of doing this: using a string array or using pointers.

The String Array

One method is to declare a storage space for the string as an array and then store the text as an ASCII string in that array as:

```
main()
{
    static char msg[]="This is a test.";
    char message[sizeof(msg)];

    strcpy(message,msg);
    printf("%s\n",message);
}
```

The *char* declaration saves an array space of 16 characters for *message* (fifteen characters plus a terminating null character). The *strcpy()* function copies the text into the *message* array. The *printf()* function then outputs the array.

Using Pointers to Access Strings

As another alternative, you could declare a pointer:

```
main()
{
    char *message;

    message = "This is a test.";
    printf("%s\n",message);
}
```

Here, the declaration allocates space for a pointer called *message*, and the first statement in the body of the program allocates space for a string and initializes the pointer to the value of the address of the first character of the string.

Initializing Variables

You can also use the declaration statement to initialize a variable to any specific value. For example, you could simplify the earlier example as:

```
/* Fahrenheit to Celsius Converter */
#include <stdio.h>
main()
{
    float fahrenheit, celsius;
    float DELTA = 32.0;
    char fahrena[10];

    printf("What is the temperature in Fahrenheit? ");
    fgets(fahrena,10,stdin);
    fahrenheit = atof(fahrena);
    celsius = (5.0/9.0) * (fahrenheit - DELTA);
    printf("The temperature is %6.1f Celsius.\n", celsius);
}
```

In this example a constant is declared and initialized. Variables can be initialized in the same way, but their value will change during the execution of the program.

There is an even better way to initialize constants: the *#define* directive. This directive permits us to define a value for any name, after which the value is substituted for the name wherever it appears in the program. No semicolon is used after the *#define* directive. (If a semicolon is used, it is considered part of the definition and can have undesirable effects.)

As an example of using a *#define*:

```
/* Fahrenheit to Celsius Converter */
#include <stdio.h>
#define CONSTANT (5.0/9.0)
main()
{
     float fahrenheit, celsius;
     char fahrena[10];

     printf("What is the temperature in Fahrenheit? ");
     fgets(fahrena,10,stdin);
     fahrenheit = atof(fahrena);
     celsius = CONSTANT * (fahrenheit - 32.0);
     printf("The temperature is %6.1f degrees Celsius\n", celsius);
}
```

Notice that constants defined in this way are generally put in uppercase to distinguish them from variables. No declaration statement is needed.

Normally all the *#define* statements are put in a separate file and added at compile time with an *#include* directive:

```
#include "const.h"
```

Here, the *const.h* file would contain:

```
#define CONSTANT (5.0/9.0)
```

This makes it easy to add, edit, or change constant values as necessary and have the change affect the entire program:

```
#include "const.h"
/* Fahrenheit to Celsius Converter */
#include <stdio.h>
main()
{
     float fahrenheit, celsius;
     char fahrena[10];

     printf("What is the temperature in Fahrenheit? ");
     fgets(fahrena,10,stdin);
     fahrenheit = atof(fahrena);
     celsius = CONSTANT * (fahrenheit - 32.0);
     printf("The temperature is %6.1f Celsius.\n", celsius);
}
```

The *#define* directive can be used with any type of constant, including strings:

```
#define MESSAGE "This is a test."
```

Type Conversions

QuickC permits the programmer to mix data types in a C expression. The following, for example, functions properly and creates no error message:

```
main()
{
    int x = 2;
    float y = 3;
    float z;

    z = x + y;
}
```

This extensive flexibility can also create problems. When data types are mixed in an expression the compiler converts the data variables to compatible types before carrying out the operation. In the previous example, the result is a float, and the integer would be converted to a float before performing the operation.

In converting downward, you must use caution. For example:

```
main()
{
    int x = 2;
    float y = 3;
    int z;

    z = x + y;
}
```

Here, the calculation is performed by converting the integer to a float, adding the floats, and then converting the float result to an integer. Then, the result (float) is too large to fit in the data type for which it is intended (int), and the value will be corrupted.

To avoid problems, try to minimize your data conversions, particularly converting from larger to smaller integer types, from an integer to a character, or between signed and unsigned types.

Other Data Types

QuickC also provides you with the provision of defining your own data types and structures. Boolean variables, complex structures, and other variations are possible. You will see more of this in other examples, particularly in Chapter 12.

Exercises

1. Which of the following are not valid variable names in QuickC and why?

    a. dollar$value
    b. sum_value
    c. 2Smith
    d. Smith2
    e. SMITH2

2. Which of the following are not valid integer values in QuickC and why?

    a. 1A
    b. 039
    c. 0x2F

3. Enter the program at the beginning of this chapter and execute it.

    a. What happens when a character is entered for a numeric value?
    b. What happens when a negative temperature is entered?
    c. What happens when an integer value is entered (no decimal point)?

4. Omit the semicolon at the end of the declaration statement. Try to compile. What type of error message do you get? What does this tell you about the compiler?

5. Restore the semicolon and move the declaration to make it the second line in the program. Compile and link again. Does it work now? What does this tell you about where you can declare variables?

6. Omit the declaration statement and try to compile. What happens? What does this tell you about declaring variables?

Answers

1. Only (c) is invalid. A name cannot start with a number.

2. Both (a) and (b) are invalid. (a) does not have a prefix, and therefore is read as decimal. The "A" is not a decimal digit. In (b), the number begins with 0 and therefore read as octal. The number 9 is not an octal value.

3. (a) It assumes an input numeric value of zero. Both (b) and (c) will work fine.

4. You will get a syntax error on the next statement. It does not compile.

5. Does not compile.

6. Does not compile. Error message suggests variable names are undefined. Variables must be declared.

4

Basic Input and Output

Almost any program you will write must include some provisions for writing and reading data. In the previous chapter, examples of both reading and writing data were included. In each case you use a *function* that was an integral part of the C language, such as *printf( )* or *fgets( )*. The C language provides several other functions that can be used for input and output. In each case, the functions occur in pairs; that is, an output function that corresponds to another input function. This chapter will introduce these basic I/O functions: *printf( )/scanf( ), puts( )/gets( ),* and *getchar( )/putchar( )*. In addition, you will find an introduction to the *fgets( )* function.

Before discussing these functions, however, let's take a basic look at what a function is and the idea of buffering input and output.

Introduction to Functions

Functions are parts of programs that perform a single operation. Most C compilers, such as QuickC, provide certain standard functions that are integral to the compiler. These names are the same in any compiler. The *printf( )* and *fgets( )* functions are examples of these.

In any program, it is necessary for the user to pass data to functions and, in return, to obtain data that is passed back. Information is passed to the function as an argument. Information is either returned as a value or as an argument. For example, with the function call:

```
printf("%s",msg)
```

The function inputs are the two arguments: the control string and the pointer to the character string. With QuickC, as with many other C compilers, the function can return a value if you use it as:

```
no_of_characters = printf("%s",msg)
```

in which case it returns the number of characters written.

For more extensive information on functions, refer to Chapter 8. You can also get QuickC help on any function by placing the cursor on the function naming your program and pressing ⟨Shift-F1⟩. For now, let's move on to how the input and output functions are used.

Buffers

Buffering is a technique that improves the efficiency of input and output functions. With any computer system, reading and writing are generally the slowest part of the program execution. By using buffering techniques, the speed of both reading and writing is improved. Buffering involves setting aside a storage place to hold data until the output device is ready for it (when writing) or the computer is ready for it (when inputting). The size of the buffer used by QuickC is shown by the BUFSIZ define statement in *stdio.h* file as 512 bytes.

The buffer becomes even more important in file operations (Chapter 13), but for now you should simply be aware that buffers are used for most input and output. It is used with all functions in this chapter. For this reason, you should always include the *stdio.h* file in all programs that use any of these functions. In Chapter 13 you learn how to use it for file operations and how you can bypass this buffer if necessary.

Formatted Output and Input: *printf()* and *scanf()*

You have already been introduced to the formatted output function—the *printf()* functions. There is also a formatted input function—the *scanf()* function. Let's look more closely at each of these.

The printf() Function

The example of the previous chapter had an output statement:

```
printf("The temperature is %f degrees Celsius\n",celsius);
```

The *printf()* is a C function name. It is a standard C output function (available in any C compiler) and has the general form:

```
printf(<control string>[,<item1>,<item2>, <itemj>,...<itemn>]);
```

The first argument is the control (or format) string and determines the format for *writing* the data or data variables. The remaining arguments are the data or data variables to be *written*. As an example:

```
printf("This is test %d\n",test);
```

The Control String

There are three components of the control string: text, identifiers, and escape sequences. You can use any text and any number of escape sequences. The number of identifiers should match the number of variables or values to be *written*.

Identifiers in the format string determine how each of the other arguments will be *written*.

```
printf("The temperature is %f degrees Celsius\n",celsius);
```

There should be one identifier for each of the remaining arguments. Each identifier begins with a percent sign (%), and a code to show the output format of the variable. Then, the %f shows a floating point number.

QuickC provides the user with nine identifier codes:

Identifier	Format
%d	decimal integer
%c	single character
%s	character string
%f	floating point (decimal)
%e	floating point (exponential-notation)
%g	%e or %f, whichever is shorter
%u	unsigned decimal integer
%o	unsigned octal integer
%x	unsigned hexadecimal integer

The first four will serve almost all your basic needs. The number is written right justified. In a later section you will learn how to write with center or left justification. This table is provided on a QuickC help screen, which is only an ⟨F1⟩ keystroke away.

Escape characters are used for control purposes. They always begin with a backslash.

```
printf("The temperature is %f degrees Celsius\n",celsius);
```

Historically, escape characters refer to control codes sent to the printer to do carriage returns, form feeds, and such. In reality the escape characters are more powerful; in fact, using them you can send almost any code to the output device that the device can recognize.

There are also several special backslash codes that can be used for controlling the output device during writing:

\a	bell
\b	backspace
\f	form feed
\n	line feed (LF)
\r	carriage return (CR)
\t	horizontal tab
\v	vertical tab
\\	backslash
\'	single quote
\"	double quote
\xhhh	The character hhh, where hhh is hexadecimal
\ooo	The character ooo, where ooo is octal.

For example, to print a backslash you could use \010 or \x008. Although it is not necessary, it's wise to use the prefix zeros to prevent the inadvertent use of the next characters and from them being assumed as part of the code. For example, \x08 will work, but if the next character is a zero the compiler will read \x080.

Tip

Always represent nonprinting characters with a backslash sequence to prevent confusing the compiler.

The following are invalid for the reasons shown:

'9'	only octal values are permitted
'\A'	undefined special value
'XYZ'	more than one character between quotes
\f	single quotes missing
''	no character between quotes

You can mix backslash codes, using multiple escape sequences as desired:

```
printf("This is printed\has two lines\n");
```

> **Note**
>
> Be careful not to confuse the backslash escape character with the forward slash used for comments and division. Remember, backslash for escape characters, forward slash for comments and division.

Any constant characters, text strings or data can be printed directly from the format string:

```
printf("The temperature is %f degrees Celsius\n",celsius);
```

Whatever text is in the format string will be printed as it appears in the format string.

You can add modifiers to the identifier to control the alignment or format. The following identifiers are accepted:

Identifiers	Meaning
\	Left justify item
NNNNN	Minimum field width
.NNNN	Formatting control. Shows digits to display to the right of the decimal.
L	The data item is *long* instead of *int*.

For example,

```
printf("The temperature is %-6.1f degrees Celsius\n",celsius);
```

displays *celsius* as left justified, in a field width of six characters, with one digit to the right of the decimal.

You can also control the format dynamically using an asterisk. You must add an argument to specify the field width.

```
width=6;
qty=34;
printf("The quantity on hand is %*d\n",width,qty);
```

If you need to use a percent sign in writing a number, use a double percent sign in the format string:

```
growth=12;
printf("Your investment has grown by %d%%\n",growth);
```

Tips

If you wish decimal points to align in a table of decimal numbers, use a modifier to output the numbers. Specify a width larger than any of the numbers.

The Example

Before continuing, try entering and using the following program to experiment with the *printf( )* function:

```
/* test program for printf function  */

#include <stdio.h>
#define TEST "This is a test string"

main()
{
    char *surname, *name;
    int letter;
    float amount;
    int width, value;

    /* Printing a constant string */
    printf("This is a test\n");

    /* Printing a constant */
    printf("%d\n",234);


    /* Printing a constant, defining a small field */
    printf("%2d\n",234);

    /* Writing a string, defining a small field */
    printf("%3s\n",TEST);

    /* Multiple value output */
    surname="Mr.";
    name="Jones";
    amount=5000;
    printf("%s %s, you have just won $%6.2f
dollars!\n",surname,name,amount);
```

continued

```
/* Dynamically controlling the field format */
width=4;
value=233;
printf("The number is %*d\n",width,value);

/* Printing the ASCII value of a letter */
letter = 'c';
printf("The equivalent ASCII for %c is %d\n",letter,letter);
}
```

Reading with the scanf() Function

The *scanf()* function is the formatted input function. This function can be used to enter machine-formatted numbers, characters, or character strings to a program. For example:

```
scanf("%f",&fahrenheit);
```

The appearance is similar to the *printf()* function, but there is a distinct difference. The general form of the *scanf()* function is a format string and one or more input variable item pointers:

```
scanf(<control string>,<item1 pointer>,<item2 pointer>, <itemn
pointer>,...<itemn pointer>);
```

Notice the difference. With the *printf()* function, the actual variables are listed. With the *scanf()* function, pointers to the variables are listed. In the previous example, the ampersand with the variable name in the argument suggests the pointer to the variable is used rather than the variable.

Note

Programmers should avoid, unless necessary, the use of the *scanf()* function for keyboard input. It should be used only for machine-formatted input. For user input, it is considered better form to use the *gets()* or *fgets()* functions (see next sections) and then convert any numbers entered using the appropriate conversion routine.

The Control String

The control string for the *scanf()* function consists only of identifiers. Most of the same identifiers used for *writing data* can also be used for *reading data*:

Identifier	Format
%d	decimal integer
%c	single character
%s	character string
%f	floating point
%e	floating point
%u	unsigned decimal integer
%o	unsigned octal integer
%x	unsigned hexadecimal integer
%h	short integer

Notice the difference from the previous list: there is no %g option, the %h option for short integers is added, and the %f and %e are equivalent, each accepting decimal or exponential input numbers.

The function returns the number of fields read. The returned value can be used as a check in a program to determine if all fields were read.

Using the *scanf()* Function

The *scanf()* function can be used for entering multiple values by using additional format codes in the control string. For example, you might have the following lines of code in a program reading preformatted addresses from an input device:

```
printf("Enter City and State: ");
scanf("%s %s",city,state);
```

Strings that are entered cannot have any white space, as any white space terminates the input reading. In the previous example, New Orleans would be an illegal city input.

In this example *city* and *state* are pointers to character arrays, and no ampersand is necessary. For numeric variables, the ampersand would have to be used, as in the previous example.

Note

Do not use the pointer method of declaring character strings for the *scanf()* function. Use the array method.

Text strings cannot be a part of the *scanf()* control string. Prompts should be written from a separate statement using the *printf()* or *puts()* functions.

The *scanf()* Function and User Input

As the *printf()* function is very useful for formatted input, you might expect that the *scanf()* function would be useful for input, particularly for numeric values. From a practical viewpoint, however, it is best not to use the function for user input. You can see why by trying the following program:

```
/* This is an example of improper scanf() use */
#include <stdio.h>
main()
{
     int  address_no;
     char name[40+1];
     char street[40+1];
     char city[20+1];
     char state[2+1];
     char zip[5+1];

     printf("Address Number: ");
     scanf("%d",&address_no);
     printf("Name: ");
     gets(name);
     printf("Address: ");
     scanf("%s",street);
     printf("City, State, Zip: ");
     scanf("%s %s %s", city,state,zip);
}
```

There are three major problems with this example:

1. The *scanf()* function reads up to, but not including, the newline character. The *gets()* function for the name reads the newline character. The result is:

```
Address Number: 3
Name: Address:
```

In other words, the program doesn't wait for you to enter the name. The *scanf()* function for the address number reads up to, but not including, the newline character. After the next prompt for the name, the *gets()* function reads the newline character still in the buffer. Since this function reads through the next newline, *gets()* thinks it has input and the program moves ahead to the address prompt.

2. With the *scanf()* function, you cannot have any white space in the input string. Once a space is read, the program assumes all the input string is read. In reading the address, no spaces could be used.

3. The behavior of the *scanf( )* function is very compiler dependent.

With a little programming work and with the use of a few QuickC functions, you could make the program work with the *scanf( )* function. It would be much better, however, to use the *fgets( )* function for all input, and the better forms for this example will be shown in later sections.

String Input and Output: *puts()* and *gets()* Functions

If you are reading and writing character strings, the easiest method is generally to use the *gets( )* and *puts( )* functions.

String Output

The *puts( )* function can be used to output a simple character string. The general form is:

```
puts(text_ptr)
```

where *text_ptr* is a pointer to the character string or an array. You must also include an *#include <stdio.h>* at the beginning of the program to enable QuickC to find the function. Here is a simple example:

```
#include <stdio.h>
main()
{
      static char array[] = "This is an array text string.";
      char    *msg = "This is a text string with a pointer.";

      puts(array);
      puts(msg);
      puts(&array[2]);
      puts(msg+2);
}
```

The result is:

```
This is an array text string.
This is a text string with a pointer.
i
i
```

The function is very simple to use but can only be used with character strings.

With a character string, *puts( )* takes less typing than the *printf( )* function. The *puts( )* function also automatically adds a newline character at the end of the output string forcing a carriage return and linefeed.

One question you might have is this: how does *puts( )* know when the end of the character string is reached? The answer is that *puts( )* reads to the next null character. This can lead to some interesting and frustrating problems if you forget to include the null character. For example, DON'T try this:

```
main()
{
    static char bad_news[] = {'H','E','L','L','O','!'};

    puts(bad_news);
}
```

Since there is no null character in the string, the output function will continue to output until it can find one somewhere in memory—which could take time and send some very interesting codes to the screen.

String Input

You can use the complement of the *puts( )* function, the *gets( )* function, for the input of character strings. As with the *puts( )* function, you must include the *stdio.h* file. The general form is:

```
gets(text_ptr)
```

Here is a simple example:

```
#include <stdio.h>
main()
{
    char name[80];

    puts("What is your name?");
    gets(name);
    printf("Your name is %s\n",name);
}
```

Notice that you can mix *puts( )* and *printf( )* functions as desired in a program.

Now here is a better form of the example of the previous section:

```
#include <stdio.h>
main()
```

continued

```
{
        int address_no;
        char address_noa[4];
        char name[40+1];
        char street[40+1];
        char city[20+1];
        char state[2+1];
        char zip[5+1];

        printf("Address Number: ");
        gets(address_noa);
        address_no = atoi(address_noa);
        printf("Name: ");
        gets(name);
        printf("Address: ");
        gets(street);
        printf("City: ");
        gets(city);
        printf("State: ");
        gets(state);
        printf("Zip: ");
        gets(zip);
}
```

This program still has a problem, however. It would be quite possible for a user to enter a name, address, city, state, or zip code that overflows the storage allocated for that variable. This could create execution problems. An even better program form would be to use the *fgets()* function, which will be discussed later.

Single Character I/O

The *getchar()* function reads the next character from the input and returns its value. The character is echoed at the output. The function has no argument.

The *putchar()* function prints a single character on the standard output device. It has a single argument, which is the output character or variable for the output character.

With both of these, you must include the *stdio.h* file.

Now we can put these together in a simple example:

```
/* GETCHAR routine */

#include <stdio.h>
```

continued

```
main()
{
    char c;
    printf("Please enter a character: ");
    c = getchar();
    putchar(c);
}
```

If you try to execute this and enter a b, you will get:

```
Please enter a character: b    <Enter>
b
```

The character you enter is echoed, and then is displayed again after the carriage return with the *putchar( )* function.

You can simplify this with:

```
/* GETCHAR routine  */

#include <stdio.h>

main()
{
    printf("Please enter a character: ");
    putchar(getchar());
}
```

This will work identically to the first example.

Now enter several characters and then press the carriage return. What happens? Only the first character is returned.

Two other character input routines are also useful:

getche()   Returns the input character without waiting for a carriage return, echoing it.

getch()   Returns input character without waiting for a carriage return. Does not echo it.

As an example, you could use either of these to capture an option from a menu routine. Both routines require the program to include the *conio.h* file. (The *getchar( )* will wait for the user to enter a carriage return after the character is entered.)

The *fgets( )* Function

One of the best methods for keyboard input is to use the *fgets( )* function to read an input character string, then use the appropriate function to convert the input if necessary. The *fgets( )* function has three arguments: the identifier for the character string, the number of characters read, and a stream, which is the source of the data and can be a file or physical device.

```
fgets(string,n,stream)
```

The QuickC language has certain previously defined external variables for standard streams:

Identifier	Device
stdin	keyboard
stdout	display
stdprn	printer port
stderr	output device for error messages
stdaux	auxiliary port

To read text (up to 80 characters) from the keyboard to a variable name, then, you would use:

```
char name[80+2];

fgets(name,82,stdin);
```

Now you can write a better form of the previous program as:

```
#include <stdio.h>
main()
{
    int address_no;
    char address_noa[5];
    char name[40+2];
    char street[40+2];
    char city[20+2];
    char state[2+2];
    char zip[5+2];

    printf("Address Number: ");
    fgets(address_noa,5,stdin);
    address_no = atoi(address_noa);
    printf("Name: ");
    fgets(name,42,stdin);
    printf("Address: ");
    fgets(street,42,stdin);
    printf("City: ");
    fgets(city,22,stdin);
    printf("State: ");
    fgets(state,4,stdin);
```

continued

```
        printf("Zip: ");
        fgets(zip,7,stdin);
}
```

General Rules for Input and Output

You have now learned three input and output function pairs for your QuickC programs. Here is a summary of when to use each. All these use standard input (stdin) or the standard output (stdout):

getchar() and putchar() — Use for the input and output of single characters.

gets() and puts() — Use for the input and output of character strings.

scanf() — Use for the machine-formatted input.

printf() — Use for versatile output control of strings or numeric values.

getche() and getch() — Use for entering single characters when you don't want to wait for a carriage return.

In addition, another input function has been introduced that can read from any type of input stream:

fgets() — Use for entering character streams from the keyboard.

For more information on input and output functions, refer to Chapter 13.

Exercises

1. Enter the example test program for the *printf()* function, compile it and execute it. What is the output?
2. Enter the example program for the *scanf()* function for reading and address. Compile and execute it. Identify the problems discussed in the text.
3. Write a program that queries for the first and last name, then displays the name in the form last name, comma, and first name.
4. Write a program in which you can enter three floating-point numbers and they are displayed in three later lines with decimal points aligned and two places after the decimal point.

Answers

1.

This is a test
234

234
This is a test string
Mr. Jones, you have just won $5000.00 dollars!
The number is 233
The equivalent ASCII for c is 99

3.

```
#include <stdio.h>
main()
{
     char first[20+2];
     char last[20+2];

     printf("Please enter first name: ");
     fgets(first,22,stdin);
     printf("Please enter last name: ");
     fgets(last,22,stdin);
     printf("%s, %s\n",last,first);
}
```

4.

```
#include <stdio.h>
main()
{
     float one,two,three;
     char onea[10], twoa[10], threea[10];

     printf("Please enter three floating point numbers ");
     fgets(onea,10,stdin);
     fgets(twoa,10,stdin);
     fgets(threea,10,stdin);
     one = atof(onea);
     two = atof(twoa);
     three = atof(threea);
     printf("%6.2f\n",one);
     printf("%6.2f\n",two);
     printf("%6.2f\n",three);
}
```

5

Arithmetic Operations

QuickC uses operators to perform actions. Operators are the verbs in a C statement. An operator defines the action that is to be performed on one or more operands.

In the previous example you used the statement:

```
celsius = (5.0/9.0) * (fahrenheit - 32.0);
```

There are four operators in this statement: /,*,- and =. C has about 40 operators available to the programmer. Some, of course, are used more than others. This chapter will examine the use of operators in statements.

Types of Operators

QuickC provides six types of operators: assignment, arithmetic, bitwise, relational, logical, and special.

The Assignment Operator

The assignment operator is perhaps the most basic of operators, and is represented by the equal sign. For example:

```
x = 34.5/2.0;
```

results in x being assigned the value of 34.5 divided by 2.0, or 17.25. In reality x is the name of a storage location. The result of the division is placed in that storage location.

With C, you can also do multiple assignments in a single statement. The following is perfectly valid if both variables are *ints*:

```
age = previous_age = 12;
```

This assigns the value of 12 to both *age* and *previous_age*.

Note

It is important to recognize that the assignment operator changes the value of the variable to the left of the operator. Do not use it to check for equality. Use a relational operator for that purpose (see separate section).

Arithmetic Operators

QuickC provides five arithmetic operators:

- **+** Plus (addition)
- **–** Minus (subtraction)
- ***** Times (multiplication)
- **/** Divided by (division)
- **%** Modulo (integer remainder)

Each performs an action with two operands. You can use them with constants or variables, and they can be a part of a function argument. For example:

```
age = first_age + 1;
```

assigns the value of one plus *first_age* to *age*. This example shows an arithmetic operator used as part of a function argument:

```
printf("%d",10+12);
```

This displays the value 22.

In any expression, spaces are nulls and can be used as necessary for clarity. The previous expression is the same as:

```
printf("%d", 10 + 12);
```

The minus sign can be used to represent subtraction or a negative number.

```
temperature = (-30);
printf("%d", 40 - 12);
```

The modulus operator can only be used for integer arithmetic. It provides the remainder of the left operand divided by the right. For example:

```
x = 25 % 3;
```

reads as 25 modulo 3, and produces a value of 1. For float or double type, use the *fmod( )* function. For example, the following returns a value of 4 to z:

```
main()
    {
    double x,y,z;

    x = 24;
    y = 5;
    z = fmod(x,y);
    .
    .
    .
    }
```

Bitwise Operators

You can also perform operations at the bit level with C. The following bit-level operators are available:

&	AND
|	OR
^	XOR
~	NOT
<<	Shift left one bit
>>	Shift right one bit

Now let's look at examples of the four primary operators.

The NOT Operator

The NOT operator changes each 0 to 1 and 1 to 0:

```
(10110) == 01001
```

The AND Operator

The AND operator produces a 1 in the corresponding output bit position only if both of the input bits in that position are 1. There is no carry.

```
(10110) & (01011) == 00010
```

The OR Operator

The OR operator produces a 1 in the corresponding output bit position if either of the input bits in that position are 1:

```
(10110) |  (01011) == 11111
```

The EXCLUSIVE OR Operator

The EXCLUSIVE OR operator produces a 1 in the corresponding bit position if either of the input bits in that position are 1, but not both:

```
(10110) ^ (01011) == 11101
```

Shift Operators

The left shift operator shifts the bits of the left operand to the left by the number of places specified by the right operand:

```
101010 << 2 == 101000
```

The left bits are lost, and the right bits moved in are filled with zeros.

The right shift operator shifts the bits of the left operand to the right the number of places specified by the right operand:

```
1010 >> 2 == 0010
```

Bits moved past the right end are lost. For unsigned data types, the bits vacated at the left are replaced by zeros.

Use the shift operators with unsigned integer types only. The behavior of the right shift with signed types is very compiler dependent.

Using Bitwise Operators

One use of the bitwise operators is to extract information from flag variables using masks. The bits of the flag variable represent on/off states, and a mask is ANDed with the variable to obtain the desired bit. This bit is then tested to see if the state is on or off.

For example, assume an adventure game in which each room has a variable *condition(room)* associated with it of eight bits. The rightmost bit indicates whether the room has light or is dark. If dark, of course, the adventurer would need a light to see any objects in the room or to move. You could then test to see if the room had light using a mask LIGHTMASK (00000001) as:

```
(condition(room) & LIGHTMASK)
```

This would mask off the right bit, which could then be tested using an if statement (see next chapter) to determine if the room had light or not.

In using bitwise operators, the following rules are used:

First Operand	Second Operand	AND &	OR |	XOR ^
0	0	0	0	0
0	1	0	1	1
1	0	0	1	1
1	1	1	1	0

A left shift ($<<$) multiplies the number by two, a right shift ($>>$) divides it by two.

Relational Operators

Relational operators are used for comparing two qualities. They are used in conditional statements (Chapter 6). There are six relational operators in C:

> Greater than

>= Greater than or equal to

< Less than

<= Less than or equal to

== Equal to

!= Not equal to

These will be more completely introduced in the next chapter, but notice here two facts:

- The result of an expression with relational operators is either true or false.
- In comparing for equality you do not use an equal sign, but a double equal sign. The double equal sign tests for equality. The single equal sign assigns a value to a variable.

As an example, suppose you wish to check for division by zero before performing a division:

```
if (b==0.0)
    printf("Cannot divide by zero.\n");
else
    c = a/b;
```

Logical Operators

Logical operators, as relational operators, are used in conditional statements (Chapter 6). Expressions with logical operators always produce a value of 1 or 0. Any nonzero value is accepted as true. Logical operators are used with relational and other operators to create expressions. For example, $x = 4 + (x < y)$ is a legal QuickC expression.

There are three logical operators:

&&	AND
||	OR
!	NOT

The && and || operators require two operands. The ! operator requires only one.

As an example:

```
if ('0' <= x && c <='9')
     printf("x is the digit %c\n");
else
     printf("x is not a digit.\n");
```

Note

Avoid trying to test a floating point variable for equality with a constant. Usually the test will fail unless the test is made after the variable is initialized.

Special Operators

There are several special operators in C. This section reviews a few of these.

The Increment and Decrement Operators

You can simplify the addition of unit quantities using the increment or decrement operators. This makes them valuable for loop counters and related functions. In its simplest form, the increment operator in a statement would look like:

```
aa = a++;
bb = ++b;
```

In the first case, *a* is incremented by 1 after the assignment takes place. In the second statement, *b* is incremented by one before the assignment takes place. The result is that if *a* and *b* were equal on starting, *bb* now has a value one higher than *aa*, and *a* and *b* both equal *bb*.

Try the following:

```
/* program to test increment operator */
main()
{
     int      a = b = 7;
     int      aa, bb;

     aa = a++;
     bb = ++b;
     printf("a = %d\n",a);
     printf("b = %d\n",b);
     printf("aa = %d\n",aa);
     printf("bb = %d\n",bb);
}
```

The result will show *bb* with a value of 8 and *aa* with a value of 7. Both *a* and *b* are now 8.

The decrement operator works in the same way:

```
aa = a--;
bb = --b;
```

In the first case, the a variable is decremented after the assignment. In the second case, the variable is decremented before the assignment.

The increment and decrement operators produce very efficient code. The *a++*; statement, for example, reduces to a single machine instruction. Use them whenever possible.

Pointer-Related Operators

The pointer-related operators are special prefix codes that are used for performing operations with pointers. There are two pointer-related operators: the address operator (&) and the indirection operator (*).

```
/* test for indirection */
#include <stdio.h>
main()
{
     int x;
     char *message;
```

continued

```
        char xa[10];

        message = "HELLO THERE. \n";
        printf("Please enter an integer: ");
        fgets(xa,10,stdin);
        x = atoi(xa);
        printf("%sThe number is %d\n",message,x);
}
```

The asterisk is used in declaring *message* to point to the address of the first character of the string. Note that message points to the address of the first character, not to the character itself. The indirection operator is used with the *scanf()* function, and an example was shown in Chapter 4.

The Comma

The comma operator can be used in a loop expression to control loop initialization. An example will be shown in Chapter 7.

The Cast Operator

You can force a change in the data type of a variable by casting it, or putting the type name in parentheses before the variable in the expression.

Casting can be explicit or implicit. For example:

```
main()
{
        int x = 3;
        float y = 5.2;
        float z;

        z = x + y;
```

This program converts the integer value of x to a float value, adds it to y, and then assigns z to the float result. This is implicit casting; that is, the casting follows the internal rules of the C compiler. This may be what you wish.

When casting is necessary, it is generally better to do explicit casting. With explicit casting, you place the type name of the result in parentheses before the variable in the expression. For example,

```
x = (int) 3.6 + (int) 4.7;
```

assigns the value of 7 to x. Both values to the right of the assignment operator are truncated before they are added.

Try the following program to see how QuickC conversions work:

```
/* Basic conversion examples */
main()
{
      float      f1=107.73, f2;
      int        i1=25, i2;

      /* convert a float to an integer */
      i2 = (int) f1;
      printf("%f converted to an integer produces %d\n",f1,i2);

      /* convert an integer to a float */
      f2 = (float) i1;
      printf("%d converted to float produces %f\n",i1,f2);

      /* divide an integer by an integer */
      i2 = i1/2;
      printf("%d divided by two produces %d\n",i1,i2);

      /* divide a float by an integer */
      f2 = f1/ (float) i1;
      printf("%f divided by %d produces %f\n",f1,i1,f2);

      /* divide an integer by a float */
      f2 = (float) i1/f1;
      printf("%d divided by %f produces %f\n",i1,f1,f2);

      /* divide a float by a float */
      f2  = f1/25.0000;
      printf("%f divided by 25.0000 produces %f\n",f1,f2);

}
```

This will produce the following output:

```
107.730000 converted to an integer produces 107
25 converted to float produces 25.000000
25 divided by 2 produces 12
107.730003 divided by 25 produces 4.309200
25 divided by 107.730003 produces 0.232062
107.730003 divided by 25.0000 produces 4.309200
```

The *sizeof* Operator

This operator returns the size of the operand to its right. It can be used with a variable or constant as:

```
x = sizeof(float);
y = sizeof(temperature);
```

As an example, the following program returns the size of each numeric type:

```
main()
{
      int a = 3;
      float b = 5.0;
      short c = 3;
      long d = 4;
      double e = 5.0;

      printf("The integer size is %d\n",sizeof(a));
      printf("The short size is %d\n", sizeof(c));
      printf("The long size is %d\n",sizeof(d));
      printf("The float size is %d\n",sizeof(b));
      printf("The double size is %d\n",sizeof(e));
}
```

The output of this program will be:

```
The integer size is 2
The short size is 2
the long size is 4
The float size is 8
The double size is 8
```

Expressions and Statements

An *expression* is any combination of operands and operators. For example,

```
celsius = (5.0/9.0) * (fahrenheit - 32.0);
```

A C *statement* is an expression followed by a semicolon. The previous expression is also a statement. Another example of a statement is:

```
printf("%6.2f",price);
```

> **Tip**
>
> Keep your expressions simple. If you need to use a complex expression, break it down to multiple statements. (With some compilers, this will increase execution speed. Optimizing compilers should permit the user to break expressions down to several simple expressions and still maintain the same execution speed. QuickC is not an optimizing compiler.)

In creating expressions, you can also use a shorthand notation to combine operations. Note the following equivalencies in C:

Long form	Shorthand
`counter = counter + 3;`	`counter +=3;`
`price = price * (old+1.00);`	`price *= oldprice+1.00;`
`a = a & b;`	`a &= b;`

The shorthand notation should be used as often as possible, as it simplifies the expression and improves the reliability of the code. The shorthand expressions can be used with arithmetic or bitwise operations.

The Precedence of Operations

With QuickC, operators are evaluated in the following order:

Operator	Type
`! -`	Unary, logical NOT, arithmetic minus
`* / %`	Arithmetic (multiplication, division)
`+ -`	Arithmetic (addition, subtraction)
`< > <= >=`	Relational (inequality)
`== !=`	Relational (equality)
`&& ||`	Logical
`= += -= *= /= %=`	Assignment

As in most languages, you can use double parentheses to group expressions.

Exercises

1. What is the value of z in each of the following expressions? Assume x is int, y and z are floating:

   a. y = 6.0;
      x = 5;
      z = y/x;

    b. z = (int) 3.0 + (int) 3.2
    c. y = 6.0;
        x = 5.7;
        z = x + y;

Answers

1. a. 1.2
    b. 6.0
    c. 11

6

Program Control: *if* and *switch* Structures

Up to now your programs contained a series of statements that were executed in a specified order. In reality, with most programs you will wish to alter the sequence in which the instructions are executed based on specified conditions. Control structures permit a program to alter its procedure dynamically based on any specified condition. This chapter will introduce you to conditional types of controls in which the program chooses one of several groups of statements based on the value of a control expression. In the next chapter, you will be introduced to iteration type controls in which a procedure is executed a certain number of times based on the value of a control expression.

Overview of Program Flow Control

An example of simple flow control might be:

```
main()
{
    int weather;
    char weathera[10];

    printf("What is the weather?\n");
    printf("\t(1) sunny \n");
    printf("\t(2) rainy \n");
    gets(weathera);
    weather = atoi(weathera);
    if (weather == 1)
        printf("Wash and wax car.\n");
    else
```

continued

```
        printf(" Go to library.\n");
}
```

If the weather is sunny, the program will request to the user to wash and wax the car; otherwise, the program will request the user to go to the library. In this example, the statements that are executed depends upon a specified condition. Here, the program selects from one of two alternative procedures or paths.

There are then two basic aspects of flow control: the *control expression* and *control structure*.

Control Expression

The program determines which statements are executed at execution time based on the value of a control expression. A *control expression* is any expression that evaluates to zero or nonzero that is used to determine the statements that are executed or the order of the statement execution.

In the previous example, the statements after the control expression are executed only if the expression evaluates to a nonzero value. If you try the following statements:

```
if (100)
    printf("Any nonzero number is true.\n");
if (-25)
    printf("This is true, too.\n");
```

both print statements would be executed, as in each case the control expression evaluates to a nonzero value.

Control Structure

There are several types of structures available for program flow control. All these are one of two types: *conditional* and *iteration (looping)*.

A *conditional control* selects one of several sets of statements to execute based on a specified condition. The most common type is the *if . . . else* structure of the example at the beginning of this chapter. This chapter is primarily about conditional type controls.

An *iteration control* executes a group of statements several times while or until a specified condition is true. Iteration controls will be the subject of the next chapter.

Types of Conditional Control Structures

There are three basic types of *conditional* controls: One-way, two-way, and multi-way.

One-Way

The simplest type of conditional control is to execute one or more statements based on whether a specified expression is nonzero:

```
if (control expression)
    <statements>;
```

If *control expression* is nonzero, then *statements* is executed. If the *control expression* is zero, then execution skips to the next statement after the if statement semicolon and *statements* is not executed (see Figure 6.1).

Figure 6.1
The One-Way Selection Structure

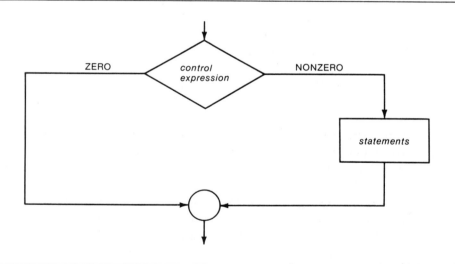

As an example:

```
if (temperature<=32)
    printf("It is freezing.\n");
```

Notice the following features of this C structure:

- The condition for the test is in parentheses after the *if*.
- There is no semicolon after the condition component; there is only one semicolon and it is at the end of the statement.
- For readability, the statements that are to be executed if the control expression is nonzero are indented from the main program body.

In a control expression testing for equality, be sure to use the double equal sign as:

```
if (temperature==32)
    printf("It right at freezing.\n");
```

This forces a test for equality. If you use the assignment operator instead (a single equal sign), you will discover a real problem. For example, try this program with its error:

```
main()
{
    int temperature;
    char tempa[10];

    printf("What is the temperature?");
    fgets(tempa,10,stdin);
    temperature = atoi(tempa);
    if (temperature=32)
        printf("It right at freezing.\n");
    printf("The temperature is %d.\n",temperature);
}
```

Here, the *if* statement resets the temperature variable to 32, regardless of what you enter. The *control expression* will always evaluate as nonzero, and the final statement will always display a temperature value of 32 regardless of whatever value you enter.

Often a single statement is executed if the *control expression* is nonzero, but you could execute several statements if they are placed within a set of curly braces to create what is known as a *statement block*.

```
if (temperature<=32)
    {
    printf("It is freezing\n");
    printf("and you better wear warm clothes");
    }
```

All the expressions within the braces will be executed if the *control expression* is nonzero.

Two-Way

In the two-way selection structure, the *control expression* determines which of two alternative sets of statements is executed:

```
if (control expression)
    statements-1;
else
    statements-2;
```

Here, if the *control expression* is not zero, *statements–1* is executed. If the *control expression* is zero, *statements-2* is executed (See Figure 6.2).

Figure 6.2
The Two-Way Selection Structure

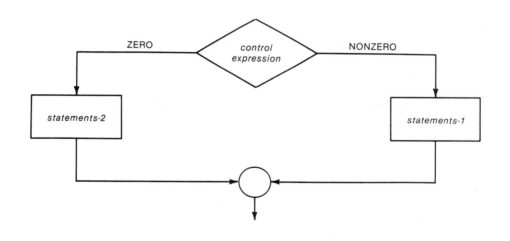

With C, there are two ways to create this structure: the *if . . . else* expression or the conditional operator.

The *if . . . else* Expression

The most conventional if structure is the *if . . . else* expression. For example:

```
if (temperature<=32)
        printf("It is freezing.\n");
else
        printf("It is not freezing.\n");
```

Here, if *temperature* is equal to or below *freezing*, *It is freezing* is displayed. If not, *It is not freezing* is displayed. At least one of the two sets of statements must be executed.

Notice the general form: neither the *if* nor the *else* line contains a semicolon. There is one semicolon at the end of the expressions for each path; that is, there are two statements. The two statement groups are indented from the main body of the program.

If there is a statement block in a path, enclose the group of statements in braces using semicolons to terminate each statement:

```
if (temperature<=32)
    {
    printf("It is freezing\n");
    printf("and you better wear warm clothes");
    }
else {
    printf("It is not freezing\n");
    printf("but watch for rain.\n");
    }
```

You can nest *if* . . . *else* clauses to any practical level, testing for additional conditions after an initial condition is met. If there are several *else* clauses, you may find it difficult to decide which *else* goes with which *if*. The general rule is that the *else* always goes with the most recent *if* unless braces dictate otherwise. There should always be a matching *if* for each *else*. All *ifs*, however, may not have an *else*. Suppose, for example, you have the following program:

```
main()
{
    int weather,day;
    char weathera[10], daya[10];

    printf("What is the weather?\n");
    printf("\t(1) sunny \n");
    printf("\t(2) rainy \n");
    fgets(weathera,10,stdin);
    weather = atoi(weathera);
    printf("What is the day?\n");
    printf("\t(1) Saturday\n");
    printf("\t(2) Sunday\n");
    printf("\t(3) Monday\n");
    printf("\t(4) Tuesday\n");
    printf("\t(5) Wednesday\n");
    printf("\t(6) Thursday\n");
    printf("\t(7) Friday\n");
    fgets(daya,10,stdin);
    day = atoi(daya);
```
continued

```
      if (day == 1)
          if (weather == 1)
              printf("Wash and wax car\n");
      else
          printf(" Go to library\n");
}
```

Here, the *else* clause really goes with the second *if*. The text string *Go to library* will only be executed if it is Saturday and the weather is not sunny. If the day is Sunday, neither *printf* expression will never be executed. How the program is indented has no effect. This means that you, as a programmer, must indent properly to ensure the program is readable as you meant it to work:

```
if (day == 1)
    if (weather == 1)
        printf("Wash and wax car\n");
    else
        printf(" Go to library\n");
```

You could even improve this even more by using:

```
if (day == 1 && weather == 1)
        printf("Wash and wax car\n");
else
        printf(" Go to library\n");
```

The Conditional Operator

There is another way to write an *if . . . else* structure. C has a conditional operator that can be used with short expressions. For example:

```
cost = (cost>10.00) ? 15.00 : 10.00;
```

is equivalent to:

```
if (cost>10.00)
     cost = 15.00;
else
     cost = 10.00;
```

The expression immediately after the equal sign is the control expression. If the control expression is nonzero, the value to the left of the colon is assigned to the variable to the left of the equal sign. If the control expression is zero, the value to the right of the colon is assigned to the variable.

Notice there are three operands used with the conditional operator: the control expression and two additional expressions. The general form is:

```
control expression ? expression-1 : expression-2
```

Multi-Way

Sometimes you may wish to choose from three or more alternative sets of statement groups.

There are two ways of accomplishing multi-way structures: using multiple *if . . . else* structures or using a *switch* structure.

The execution of the statement groups may be mutually exclusive or inclusive. If only one condition can be met and only one of the statement groups can be executed, the structure is said to be mutually exclusive. If two or more conditions or statement groups can be executed, the structure is inclusive.

Using Nested *if*s

You can nest *if . . . else* statements to create a multi-way structure. Here, the general form becomes:

```
if  control-expression-1
     statements-1;
else if control-expression-2
     statements-2;
else if control-expression-3
     statements-3;
:
else if control-expression-n
     statements-n;
else
     statements-4;
```

Figure 6.3 shows the general flow for this type of structure.

You can always create complex multi-way structures using nested *if . . . else* expressions. The conditions can involve different variables in the testing or other complex relationships.

For example, here is an example of a mutually exclusive structure:

```
main()
{
     int score;
     char grade;
     char scorea[10];

     printf("What is the score? ");
     fgets(scorea,10,stdin);
     score = atoi(scorea);
     if (score>=90)
          grade='A';
     else if (score>=80 && score<90)
```
continued

Figure 6.3
The Multi-Way Structure

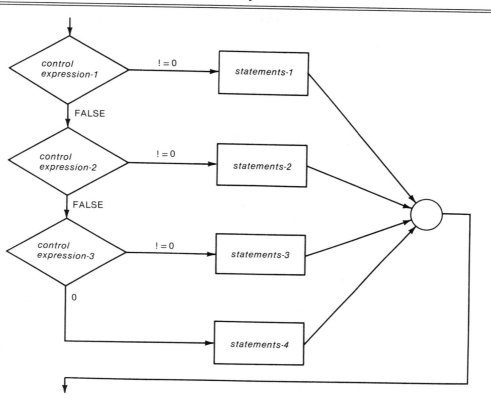

```
        grade='B';
   else if (score>=70 && score<80)
        grade='C';
   else if (score>=69 && score<70)
        grade='D';
   else
        grade='F';
   printf("The grade is %c\n",grade);
}
```

In this example only one condition can be met and one statement group executive, so the structure is mutually exclusive.

For multi-way structures, many programmers prefer adding braces for even one statement to improve the readability and make it easier to follow if it is necessary to add multiple statements in the block later:

```
if (score>=90)
```

```
        {
        grade='A';
        }
else if (score>=80 && score<90)
        {
        grade='B';
        }
```

In other cases you may wish the statement groups inclusive. For example, here is a simple program to calculate a utility rate based on a variable rate structure:

```
#define HIGH = 950
#define LOW = 300
#define RATE1(pwr) (.05*pwr)   /* rate for <= LOW kwhrs */
#define RATE2(pwr) (.06*pwr)   /* rate for HIGH-LOW kwhrs */
#define RATE3(pwr) (.07*pwr)   /* rate for >HIGH kwhrs */
main()
{
        float kwh,cost,x;
        char kwha[10];

        cost = 0;
        printf("What is the power usage in kwh? ");
        fgets(kwha,10,stdin);
        kwh = atof(kwha);
        if (kwh<=LOW)
                cost = RATE1(kwh);
        else {
                cost = RATE1(LOW);
                if (kwh<=HIGH) {
                        x = kwh-LOW;
                        cost = cost + RATE2(x);
                }
                else {
                        x = HIGH-LOW;
                        cost = cost + RATE2(x);
                        x = kwh-950;
                        cost = cost + RATE3(x);
                }
        }
        printf("The total cost is %6.2f \n",cost);
}
```

In this example the conditions are inclusive; that is, one or more conditions may be true.

The *switch* Structure

You can also use a QuickC *switch* structure to accomplish multi-way branching. Here is a simple menu program using a with a *switch* multi-way structure (this is a very simple menu program here—it will be developed better later):

```
#include <stdio.h>
main()
{
    char option;

    printf("MAIN MENU\n\n");
    printf("\t(1) Add a name\n");
    printf("\t(2) Edit a name\n");
    printf("\t(3) List names\n");
    printf("\t(4) Exit to DOS\n\n");
    printf("Please enter desired option: ");
    option = getchar();
    switch(option)
    {
        case '1' :
            printf("Option 1 selected\n");
            break;
        case '2' :
            printf("Option 2 selected\n");
            break;
        case '3' :
            printf("Option 3 selected\n");
            break;
        case '4' :
            exit(0);
        default :
            printf("Illegal option selected\n");
    }
}
```

Notice several things about this structure:

- The switch statement consists of the keyword *switch* with the control expression in parentheses, followed by a statement.
- The *case* keyword is used to check the control expression for a value. The expression is terminated by a colon.
- The *break* statements force an exit from the structure once any condition is met.

- A *default* test is optional and can be used to trap conditions not meeting any *case* condition.

Tip

Since both nested *ifs* and *switch* structures can be used for multi-way, the user is faced with the choice between the two. With the QuickC *switch* structure, the control expression must evaluate to a *int, short, long,* or *char* type. Pointers and floats are not allowed. The *case* keyword must be followed by a constant expression; that is, the expression must evaluate to a value that is constant at compile time.

Comparing Strings

When comparing text strings using relational tests, a special C function must be used. C provides several functions for this purpose.

The most general function is the *strcmp( )* function, which compares two strings and returns a zero if the strings are equal. Using this function, we can rewrite the first example of this chapter as:

```
main()
{
    char weather[10];

    printf("What is the weather? ");
    fgets(weather,10,stdin);
    if (0 == strcmp(weather,"sunny"))
        printf("Wash and wax the car.\n");
    else
        printf("Go to library.\n");
}
```

For more information on comparing strings, see Chapter 11.

Tips for Writing Control Code

Here are a few common mistakes that could plague your early C programming:

- Be sure *not* to use a semicolon after the control expression of an if structure. If the semicolon is used after the control expression, the next statement will always be executed regardless of the value of the control expression.

- The following is incorrect:

```
if (a == 2 || 5 || 7)...
```

the correct form is:

```
if (a == 2 || a == 5 || a == 7)...
```

In the former case, the control expression always evaluates to nonzero, regardless of the value of a.
- Remember to use the double equal sign to test for equality. A single equal sign is an assignment operator in C.
- Use indenting properly to control the readability of the structure.
- Use braces in a consistent way. One method here is to try to keep the closing brace under the opening brace. Using this rule makes it easier to see which braces match.
- There is a *goto* in C, but you should seldom, if ever, need to use it. If you think you need to use it, evaluate why you believe it is necessary and see if another alternative could be used.

Exercises

1. Which of the following conditions are true?

    a. 'a' < 'f'
    b. 3 < 20
    c. 'a' < 'A'
    d. 50 > 7 && 8 > 9
    e. 50 > 7 || 8 > 9
    f. 23
    g. –2
    h. !15

2. What does the expression (a==2 || 5 || 7) evaluate to if a is 5?

3. Write a program that requests two input integer numbers, then tests the numbers to see if the first is evenly divided by the second. If this condition is true, display a message to show this. Otherwise, display a message that it is not true.

Answers

1. All but e and h are true.
2. FALSE
3.

```
main()
{
    int one, two;
    char onea[10], twoa[10];

    printf("Please enter two numbers: ");
    gets(onea);
    gets(twoa);
    one = atoi(onea);
    two = atoi(twoa);;
    if (one % two == 0)
        printf("Evenly divided\n");
    else
        printf("Not evenly divided\n");
}
```

7

Program Control: Iteration Structures

There is a second type of control structure: the loop or *iteration* structure. *Iteration* structures permit the program to execute a group of statements a specified number of times based on a certain condition. Each execution of the group of statements is called an *iteration*, or loop.

There are two basic types of iterations, depending upon when the condition is tested. The *while* iteration checks a *control expression* before executing the loop. The *for* construction can be used as an alternative for the *while* loop. The *do . . . while* checks a *control expression* at the end of the loop.

The *while* Construction

The *while* construction executes a group of statements as long as a *control expression* is true. The *control expression* is tested before executing the statements (Figure 7.1). The general form is:

```
while control expression
     statements;
```

The program begins by checking *control expression*. If *control expression* is non-zero, *statements* is executed. Otherwise, the program continues with the next statement after the semicolon. As with other *control expressions*, you can use brackets to show a statement block is to be executed if the condition is nonzero.

Notice that *control expression* is tested before any statements are executed; therefore, if *control expression* is zero no statements are executed. Generally the statements alter the value of the *control expression*. Notice that the *while* construction is very similar to the *if* construction, except that the *if* construction only permits a single iteration whereas the *while* construction permits any number of iterations.

As an example, try the following program:

Figure 7.1
The *while* Construction

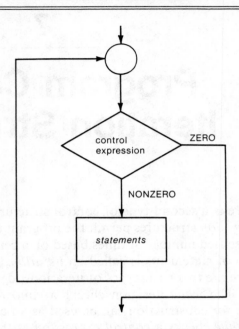

```
/* WHILE Loop Example */
#include <stdio.h>
main()
{
    static char msg[17] = "This is a cycle.";
    int ctr;

    ctr = 1;
    while (ctr++ <= 6)
        printf("%s %d\n",msg,ctr);
}
```

The program will produce the following output:

    This is cycle 1
    This is cycle 2
    This is cycle 3
    This is cycle 4
    This is cycle 5
    This is cycle 6

Notice that the value of a variable is a part of the *control expression* and is changed each iteration. Eventually the variable value reaches six and the loop execution is terminated. The *control expression* is tested before executing the statements in the loop.

Note

In creating an iterative construction, always be sure you have a terminating condition. Otherwise, the loop will continue to execute indefinitely. There must be some way for the *control expression* to eventually reach a value of zero.

Now let's try a more practical example. This program calculates the greatest common denominator of two input numbers:

```
/* Program to find the greatest common denominator */
#include <stdio.h>
main()
{
     int first,second,x;
     char firsta[10],seconda[10];

     printf("Please enter two positive integers\n");
     fgets(firsta, 10, stdin);
     fgets(seconda, 10, stdin);
     first = atoi(firsta, 10, stdin);
     second = atoi(seconda);
     while (second != 0)
          {
          x = first % second;
          first = second;
          second = x;
          }
     printf("The greatest common denominator is %d\n",first);
}
```

The program uses an algorithm developed by Euclid many years ago. If *second* is zero, we've finished our work and the *gcd* is equal to *first*. If *second* is not zero, calculate:

```
x = first modulo second
second = x
```

and try again. A sample output could look like this:

Please enter two positive integers

26

39

The greatest common denominator is 13

Now try another example. This program will permit you to enter a series of numbers and then displays the average of the numbers:

```
/* Program to calculate an average of several input numbers */
#include <math.h>
#include <stdio.h>
main()
{
    int ctr = 0;
    double number, average, sum;
    char numbera[10];

    sum = 0.0;
    number = -1.0;
    printf("Please enter the input numbers, \n");
    printf("terminating with a zero.\n");
    while (number != 0)
        {
        fgets(numbera, 10, stdin);
        number = atof(numbera);
        sum = sum + number;
        ctr++;
        }
    average = sum/(ctr-1);
    printf("The average is %f\n",average);
}
```

In this example the input numbers are read and summed in a *while* loop. As soon as a zero is entered, the *while* loop is terminated on the next iteration without executing the statements in the loop. The average is then calculated and displayed.

The readability of the example, however, is poor. In this type of problem it would be better to test for the condition after the input number is read. That would eliminate the need for the somewhat crude initialization (number = -1) and the extra iteration. We can put the test at the end of the loop using a *do . . . while* construction.

The *do . . . while* Construction

The *do . . . while* construction executes a group of statements and then checks a *control expression*. If the *control expression* is nonzero, the group of statements is executed again; if zero, the program exits the loop. Figure 7.2 shows the general structure. Notice the similarity to the *while* construction except that the test is at the end of the loop. For this reason the group of statements will always be executed at least once.

Figure 7.2
The *do while* Construction

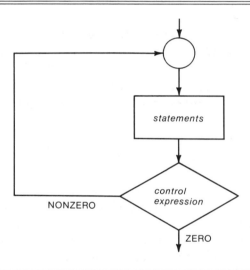

The general form of the *do . . . while* construction is:

```
do
     statements
while (control expression);
```

As with the *while* statement, you can use a statement block if the group is enclosed in braces.

Now you can rewrite the example of the previous section as:

```
/* Program to calculate an average of several input numbers */

#include <math.h>
#include <stdio.h>
main()
{
```
continued

```
        int ctr=0;
        double number,average,sum;
        char numbera[10];

        sum = 0.0;
        printf("Please enter the input numbers, \n");
        printf("terminating with a zero.\n");
        do   {
             fgets(numbera, 10, stdin);
             number = atof(numbera);
             sum = sum + number;
             ctr++;
             }      while (number != 0);
        if (ctr != 1)
             {
             average = sum/(ctr-1);
             printf("The average is %f\n",average);
             }
        else
                printf("There were no numbers entered\n");
}
```

Notice the improved clarity of the program. It is no longer necessary to initialize *number*, as no test is made until an input is received. The test is at the end of the loop, and the program exits the loop if the test is true. The counter has already been incremented at that time, so this must be considered when the average is calculated. Braces are used to show that the group of statements are all a part of the loop.

The *for* Construction

The *for* construction is used to execute a group of statements a specified number of times. The general form of the for construction is:

```
for (initializing_expression; control_expression; step_expression)
      statements;
```

Notice there are three expressions inside the parentheses, and they are separated by semicolons. The first expression is an initializing statement. The second is the *control expression*. The loop continues as long as the *control expression* is non-zero. The third expression controls the step.

Using the for *Construction*

As an example, you can rewrite the first example of this chapter as:

```
/* FOR Loop Example */
#include <stdio.h>
main()
{
    char *msg;
    int ctr;

    msg = "This is cycle ";
    for (ctr=1; ctr < = 6 ; ctr++ )
        printf("%s %d\n",msg,ctr);
}
```

Notice how much more compact the code is now. Inside the parentheses are the three expressions: the initializing statement, the *control expression* for testing, and the step statement that was formerly a part of the loop. The expressions are separated by semicolons. If any one of these is not used, it should be blank:

```
/* FOR Loop Example */
#include <stdio.h>
main()
{
    char *msg;
    int ctr;

    ctr = 1;
    msg = "This is cycle ";
    for ( ; ctr <= 6 ; ctr++ )
        printf("%s %d\n",msg,ctr);
}
```

As before, you can use a statement block in the loop if the statements are put in braces:

```
/* FOR Loop Example */
#include <stdio.h>
main()
{
    char *msg;
    int ctr;
```

continued

```
        msg = "This is cycle ";
        for (ctr=1 ; ctr <= 6 ; ctr++ )
              {
              printf("%s %d\n",msg,ctr);
              printf("End of this cycle");
              }
    }
```

Other Variations

As you can imagine, the for construction is much more versatile than the similar statement in most other languages.

- As with most languages, you can increment or decrement the counter and use a step function:

```
for (ctr=10; ctr>0 ; ctr-=2 )
      printf("%d\n",ctr);
```

- You can also use geometrically increasing steps or any legal expression as the third component:

```
for (ctr=1; ctr<10; ctr *= 2)
      printf("%d\n",ctr);
```

- You can use some other variable in the condition test other than the loop variable:

```
oldprice = 3.00;
for (ctr=1; price<10.00; ctr++)
        {
        price = oldprice + ((ctr*oldprice)/10.00);
        printf("%6.2f",price);
        }
```

- You can omit an expression in the statement as long as the loop has some way to terminate. For what *ctr* value, for example, will the following terminate?

```
result = 0;
for (ctr=1,result<10;)
      result = result*ctr;
```

- You can change the step expression dynamically while the loop is executing. For example, assume:

```
temp = 1;
for (ctr=1; ctr<10; ctr= temp*ctr)
    {
    if (ctr>5)
        temp = 2;
    printf("%d\n",ctr);
    }
```

Here, after the first five iterations, the step is changed to a larger value.

Designing with Iterative Control

This chapter described three types of loop control: the *while*, the *do . . . while*, and the *for*. Which construction to use in a given situation depends upon the application. For example, deciding between the *while* and *do . . . while* depends upon when you wish to do the test. In probably about 90% of applications, the *while* is preferred over the *do . . . while*. One reason for this is that with the *while*, the program statements can be skipped if the test fails. With the *do . . . while*, the statements will always be executed at least once.

Exercises

1. Write a program that reverses the digits of a positive integer input number. Hint: The right digit is equal to the number modulo 10. Write it first as a *while* construction, then rewrite it using a *do . . . while* construction.

2. Write a program that displays the sum of the digits of an integer input number.

Answers

1.

WHILE:

```
#include <stdio.h>
main()
{
    int num,right;
```

continued

```
        char numa[10];

        printf("Please enter an integer: ");
        fgets(numa, 10, stdin);
        num = atoi(numa);
        while (num !=0)
            {
            right = num % 10;
            printf("%d",right);
            num = num / 10;
            };
        printf("\n");
    }
```

DO WHILE:

```
    #include <stdio.h>
    main()
    {
        int num,right;
        char numa[10];

        printf("Please enter an integer: ");
        fgets(numa, 10, stdin);
        num = atoi(numa);
        do  {
            right = num % 10;
            printf("%d",right);
            num = num / 10;
            } while (num != 0);
        printf("\n");
    }
```

2.

```
    #include <stdio.h>
    main()
    {
        int num,right, sum=0;
        char numa[10];

        printf("Please enter an integer: ");
        fgets(numa, 10, stdin);
        num = atoi(numa);
```

continued

```
do   {
     right = num % 10;
     sum = right+sum;
     num = num / 10;
     } while (num != 0);
printf("The sum is %d \n",sum);
}
```

8

Using Functions and Macros

When a company builds a complicated machine, like a computer, they don't start from scratch with the raw materials such as silicon, steel, and plastic. They assemble the computer from previously constructed parts, such as the power supply, function boards, and the main circuit board. Each of these parts, in turn, is also quite complicated. They aren't assembled from raw materials, but from still simpler parts such as integrated circuits, resistors, and capacitors.

You can apply the same principle to building computer programs. Instead of trying to build your program from the raw materials offered by a particular programming language, you can build a program out of separately constructed parts. Each of these, in turn, can be built of still simpler parts, until you reach the level of the basic language statements of that particular program. The parts out of which you build programs are called *functions* and *procedures*.

What is more, these functions and procedures have two very desirable properties that are not shared with the example of building a computer. First, using a function does not "use it up." You can use the same function as many times as desired in a program, but the compiler will only add it to the program once. Second, whereas the computer parts must be manufactured before the computer, the functions can be written either before or after the main program is written.

The creation and the use of functions with the C language is one of the most important features of the language.

The Function

Functions relate a dependent variable to one or more independent variables. The variables are said to be the arguments of function. You have already used several functions in your programs. For example, the *printf()* function has the form:

```
printf(format_string,argument1,argument2,arg umentᵢ ... argumentₙ)
```

The arguments are *format__string,argument₁,argument₂ to argumentₙ.*

Although nothing about a return value from this function has been mentioned, the QuickC version does return a value—the number of characters written. You could also write the function as:

```
h = printf(format_string, argument1, argument2, argumentᵢ...argumentₙ)
```

After execution, the variable *h* would then be set to the number of characters sent to the display. The return value is often used to show an error if one occurred during the function execution.

In any program you write, *main( )* is also a function. When the program is started, a hidden routine is initiated. This is the C support start-up module. The hidden routine, in turn, calls the function *main( )*. Like any other function, *main( )* returns a value. As we shall see later, there is also a way for the user to pass values to *main( )*.

The *main( )* function, in turn, can call other functions. Any application program is really a hierarchy of functions, with the hidden routine being topmost. This routine calls *main( )*, which then eventually calls other functions (see Figure 8.1).

Figure 8.1
The Structure of a C Program

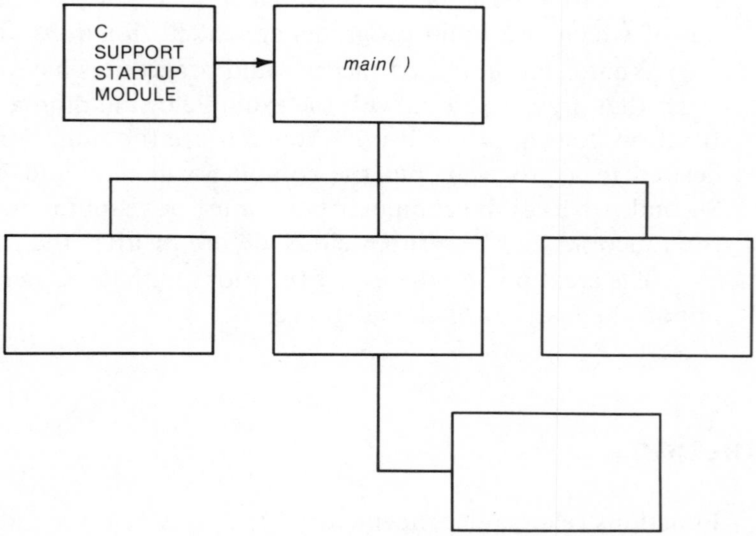

Why Functions Are Important

The basic C language is really a medium-level language; that is, each statement compiles to one or very few lines of code. For this reason C is often called a portable assembly language.

Now if you had to write all your programs in the very basic C language, it would take a long time to write even a simple program. There are many things that you do over and over again in many programs. For example, in almost every program you will do writing and reading. Why write the code for this each time you write a program? That is why almost any C compiler has a *printf( )* function in its library that is ready to do the output work for you.

Types of Functions

There are basically three types of functions you can use: functions in the QuickC library that came with your compiler, commercial functions, and functions you write.

QuickC Functions

The QuickC product includes an extensive library of over 350 functions that you can use for many purposes. These include the basic C functions (such as *printf( )*) that almost any C compiler has as well as some exciting graphic functions that enable you to add graphics to your application. Appendix B contains a summary of this library.

With many of these functions, you need to add a line at the beginning of the program to include one or more files as:

```
#include <stdio.h>
```

This instructs the compiler to look in the include file *stdio.h* file for the definitions needed by the function (such as buffer size, structure definitions, and so forth). The number and names of the include files needed for a particular function depend on the function and are listed for each function in the library manual that came with your QuickC. The include files are simple text files, and you can even create your own include file for the functions you write. The compiler reads include files as a part of the input compiled source code. You can view an include file using the view include command on the QuickC menu.

The left and right arrows show the path the search should use for the file, and that it should omit the current directory and follow the current path. If you use quote marks as:

```
#include "mail.h"
```

this suggests the path the search for the file should begin with the current directory and then follow the current path designation.

Commercial Function Libraries

You can also purchase libraries of functions from various suppliers (such as Lifeboat) that add database management support, various types of menus, and other utilities (see Appendix G).

Writing Your Own Functions

You will find many cases in which you are entering the same lines of code to one program you entered earlier to another program or, even worse, entering the same lines of code several times to the same program. Then, you would want to write your own functions, keeping them in a library, and using them often as routines in your application programs.

Using Functions

Functions save you work. Each function represents several lines of code. Using the same functions in many programs eliminates the necessity of having to add the code to each program you write. In fact, the function does not even have to be written in C. It could be written in any compiler language that is compatible with Microsoft's linker. This includes Microsoft's QuickBASIC, assembly language or even a C compiler from another manufacturer. To some extent, you can mix functions written in several languages, taking advantage of the best of each language.

Note

This is a more ideal concept than practical reality. You probably won't have much trouble mixing object modules from various Microsoft compilers, but use caution in extending this to compilers from other manufacturers. The object module conventions may be compatible.

Functions, then, give you the capability of converting the medium-level C language to a powerful high-level language of your own making. Once this "language" is created, you can build many applications from your creation. As an example, if you like to create object-oriented adventure games, you can create powerful functions to support the objects and actors you use in your games. A good example of this is David Betz's "An Adventure Authoring System" in *Byte* (May, 1987) which was written in C. If you like animation, you can build functions to support this. You can also write database managers, spreadsheets (Lotus 1-2-3 was initially written in C), word processors, or whatever. In each case, the developer created functions that were application-specific.

Finally, functions are an extension of structured programming techniques (see Part III). Functions should have a single entry and exit.

Let's review, then, the advantages of functions:

1. Development time and cost is reduced, as functions already written and debugged are portable to other programs and C compilers.

2. You can create your own high-level language that is application-oriented and can be used for many applications.

3. Functions improve the readability of the program, as each function has a single purpose.

Don't be hesitant, then, to use functions wherever you can in your programs. Build up your own libraries. Purchase those that are relevant to any program you are developing.

This chapter will introduce you to the basics of writing functions. With QuickC, you can also create libraries of functions that you use often and access them automatically on starting QuickC.

Tip

Use as many functions as you can in your program. Check public domain libraries for ones you can use. Purchase ones that are relevant to your applications. Write your own and build your proprietary library.

A Simple Function

Now try your hand at a simple program that uses a function. This is a very simple program that displays a message, initiates a delay, then displays another message:

```
/* Program to test a delay function */
#include <stdio.h>
main()
```

continued

```
    {
        void delay();

        printf("Starting\n");
        delay();
        printf("Ending\n");
    }

/* DELAY function */
void delay()
{
    unsigned int i, j, n;

    n = 1000;
    for (i=0; i<n; i++)
        for (j=0; j<n; j++);
    return;
}
```

This is a very simple example, but it does illustrate some important features of writing any function:

1. The function name is followed by two parentheses. There are no arguments here, but even when no arguments are used the two parentheses must be there. This enables the compiler to distinguish between variables and function names.

2. The function return value is declared in the calling program. If you don't declare it, the return value is assumed *int*. Even if you don't plan to use any return value, it is still a good idea to declare the function. This gives some protection and returns an error message if you use the function improperly. Here, there is no return value, and the function return value is declared as *void*.

3. When the function itself is written, there is no semicolon after the function name. This tells the compiler you are defining the function, not using it. (In the main program, where you are using it, a semicolon follows the function name.)

4. When writing the function, the return value (*void* here) is declared and must match the declared return value of the calling function.

5. The function, like the main program, uses an opening and closing brace.

6. Variables used in the function are defined inside the braces. The variables are local to the function. If a variable by the same name exists outside of the function in the main program or another function, it is not the same variable.

7. Function names follow the same rules as variable names: they must start with a letter or underscore, you can use digits after the first letter, you cannot use spaces in the name, and with QuickC only the first 31 characters are significant.

In this example the function creates a delay with a length defined by the variable *n* in the function. This controls two loops, one inside the other. The total number of loop iterations is n^2.

Now let's take the example one step further by enabling the calling program to define the length of the delay:

```
/* Program to test a delay function */
#include <stdio.h>
main()
{
    void delay();

    printf("Starting\n");
    delay(1000);
    printf("Ending\n");
}


/* DELAY function */
void delay(n)
unsigned int n;
{
    unsigned int i,j;

    for (i=0; i<n; i++)
        for (j=0; j <n; j++);
    return;
}
```

Here, we have added a single argument, and this argument enables a value to be passed to the function to control the length of the delay. The actual value is passed to the variable n in the function. This variable, as before, controls the number of loop iterations.

Note

The argument values in the function are declared before the first brace. Other variables in the function are defined after the first brace.

You could also write this program as:

```
#include <stdio.h>
main()
{
      unsigned int c;
      void delay();

      printf("Starting\n");
      c = 1000;
      delay(c);
      printf("Ending\n");
}
```

Here, the argument variable in the main program enables a value to be passed to the function. The arguments, as you can see in this example, can have different names. Even if they are the same name, they are not the same variable. If the function has more than one argument, the values are passed matching argument for argument (see Figure 8.2). Both the program and the function must have the same number of arguments for the function.

Figure 8.2
Passing Argument Values to a Function

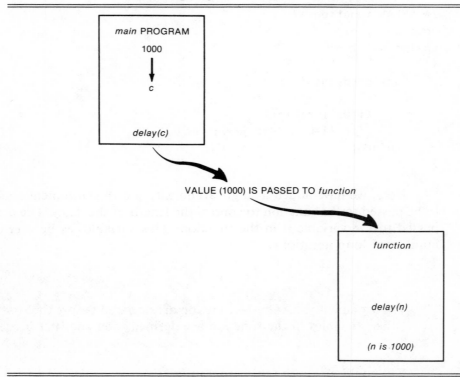

Here is a third way to write the same program:

```c
#include <stdio.h>
main()
{
    void delay();

    printf("Starting\n");
    delay(500*2);
    printf("Ending\n");
}
```

Here, the result of the calculation is passed to the function, not the formula.

Returning Values Using the *return()* statement

Sometimes you are using a function to calculate one or more dependent variables from one or more independent variables. For example, assume we wish to calculate the area of a circle when the radius is known using a function (Figure 8.3).

To do this, the *return* statement is used to return the area value as:

```c
/* CIRCLE function */
#include <math.h>
#include <stdio.h>
main()
{
    double radius, area, circle();
    char radiusa[10];

    printf("Please enter radius: ");
    fgets(radiusa,10,stdin);
    radius = atof(radiusa);
    area = circle(radius);
    printf("The area is %12.4f\n",area);
}

/* function to return area of circle from radius */
#define PI 3.141593
double circle(r)
double r;
{
    double a;
```

continued

```
    a = PI * r * r;
    return(a);
}
```

Figure 8.3
Calculating the Area of a Circle

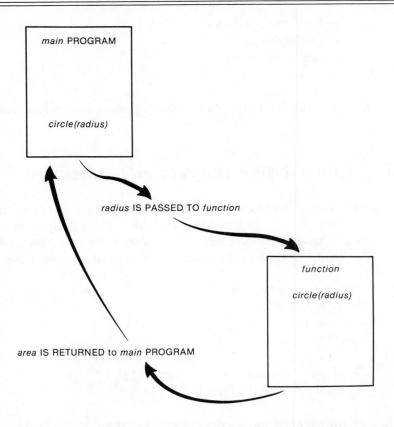

The radius of the circle is passed to the function as an argument. The area is then calculated. The return statement does two things: it terminates the function, and it returns a value to the calling program. Any statements after the return will not be executed. The return statement has the form:

```
return (expression);
```

where *expression* evaluates to a value which is then passed back to the main program. With return, you can only send one value back to the calling program. If there are no values to be passed back, you can use return; to cause a simple termination (see the previous *delay( )* example).

Notice that *circle(r)* must be declared in the *main( )* program. This declaration defines the type of the value that will be returned from the function.

In this example, the variable a is assigned to the returned value. If you fail to declare the return value of the function in the program it is used, the value will be returned as an *int* type.

The *atof( )* function is used in this example to convert the string entered by the user to a floating point number of the double type. When using this function, always be sure to include the *math.h* file.

You could write this same program in a shorter form as:

```
/* Using the CIRCLE function */
#include <math.h>
#include <stdio.h>
main()
{
    double radius, circle();
    char radiusa[10];

    printf("Please enter radius: ");
    fgets(radiusa,10,stdin);
    radius = atof(radiusa);
    printf("The area is %12.4f\n",circle(radius));
}


/* function to return area of circle from radius */
#define PI 3.141593
double circle(r)
double r;
{
    return( PI * r * r;);
}
```

Returning Multiple Values

Now assume the objective is to create a function that will swap two integer values. This is useful with sort programs, which generally do swaps in sorting and must return two values. For this purpose we need the function to be able to accept two input values and return two output values. We might imagine we would pass two integers to the function and two would be returned. This won't work, but let's see why:

```
#include <stdio.h>
main()
```

continued

```
{
     void swap();

     int a,b;
     a = 3;
     b = 5;
     swap(a,b);
     printf("%d %d",a,b);
}
void swap(a,b)
int a,b;
{
     int c;
     c = a;
     a = b;
     b = c;
   return;
}
```

This looks like a typical subroutine in any language, but if you try it, you will find it doesn't work. This is a very easy mistake to make, and the problem is simple—a function doesn't change any variable in the main program if a variable value is passed to the function from the main program. The variable in the main program remains unaltered. If you want to change a variable in the main program, you must pass the *address* of the variable as an argument to the function, not the variable. Use this address to access the value and change it.

In this example remember that the *a* and *b* in the function are not the same as the *a* and *b* in the main program. The function doesn't do anything to the values of *a* and *b* in the main program.

You can get this program to work so that you can modify the variables in the main program by changing it so it will pass the *addresses* of the variables instead of the variable values:

```
/* SWAP  to swap two integers */
#include <stdio.h>
main()
{
     int x,y;
     void swap();

     x = 3;
     y = 5;
     swap(&x,&y);
     printf("x now equals %d, y now equals %d\n",x,y);            continued
```

```
}
/* the swap function */
void swap(x1,x2)
int *x1,*x2;
{
    int temp;
    temp = *x1;
    *x1 = *x2;
    *x2 = temp;
    return;
}
```

Now the addresses (integer pointers) of the variables to swap are passed to the function as *&x* and *&y*. This means that x1 and x2 in the function are integer pointers, or the pointers to the addresses of the variables to swap. A variable temp is used to hold one of the values. The asterisk operator is used to recover the actual values, which are then swapped.

Here is a brief generalization of the use of the *&* and *** operators for this purpose:

```
&foo is the address of variable foo.
pointer_foo is &foo
*pointer_foo is the value stored at &foo, or foo.
```

This example illustrates how you can return two or more values from a function. For example, you could write a program that returns the square, cube, and fourth power of a number as:

```
/* returns the first four powers of a number */
#include <stdio.h>
main()
{
    int number,square,cube,quad;
    char numbera[10];
    void power();

    printf("Please enter an input number: ");
    fgets(numbera,10,stdin);
    number = atoi(numbera);
    power(&number,&square,&cube,&quad);
    printf("%d squared is %d\n",number,square);
    printf("%d cubed is %d\n",number,cube);
    printf("%d to the fourth power is %d\n",number,quad);
}
/* the power function */
```

continued

```
void power(no,sq,cu,qu)
    int *no, *sq, *cu, *qu;

{
    *sq =  *no * *no;
    *cu = *no * *sq;
    *qu = *no * *cu;
    return;
}
```

In this example the function is called with a pointer to the number. The function calculates the powers and returns the pointers to the second, third, and fourth powers as the remaining arguments.

Recursion

C permits you, if you wish, to define a function partially in terms of itself. A function is said to be recursive if it is defined in terms of itself, or calls itself.

The most common example is the use of recursion to create a factorial function. In particular, the function *factorial(n)* should return the product of all integers 1 through *n*. More specifically:

```
factorial(1) = 1
factorial(2) = 2
factorial(3) = 6
factorial(4) = 24
```

and

```
factorial(n) = n!
```

This can be written in a QuickC program as:

```
/* FACTOR - Program to compute the factorial of a number */
#include <stdio.h>
main()
{
    unsigned factorial();
    unsigned  x,y;
    char numbera[10];

    printf("Please enter input number: ");
    fgets(numbera,10,stdin);
    x = atoi(numbera);
```

continued

```
        y = factorial(x);
        printf("The factorial of %u is %u\n",x,y);
        exit(0);
}


unsigned factorial(n)
unsigned n;
{
        if (n <= 1)
             return(1);
        else
             return(n * factorial(n-1));
}
```

The example shows the *factorial(n)* function with a *main( )* program to test the function. The *factorial(n)* function calls a copy of itself, which in turn calls a copy of itself until it is called with the value 1 (Figure 8.4).

In recursive calls, the program does not call itself, but a copy of itself. The program winds down until a specified condition is met (n=1 in this example), and then unwinds through each invocation again. There must be a terminating condition or the program will call indefinitely.

Here are some general program design rules with recursion:

1. Recursion improves the efficiency of some types of programs (as the last example), but does make the program difficult to read and understand. Use sparingly.

2. Make the recursive function do its work on the way down, not on the way up; that is, avoid the use of statements in the function after the recursive call.

3. Minimize variables and complex structures in the function.

Command Line Arguments

As the primary program module *main( )* is also a function, you might expect to be able to pass argument values to the main function in starting the program. QuickC provides a method of doing this by using two arguments with the call *argc* and *argv*. For example, the following will work to pass one command line argument to the program:

```
#include <stdio.h>
main(argc, argv)
int argc;
char *argv[];
```

continued

Figure 8.4
Using Recursion

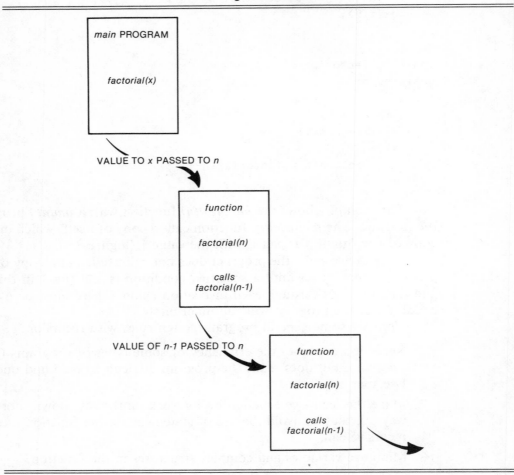

```
        {
        int rflag = 0;
        int     debugflg=0;

        while (--argc > 0)
            {
            ++argv;
            if (**argv != '-')
                break;
            switch(argv[0][1])
                {
                case 'r' :
                    ++rflag;
```

continued

```
                    continue;
            case 'd' :
                    ++debugflg;
                    continue;
            default :
                    printf("unknown flag: %c\n",argv[0][1]);
                    continue;
            }
        }
    }
```

The *argc* argument defines the argument count, and *argv* is an array of pointers to the argument values. Now you can initiate a restore function from an adventure program in QuickC as:

```
C:\adv -r
```

Using Macros

In C, procedures can be written either as functions or macros. If the procedure is simple, it can be defined by a *#define* statement instead of writing it as a function and used in this way. For example, here is a macro that returns the cube of a number:

```
/* MACRO definition */
#include <stdio.h>
#define CUBE(a)  ((a) * (a) * (a))
main()
{
    int no,y;
    char noa[10];

    printf("Please enter an input number: ");
    fgets(noa,10,stdin);
    no = atoi(noa);
    y = CUBE(no);
    printf("The cube of %d is %d.\n",no,y);
}
```

When this program is compiled, the formula defined in the *#define* statement is substituted in the program for *CUBE(no)*. This calculates the cube, which is then displayed.

> **Note**
>
> In defining a macro, be sure the case of the function name in the program matches that in the *#define* statement.

Macros Versus Functions

When should macros be used, and when should you create a function instead? Here are two primary considerations:

- Macros are faster than functions to execute. Whenever a function is used, it must be called each time it is executed. Values or addresses must be passed to the function and values returned. Macros, in contrast, are program code substitutions.

- Functions can reduce the length of the program. When the program is compiled, whatever is in the *#define* statement is substituted at compile time for each instance. There is no call to any function, with the overhead with saving the return address on a stack. Macros, however, are at a disadvantage if the same macro is used several times in the program. Then, the *#define* statement will cause the program to be expanded for the substitution each time the macro is used, resulting in a larger program. In contrast, functions are only added once to the program.

Macros are also better for short routines that can be put on a single line. You can put a long routine in a macro, but it will be difficult to read and understand.

You cannot use pointers as arguments with macros, but they can be used to support multiple return values.

Macros do have some good points, however. You can use them with any type of argument. They only define a substitution, and do not have type-specific arguments. You can use the same macro with *char, int, short,* or *long* data types. This makes them particularly useful if you need to use the same procedure with different types of arguments.

Keeping this in mind, let's return to the *getchar( )* and *putchar( )* routines used in Chapter 4. As mentioned in that chapter, these are defined as macros in the *stdio.h* file that came with QuickC. If you examine this file, you will find:

```
#define getchar() getc(stdin)
#define putchar(c) putc(c),stdout)
```

This means you use them as macros. It you wish to use them as functions, QuickC provides the *fgetchar( )* and *fputchar(c)* functions which are identical to *getchar( )* and *putchar(c)* respectively, but operate as functions. You may use either in your program. In using either the macro or function versions you must include the *stdio.h* file in the program. You can include the definitions needed for your macros that you write as a part of an include file at the beginning of your program. In the mailing list program of Part III of this book, you will see an example of this.

Types of Macros

There are three basic types of macros: expression macros, definition macros, and function macros. The following program shows an example of each:

```
#include <stdio.h>
#define TWELVE 12
#define PRINTX(x)  printf("The answer is %d\n",x)
#define CUBE(y) ((y)*(y)*(y))
main()
{
    int x, y, z;
    x = TWELVE;
    z = CUBE(x);
    PRINTX(z);
}
```

The second *#define* in this program defines a function macro. This is a routine that emulates a function. The function macro returns a single output value for given input values. Remember, however, that it does not behave like a true function (see Table 8.1). Unlike a function, there are no calculations, only substitutions. A function call passes the value of the argument to the function during program execution. A macro call does only substitution during the compile process.

Table 8.1
Macros Versus Functions

Macros	Functions
Faster than functions.	Slower than macros.
Generic and can accept multiple types	Can accept only a single data type.
Expands a program each time it is used	Expands a program only once, even when used many times.
Can have side effects	No side effects
Does not support recursion	Supports recursion

Table 8.1 (cont.)

Macros	Functions
Difficult to debug	Easy to debug
Not modular or hierarchical	Modular and hierarchical
Returns a single value	Can return multiple values
Flexibility for expression or statement substitution	No expression or statement substitution.
Expands program each time it is invoked	Expands program only a single time, regardless of the number of times invoked.

There are two other types of macros that also prove useful. The first #*define* shown, the definitional macro, equates a variable name to a value. Wherever the variable name occurs in the program, the compiler substitutes the value. The third #*define* creates an expression macro. In this case, a frequently used expression is reduced to a single variable name. None of the macros end with a semicolon.

Tips for Using Macros

Here are a few tips in the use of macros:

- You can use substitutions within substitutions; that is, you can expand a term in a definition with another term:

```
#define TWELVE 12
#define ACE(x) (TWELVE * (x))

main()
{
    int x,y;
    x = 4;
    y = ACE(x);
    printf("%d",y);
}
```

This is dangerous, however, and should be avoided unless necessary. The results are unpredictable.

- Keep the macros in include files and use an #*include* directive to add them to the program.
- You can create a macro that is longer than one line by using the backslash operator at the end of the line to show a continuation. You can also use curly braces, putting each statement of the macro on a separate

line and ending each with a semicolon. As a general rule, however, keep your macros to a single line.

- Avoid recursion in macros.

Exercises

1. List the functions you used in the first six chapters. Why are they functions?
2. Write a swap function to switch two floating point values.
3. Write a function that will return the cube of an input value.
4. What is the maximum input value that can be used in the factorial recursion example shown? Why? Can you modify it to work with larger input values?
5. What are three advantages of using functions (over macros)?
6. What is an example of a function that has no input or output?

Answers

1. *printf( ), fgets( ), scanf( ), power( ), puts( ), gets( ), getchar( ), putchar( ), getche( ), getch( ).*

2.

```
/* SWAP  to swap two float */
main()
{
     float x,y;
     void swap();

     x = 3.0;
     y = 5.0;
     swap(&x,&y);
     printf("x now equals %f, y now equals %f\n",x,y);
}
/* the swap function */
void swap(x1,x2)
float *x1,*x2;

{
     float temp;
     temp = *x1;
     *x1 = *x2;
     *x2 = temp;
```

continued

```
        return;
    }
```

3.

```
main()
{
      int in;
      int cube();
      char ina[10];

      printf("Please enter a number: ");
      fgets(ina,10,stdin);
      in = atoi(ina);
      printf("The cube is %d\n",cube(in));
}
int cube(x)
int x;
{
      return(x*x*x);
}
```

4. The minimum input value is 8. To modify for higher values:

```
/* FACTOR - Program to compute the factorial of a number */
main()
{
      long factorial();
      long x;
      long y;
      char xa[10];

      printf("Please enter input number: ");
      fgets(xa,10,stdin);
      x = atol(xa);
      y = factorial(x);
      printf("The factorial of %ld is %ld\n",x,y);
      exit(0);
}

long factorial(n)
long n;
{
if (n <= 1)
```

continued

```
        return(1);
    else
        return(n * factorial(n-1));
}
```

5. a. They support modular programming (macros do not).

    b. Functions use less memory than macros if used several times in a program.

    c. Functions permit keeping function variables separate from the main program.

    d. Debugging is simplified, reducing development time.

6. The first delay function in this chapter has no input or output.

9

Managing the Storage of Variables

QuickC provides great flexibility in controlling how variables are used. It is the programmer who manages how variables are used, not the language. This puts more power at the hand of the programmer, but also requires knowledge of the programmer about how to use this power. This chapter will introduce you to the basic ideas of managing the storage of variables. You will also learn more special variable types and other variable management techniques.

You have already learned two attributes of a variable: type and value. To identify the type of variable, you use a declaration statement. Variables are given values by the process of assignment, either in the declaration statement or in the body of the program. Now let's look at a third attribute of a variable: its *storage class*.

Storage Classes

Variables you have used in the first eight chapters were local; that is, known only to the functions containing them. In Chapter 8, for example, you used a function to return multiple values. In doing this, you had to use pointers, as the value could not be passed back as an argument. If the main program had a variable named *cube* and the function had a variable named *cube*, they were two separate variables to the program.

There is a way, however, to make a variable common to both the main program and the functions. You can do this by using a different storage class for the variable; that is, making the variable global. A global variable is a variable known to several functions. You can create global variables by declaring the variable before the main program, then using the *extern* keyword as a part of the variable declaration in each function in which it is used. The program then becomes:

```
/* returns the first four powers of a number */
#include <stdio.h>
int number, square, cube, quad;
main()
{
    extern int number, square, cube, quad;

    void power();
    char numbera[10];

    printf("Please enter an input number: ");
    fgets(numbera,10,stdin);
    number = atoi(numbera);
    power();
    printf("%d squared is %d\n",number,square);
    printf("%d cubed is %d\n",number,cube);
    printf("%d to the fourth power is %d\n",number,quad);
}
/* the power function */
power()
{
    extern int number, square, cube, quad;
    square =  number * number;
    cube = number * square;
    quad = cube * number;
    return;
}
```

Notice that the function no longer has any arguments, nor are they needed. There is no returned value or address. Four global variables are defined before the main program. These are used by both the main program and the function. The *extern* keyword in the main program and function references the global variables. Declaring the variable external to the functions using it and using the *extern* keyword to reference the function changes the storage class of the variable, a third attribute of every variable you use. The storage class of a variable defines its scope (the availability of the variable to other functions) and how long the variable remains in memory. As this example shows, it opens a real opportunity. There are, however, also hidden dangers of declaring a variable this way. This chapter will help you see both the benefits and dangers of sharing variables between functions and illustrate how it is done.

Every variable has a storage class, whether or not it is declared explicitly. C provides four storage classes for variables: automatic, external, static, and register. The class for a variable is defined when you declare it. If you do not declare it explicitly, the class defaults to automatic. All the programs in the first eight chapters used automatic variables. Now let's look at each of the four storage classes.

Automatic

Automatic is the default storage class for a variable. If you omit any keyword for the storage class, the storage class is assumed as automatic. You can also specifically define the storage class using the auto keyword.

```
#include <stdio.h>
main()
{
    auto int x, y, z;

    x = 3;
    y = 4;
    z = x + y;
    printf("The sum is %d",z);
}
```

Any variable declared as automatic is only available to the statements in the function of which it is a part. The variable is not available to any functions called by the function or to any statements outside of the defining function. If the same name is used in another function, it is assumed as a different variable and has a different memory location.

The scope of an automatic variable is local to the function of which it is a part. The variable is declared immediately after the opening brace of the function. The variable comes into existence when the function is called. When the function returns control to the calling program, the variable ceases to exist and no longer takes memory space. An automatic variable in the *main()* procedure, for example, becomes active when the procedure is started. It is not available in any called function, but is still active when the function returns control to the *main()* procedure. Since an automatic variable only uses memory space when its function is active, using automatic variables saves memory space.

External Variables

Global variables are variables available to all functions and modules of a program. Semiglobal variables are variables used by two or more modules or functions. You can create global or semiglobal variables by defining them outside of the first routine that uses them and then using the *extern* keyword in any subsequent modules and functions that use the variables to refer to the global definitions.

```
#include <stdio.h>
int x=3, y=4;
main()
{
    extern int x,y;
    int z

    z = x + y;
    printf("The sum is %d",z);
}
```

It is not necessary to use the *extern* keyword if the variables are used in the same file as the declaration and in the function immediately following the declaration. For example, in the previous case the keyword is not needed. It is still a good idea, however, to include the keyword to improve the readability of the program.

In this example variable is declared before the *main()* procedure. You can also initialize it now if you wish. The *extern* reference in the main program or any subsequent functions does not declare the variable again, but simply tells the compiler to use the variable that was previously declared with its present value. A statement with an *extern* keyword always refers to a previous declaration.

Use external variables for global values that you use in your programs. For example, if your company name is displayed on several screens, it could be put in a global variable and used for the entire program. In the same way, the default drive to use could be stored as a global variable.

One word of warning: use global values with caution (see later in this chapter). They are gluttons for computer memory, they do not make functions portable, and programs with a lot of global values are difficult to debug because so many of the modules can affect the variable.

Using external variables raises some real dangers that can trap the unwary programmer. For example, suppose you wrote the previous example as:

```
/* Don't do it this way */
#include <stdio.h>
short number, square, cube, quad;
main()
{
    extern int number, square, cube, quad;
    ⋮
```

The variables are declared globally as short, and then accessed within the function using the *extern* keyword as *int*. The results are unpredictable and will vary with the compiler. As a first step to preventing this type of problem, declare all globals in one place, and that should be in the include file. In this file, a comment statement should label them as globals. An even better idea is described later in Chapter 16.

Static Variables

The static variable is a variable that doesn't disappear when the function returns control to the calling program. The scope is the same as with an automatic variable; that is, the variable is local only to the block of which it is a part. The difference is that when the function returns, the variable value is not lost and is available if the function is called again. Let's look at an example to clarify this:

```
/* AUTO variable test */
#include <stdio.h>
main()
{
     int ctr;

     void counter();

     for (ctr=0;ctr<5;ctr++)
          counter();
}
void counter()
{
     static int y = 1;
     int x=1;
     printf("x = %d   y = %d\n",x,y);
     x = x +1;
     y = y + 1;
     return;
}
```

If you try this little example, you will get the following output:

x = 1 y = 1
x = 1 y = 2
x = 1 y = 3
x = 1 y = 4
x = 1 y = 5

In this example the function counter is called five times from the main program. The variable *x* is an automatic variable, its value (and the storage area for the variable) is lost each time the function returns to the main program. The variable *y* is a static variable. When the function returns, the value of *y* remains set to the previous value and is not reset by the declaration statement. The function does not release the memory space for the *y* variable on exiting the program. Both *x* and *y* are local only to the function in which they are used. All static variables have memory allocated to them as long as the program is running.

You can make a static variable global by putting it before the function in which it is used and using the *extern* keyword in the functions to refer to it:

```
/* AUTO variable test */
#include <stdio.h>
main()
{
     int ctr;

     void counter();

     for (ctr=0; ctr<5; ctr++)
          counter();
}
static int y = 1;
void counter()
{
     extern static int y;
     int x=1;
     printf("x = %d   y = %d\n",x,y);
     x = x +1;
     y = y + 1;
     return;
}
```

Register Variables

The computer processor chip has several internal registers that can be used for temporary storage. These are useful sometimes because accessing a register to get a variable value is much faster than trying to access a memory location for a variable value. Use register variables when the variable will be accessed often. Register variables are particularly useful for loop counters:

```
#include <stdio.h>
main()
{
     register int ctr;
```

continued

```
    void counter();

    for (ctr=0; ctr<5; ctr++)
        counter();
}
```

In using register variables, you are making a request that may be fulfilled. A register will only be used if one is available. If no register is available at the time, the variable reverts to an automatic variable.

Register variables can only be used for *char, short,* and *int* data. They cannot be used with *long, float*, or *double* as a register is only 16 bits (2 bytes) in size.

Special Data Types

C provides several special data types that are useful for many applications.

The enum *Type*

The *enum* keyword can be used to define a list of valid values for an identifier. For example:

```
enum flag {true,false};
enum flag delete_flag, update_flag;
```

Two statements are used. The first declares the variable type *enum* flag as one that can have one of two values: *true* or *false*. Note that enum flag is not a variable, but variable type. The second statement assigns the two variables *delete_flag* and *update_flag* as *enum* flag type.

Here is another variation:

```
enum days {sun,mon,tue,wed,thu,fri,sat};
enum      days       today;
```

Here *enum* days is a variable type that can have any one of seven values—the days of the week. The second statement declares today to be of that type.

Here is an example of using the *enum* keyword:

```
#include <stdio.h>
main()
{
    enum month {jan,feb,mar,apr,may,jun,jul,
```

continued

```
        aug,sep,oct,nov,dec} ;
    enum month now_month;

    now_month = jun;
    printf("The present month number is %d.\n",now_month);
}
```

This declares the variable *now_month* to be of the *enum month* type, which can have any of twelve values. Internally, C tracks the list with an integer value assigned to each item, which means the *enum month* variable must be printed with *%d*.

If you try this example, you will get:

```
The present month number is 5.
```

which is not correct (it should be 6). The reason is that C starts the list numbering from zero, so *jan* is assigned the value of 0. You can, however, reassign any or all values. To get this program to work, simply reassign the first month:

```
#include <stdio.h>
main()
{
    enum month {jan=1, feb, mar, apr, may, jun, jul,
        aug, sept, oct, nov, dec} ;
    enum month now_month;

    now_month = jun;
    printf("The present month number is %d.\n",now_month);
}
```

You can only use integer values for assignments, but the use of both negative and positive integers is permitted. You can put assignments on multiple list values, and unassigned list items are numbered sequentially from the last assigned list item. (These assignment rules vary with compilers and are not too portable.)

The use of the *enum* keyword is somewhat limited, as QuickC still assumes the variable to be an integer value. The *enum* keyword also has limited portability. Some C compilers will not permit arithmetic expressions with *enum*-declared variables. The primary advantage is that the program is more readable. For example, you might have a menu structure and switch on any of several *enum* variable values. You can also use them in logic decisions to improve readability:

```
enum available_colors {blue,green,red};
enum available_colors color;

color = red;
if (color == red)
    printf("You picked red, one of the available colors.\n");
```

The void *Keyword*

Good programming style requires that the programmer always define type of variable returned from a function, even when nothing is being returned. For example, from Chapter 8 the short program that returns the powers could better be written as:

```
#include <stdio.h>
main()
{
    void power();
    int number,square,cube,quad;
    char numbera[10];

    printf("Please enter an input number: ");
    fgets(numbera,10,stdin);
    number = atoi(numbera);
    power(&number,&square,&cube,&quad);
    printf("%d squared is %d\n",number,square);
    printf("%d cubed is %d\n",number,cube);
    printf("%d to the fourth power is %d\n",number,quad);
}

/* the power function */
    void power(no,sq,cu,qu)
    int *no, *sq, *cu, *qu;

{
    *sq =  *no * *no;
    *cu = *no * *sq;
    *qu = *no * *cu;
    return;
}
```

This tells the user immediately that no return value is expected.

Modifiers

C provides certain modifiers that can also be used in a declaration. These are not really types, but modify other types.

If a variable could be modified from outside the program, it should also be declared with the *volatile* modifier. This will prevent the compiler from doing certain optimizing that could do strange things with the data. Variables used for modem and clock data are typical candidates for this modifier.

Variables that cannot change during program execution can be locked to a value with the *const* modifier. The attempt to hold a variable constant may seem a contradiction, but it is really a protection for the programmer against unintentional program execution modifying something that shouldn't get modified. The best candidates here are arrays. As you will see in the next chapter, you cannot pass array values to a function, only the address of any array. Array functions, then, modify the original array data.

For example, suppose you were creating a function that writes an error message, with a pointer to the message string passed to the function. You could then begin your function as:

```
int errmsg(string)
const char *string
{
    ⋮
```

Here, *string* is a pointer to an array of characters. Now the *errmsg( )* function can use *string*, but cannot alter it.

Symbolic Data Types

If you have a complex data declaration that is used several times for several variables, it is often better to define it with a symbolic name and use the name to declare each variable. You can assign a symbolic name to a declaration by using the *typedef* keyword:

```
typedef int CTR;
CTR i, j, k;
```

In this example the word CTR is defined as *int*. This symbolic declaration can then be used in subsequent variable declarations. As an example, suppose you planned to declare your integers *int*, but later wanted to change all of them to a *short* type. This would be easy if you created a *CTR* type and used it to declare your integers. Then, by changing the one *typedef* statement, you could switch all your integers from *int* to *short*.

We could also have done this with a define statement:

```
#define CTR int
```

The *typedef* keyword, however, is more powerful than a *#define* statement concerning variables. For example, you could define a string type as:

```
typedef    char         STRING[81];
STRING                  last, first, address, city, state;
```

This has the same effect as:

```
char last[81], first[81], address[81], city[81], state[81];
```

Here, you could not have used the *#define* statement to create an equivalent. You are not defining a new variable type, only a new name for a variable type that already exists. Unlike a *#define* statement (which is processed before compiling by a preprocessor), the *typedef* statement is processed during the compiling.

Here is a similar application:

```
typedef char     *STRING;
STRING            last, first, address, city, state, buffer;
```

Again, this could not be done with a *#define* statement. Another application is for the assigning of a name to a complex data structure that will be used for several variables (see Chapter 11). The structure is defined once, given a name, and then used to declare several variables.

In using symbolic names, remember the following rules:

1. Put the symbolic name in capital letters to distinguish it from other variables.

```
typedef CTR      int;
```

2. Use the *typedef* statement as you would a declaration—put it inside the function for local variables, outside for global variables.

```
test()
{
     typedef CTR      int;
     CTR              counter;
     :
     :
}
```

3. You cannot define the storage class of a variable with a *typedef* statement.

4. Use the *typedef* keyword to improve readability and to reduce the need for multiple entry of complex declarations.

Stack Management

Automatic variables are kept on a stack. A stack is a continuous series of memory locations that function much like a stack of cafeteria trays. The last piece of data pushed on the stack is always the first off when the stack is popped. Global variables, in contrast, are stored in a separate data segment area. Knowing how the stack works is important for efficient C programming. When a function is called, the stack is used to save the return point in the calling program and the arguments for the function. As local variables are declared, they are pushed to the stack. Once the function has finished its work, the local variables are lost (freeing up stack space) and the return address is used to get back to place in the calling program from where the function was called. Using automatic variables keeps the variables local and conserves memory, as they only need storage while the function is active.

Techniques for Managing Variables

The golden rule of managing variables is to keep the scope as small as possible. The temptation is to use global variables and external references to pass values to and from a function. This gives the appearance of simplifying the program, as in the first example of this chapter. This appearance, however, is deceiving. The function then becomes locked to special variable names and a single program, and is no longer portable to other C programs you may develop.

If you are using a global variable, sometimes it is only necessary to use it for two or three functions. Then, you can define the variable before the first function in which it is used, keeping it semiglobal. (This only works if the function group using the variable is compiled as a group.) A good example of this is a set of two or three modules that work together as a single function. Then, you could create semiglobal values that are shared by the functions, yet the unit acts as a single function with complete portability. Values and addresses are passed to and from the unit using arguments.

Avoid *overloading* and *superseding* of variables. Overloading refers to the practice of using one variable for several purposes, such as a single variable x over and over again for various purposes. Its meaning at any one time depends on the context of the program.

Superseding refers to the redeclaring of a variable. The new declaration supersedes the original. For example, a variable defined as global might be temporarily redefined as automatic. The results are unpredictable, and vary with the compiler. The result is a loss of portability if the program works at all.

Table 9.1 shows a summary of the four storage classes. Here are some good general rules:

1. Keep the scope of your variables as small as possible. Pass values and addresses with arguments and return values, not by using global

variables. This keeps your functions portable and you can use them in other programs. It also simplifies debugging.

2. Don't use the same variable name for two different variables. If *square* is used as an auto variable in the main program, don't use the same name for an auto variable in a function. If you need to use a similar variable locally, use a consistent naming convention as:

counter   global variable

l_counter   local variable

3. Don't initialize a variable unless necessary. For example, it is not necessary to initialize a *for . . . else* loop counter, as the *for . . . else* construct initializes the counter.l_counter.

```
/* Don't do this */
int ctr = 0;

for (ctr = 0; ctr <10; ctr++)
:
```

4. Put global variables in the include file and label them as such.

5. In declaring a static array, you can omit value for the array size if you initialize it.

For example, instead of:

```
static char msg[16] = "Hello out there";
```

use:

```
static char msg[] = "Hello out there";
```

This saves you the need to count the characters.

6. Use register variables for loop counters.

7. Avoid superseding a declaration. Do not redeclare a variable you have already declared. Note: the *extern* keyword does not redeclare a variable, but only references a variable already declared.

8. Avoid overloading, or trying to minimize variables by using a variable name for multiple purposes.

9. Keep declarations at the beginning of the block in which they are used.

10. References to external variables in a function should be before local declarations.

Table 9.1
Storage Class Summary

Storage Class	Keyword	Duration	Scope
automatic	auto	temporary	local
external	extern	permanent	global
static	static	permanent	local
static	external static	permanent	global
register	register	temporary	local

More on Typing

QuickC provides the user with a large amount of flexibility in declaring variables, but it is up to the user to take advantage of it properly. This chapter contained only the basics of declaring variables. The next two chapters will describe the typing of arrays and special data structures.

Exercises

1. Examine the following program:

```
#include <stdio.h>
main()
{
        enum av_colors {blue,green,red};
        enum av_colors color;
        char colora[10];

        printf("Please enter a color: ");
        fgets(colora,10,stdin);
        color = atoi(colora);
        if (color == red)
                printf("You picked the red color");
}
```

    a. What data do you need to enter to get the text answer message?

    b. What happens with QuickC if you enter an illegal value?

2. Why would you use each of the following data types?

    a. *enum*

b. *typedef*

c. *void*

Answers

1. a. You need to enter the value 2.

   b. There is no output message. Illegal *enum* values are not trapped.

2. *enum*—to improve readability

   typedef—to simply multiple declarations of complex variables. Also improves readability.

   void—to declare a function with no return value.

10

Arrays and Pointers

For many types of applications, you wish to store a list or table of data in memory. The computer can then refer to any item of the list quickly.

A good application of this is the problem of printing addresses by zip code. The addresses may be stored in a random order on the disk, but it would be quite time-consuming to sort the disk addresses to the new order. Using an array, you print the addresses in zip code order quickly:

- Concatenate each record's zip code and its corresponding record number and store these to an array (Figure 10.1).
- Sort the array, which would put the array items in zip code order.

You could then use the sorted array to retrieve the addresses in zip code order: examine each array item in turn, strip off the record number, and then use this record number to retrieve the address from the disk for printing.

Arrays and QuickC

An array is a special type of data structure, a method of organizing data. A QuickC *array* is a variable that holds multiple values in an ordered sequence. The values are called the *elements*, and must all be of the same data type. Whenever *iterative* structures are used, arrays are often used with them.

Arrays offer the advantage of quick access to specific data. The reason for this is that the subscript in the array variable name is used to identify the element to which you are referring. Let's look at an example. You have already used one type of array:

```
#include <stdio.h>
main()
{
```

continued

```
char msg[40] = "This is a test.\n";

printf("%s",msg);
}
```

Figure 10.1
Using an Array for Ordering Addresses

		FILE		
ARRAY	#	Record		
[4] [10027]	1	Bill	Baker	20783
[3] [10471]	2	Charleen	Brown	99701
[1] [20783]	3	Jack	DeWitt	10471
[5] [60604]	4	Carl	Lemmon	10027
[6] [92049]	5	Barry	Linter	60604
[2] [99701]	6	Sue	Able	92045

In this example *msg* is declared as an array of 40 characters. In declaring it, you are defining the type of each element of the array (*char*) and the length of the array. All elements of the array must be of the same type. The array, like any variable, also has a storage class. Then it defaults to automatic. The brackets in the declaration identify it as an array, and the number within the brackets (40) shows the size of the array.

In the body of the program, you can use the brackets with a subscript to refer to any element of any array. In the previous example, the fourth element of the array is the character *s*. The subscript number always starts from zero in C so:

```
msg[0] = "T"
msg[1] = "h"
msg[2] = "i"
msg[3] = "s"
```

This makes it easy to locate any element of the array quickly.

In the same way, you can create an array of integers, real numbers, or any other type of data structure:

```
int        partno[25];
float      price[25];
```

Here, an integer array of 25 part numbers is defined and is a floating point array of 25 prices. You must use a constant to declare the array. You cannot declare the size of the array with an expression containing a variable (you can, however, use a constant expression). Arrays can be of a single dimension (as shown here) or, as we shall see later in this chapter, multidimensional. Here are a few examples:

```
#define ANYSIZE 100
int illegalsize;
int myint[100];          /* OK */
int myint[ANYSIZE]       /* OK */
int yourint[illegalsize] /* not ok */
```

Initializing Arrays

In declaring variables, you discovered you could initialize the variable when it was declared as:

```
int flag = 1;
```

You can do the same with arrays *only* if the array is static or declared externally. For example, here is a simple program to calculate the mean of a group of numbers using a static array:

```
#include <stdio.h>
main()
{
    static float values[]={12.0,6.0,7.0,3.0,15.0,10.0,18.0,5.0};
    int index, size;
    float sum, temp;
    float mean;

    sum = 0.0;
    size = sizeof(values /(sizeof (float)) ;
    for (index=0; index < size; index++)
        sum += values[index];
    printf("The mean is %f\n", sum/size);
}
```

The array is declared as *static float* and initialized. Notice that the initial values are placed between braces. The number of array elements is calculated by dividing the size of the array by the size of each element of the array. To obtain the mean the elements are summed, then divided by the array size.

Here is the same program with the array declared externally:

```
#include <stdio.h>
float values[]={12.0,6.0,7.0,3.0,15.0,10.0,18.0,5.0};
main()
{
      extern float values[];
      int index, size;
      float sum, temp;
      float mean;

      sum = 0.0;
      size = 8;
      for (index=0; index < size; index[+]+)
            sum += values[index];
      printf("The mean is %f\n", sum/size);
}
```

In either case, the array variables remain in memory occupying memory space during the entire execution of the program. Moreover, as we shall see later, if you call a function that operates on an array (such as a function to print a character string), you must pass the address of the array to the function rather than the value. With most functions you pass a copy of the data, which is used by the function. With arrays, you are passing the address of the array and the function operates on the data itself.

Arrays of class automatic are created out of stack space and are not cleared to zero on starting. For this reason, you should always initialize any automatic class arrays. Arrays that are declared static or external are cleared by the C runtime start-up code.

Another way to initialize a local array is to use the *memset( )* function. For example:

```
char first[25+1];
memset(first,'\0',sizeof(first));
```

Inputting to an Array

Now suppose we wish to enter data to an array that has been previously defined. This could be done for the previous example as:

```
#include <math.h>
#include <stdio.h>
#define MAXSIZE 20
```

continued

```
main()
{
    double values[MAXSIZE];
    int index = 0, size;
    double sum = 0.0;
    char inputa[10];

    do {
        printf("Please enter a number: ");
        fgets(inputa,10,stdin);
        values[index] = atof(inputa);
        } while (values[index++] != 0.0);
    size = index - 1;
    for (index=0; index < size; index++)
        sum += values[index];
    printf("The mean is %f\n", sum/size);
}
```

The maximum size of the array here is defined using a *#define* statement. The array is declared automatic (it can be declared automatic since it is not initialized). The values are entered with a *do . . . while* loop. The array will permit the entry of any number of values up to the maximum (20 in this example), so some means must be provided to determine when all input values have been entered. Then, the entry of zero terminates the entry. C also does not check to see if the maximum size of the array has been exceeded (20 here). For most programs, you should check the number of entries and be sure the maximum array size is not exceeded.

Pointers and Arrays

The use of arrays requires expertise in the understanding of how C uses pointers. For the moment, remember that the following is true in C:

```
*foo refers to the data stored at address foo.
&foobar refers to the address of foobar.
```

The array name represents a pointer to the first element of an array; that is, the address of the first pointer. You can then say that:

```
foo == &foo[0]
```

Now let's look at an array example using pointers:

```
/* ARRAYPTR Array pointer demonstration */
#include <stdio.h>
main()
{
    int     partno[4], *pts, index;
    float       price[4], *ptf;

    pts = partno;
    ptf = price;
    for (index = 0; index <4; index++)
        printf("base + %d: %10d %10d\n",
            index, pts+index, ptf+index);
}
```

If you run this, the output will look like:

```
base + 0:         5228       5208
base + 1:         5230       5212
base + 2:         5232       5216
base + 3:         5234       5220
```

There is an interesting aspect of C here that is very important to understand. The pointers *pts* and *ptf* are not declared. Instead, we define that data to which these point: *pts* and *ptf*. Afterward, when the pointer is incremented, the pointer is incremented by number of storage units, not by the actual value of the index. Adding 1 to a *float* pointer increments it by four, and adding 1 to a *short* pointer increments it by two (Figure 10.2).

Note

Whenever a pointer is incremented or decremented by an integer type, C scales the value of the pointer by the *sizeof* the object pointed to. This ensures that the compiler uses the sizeof functionality built into itself, and incrementing the pointer by 1 will always point to the next data item regardless of the size of the item.

As a result, the following conditions are all true:

```
partno + 2 == &partno[2]
*(partno+2) == partno[2]
```

In the first condition the two addresses are the same, in the second the two values are identical.

Figure 10.2
Pointers and Array Storage

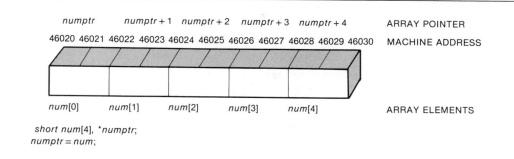

Using Arrays in Functions

Arrays can be used either in the body of a function or as arguments. The previous discussion applies to any array used in the body of a function. Passing arrays as arguments, however, involves some special precautions that must be addressed by the programmer.

As an example, let's return to the problem of sorting, which was mentioned at the beginning of the chapter. This is a very common use of arrays, so much so that most programmers create a collection of array sort functions for various types of applications. Here is an example of using a sort function for sorting a series of input float numbers:

```
#include <math.h>
#include <stdio.h>
#define MAXSIZE 20
main()
{
    static double values[MAXSIZE];
    int index = 0, size;
    double sum = 0.0;
    char inputa[10];

    printf("\33[2J");      /* clear screen */
    do {
        printf("Please enter a number: ");
        fgets(inputa,10,stdin);
        values[index] = atof(inputa);
        }
```

continued

```
            while (values[index++] != 0.0);
            size = index - 1;
            sort(values,size);
            printf("The sorted list:\n");
            for (index=0; index < size; index++)
                {
                sum += values[index];
                printf("%f\n",values[index]);
                }
            printf("The mean is %f\n", sum/size);
}


/* BUBBLE sort routine */
/* sorts an array of floats */
sort(array,size)
double array[];
int size;
{
        int i, j, temp;
        for (i = 0; i<size-1; i++)
            for (j=i+1; j<size; j++)
                if (array[i] > array[j])
                {
                temp = array[j];
                array[j]=array[i];
                array[i] = temp;
                }
}
```

This is a modified version of the earlier program that calculates the mean. The difference is that the input numeric array is sorted in ascending order and then listed before the mean is displayed.

The sort technique used here in the function is known as a bubble sort. The function starts by trying to find the smallest item in the list and putting it as the first element of the array. The procedure is then repeated with the remainder of the list, putting the next smallest item as the second element of the array. This continues until the entire list is in ascending order. The bubble sort is one of the easiest to program, but is one of the least efficient. For larger lists, you would probably wish to use a better algorithm.

The outer loop, with the *i* index, determines which element of the array will be used for comparisons. It starts with the first array element. The inner loop, with the *j* index, steps through the remaining array items comparing each with the first. If the comparison shows the elements are out of order, a swap is initiated. To initiate a swap, it is necessary to first store one item in a temporary location.

Remember that it is the original array that is swapped, not a copy of the array. This saves C the time of dragging all the array values into an array in the function and then returning all the sorted values. There is also a danger, as if the function is improperly designed it can destroy the original array values.

Character String Arrays

String arrays should be handled carefully in C. Remember that you can declare a character string by either using an array or a pointer:

```
char msg1[40];
char *msg2;
```

The first method actually reserves space for the character string array. The second only declares a pointer to a character. You can use the *scanf( )* function to read input characters to an array declared the first way. You would get an error message trying to use *scanf( )* to input values for a variable declared the second way, as the declaration reserved no storage for the array.

A character string is always stored with a null character ('\0'), whether it is specified or not. The following two are identical:

```
static char msg[5] = "Test";
static char msg[5] = {'T', 'e', 's', 't','\0'};
```

Notice that the array size specification must include space for this null character. If you use a larger array size, the extra elements are initialized to zero in each of the previous cases. If you omit the array size, it is assumed as the number of initializing characters. If you use QuickC library's *strlen( )* function to return the length of the string, it will not include the null character in the count.

For using string arrays, then, the programmer should observe the following precautions:

- Be sure that any function or operation that creates a string also creates the null character at the end. For example:

  ```
  char msg[3+1];
  char[0] = '1';
  char[1] = '2';
  char[2] = '3';
  char[3] = '\0';
  ```

- Before copying a string array, be sure the source string (with null character) is less than or equal to the size of the destination array. For example:

```
char oldname[21+1];
char msg[19+1];

strncpy(msg, oldname, sizeof(msg)-1);
msg[19] = 0;
```

- Be sure the null character is copied when a string is copied (see last example).

Multidimensional Arrays

You can also create arrays of multiple dimensions by using a set of square brackets for each dimension:

```
int values[2][3];
```

You can also initialize the array if it is external or static:

```
#include <stdio.h>
main()
{
    static int values[2][3] = {{0,1,2},{3,4,5}};

    printf("%d",values[0][2]);
}
```

In this example the program would display the output value of 2.

Now let's try an interesting experiment by trying to modify the sort function used earlier to work with a multidimensional array. Here, the array is used to store the codes for each salesperson and their corresponding sales total. The program will permit us to enter each sales code and sales total, then uses a sort function to sort them in decreasing sales volume. The program then displays the output list.

```
#include <math.h>
#include <stdio.h>
#define ROWS 20
#define COLUMNS 2
main()
{
    static double sales [ROWS] [COLUMNS];
    int index = 0, size;
    char agent_number[10], agent_sales[10];
```

continued

```
    printf("\33[2J");    /* clear screen */
    printf("Please enter salesperson number and\n");
    printf("sales. Enter two zeros to terminate:\n\n");
    do {
        printf("Enter agent number: ");
        fgets(agent_number,10,stdin);
        printf("Enter agent's sales: ");
        fgets(agent_sales,10,stdin);
        sales[index][0] = atof(agent_number);
        sales[index][1] = atof(agent_sales);
      }
    while (sales[index++][0] > 0);
    size = index - 1;
    sort(sales,size);
    printf("The sorted list:\n");
    for (index=0; index < size; index++)
        printf("%3.0f %6.2f\n",sales[index][0], sales[index][1]);
}
/* BUBBLE sort routine */
/* sorts an array of floats */
sort(array,size)
double array[][COLUMNS];
int size;
{
    int i, j, k;
    double temp [COLUMNS];

    for (i = 0; i<size-1; i++)
        for (j=i+1; j<size; j++)
            if (array[i][1] < array[j][1])
                {
                for (k=0; k<COLUMNS; k++)
                    temp[k] = array[j][k];
                for (k=0; k<COLUMNS; k++)
                    array[j][k] = array[i][k];
                for (k=0; k<COLUMNS; k++)
                    array[i][k] = temp[k];
                }
}
```

Here is a sample execution of the program:

```
Please enter each salesperson number and
sales. Enter two zeros to terminate:
```

```
Enter agent number: 007            <Enter>
Enter sales for this agent: 12.0   <Enter>
Enter agent number: 100            <Enter>
Enter sales for this agent: 48.00  <Enter>
Enter agent number: 125            <Enter>
Enter sales for this agent: 6      <Enter>
Enter agent number: 167            <Enter>
Enter sales for this agent: 23.0   <Enter>
Enter agent number: 0              <Enter>
Enter sales for this agent: 0      <Enter>
```

The sorted list:

```
100   48.00
167   23.00
007   12.00
125    6.00
```

The two-dimensional array is declared in the main program by defining two constants *rows* and *columns*. The corresponding codes and sales volumes are entered to the array, after which the function is called and the array sorted.

Notice that the function now has lost some of its independence, as some information used by the function (*columns* and *rows*) must now be passed as constants without using arguments. You can pass the size of a one-dimensional array to a function in C, but with two or more dimensions only the first subscript can be passed.

The temporary storage in the function for swapping must now be to an array, as each element of a row must be swapped if a row is swapped. Notice how this temporary array is defined (compare it with the last sort example).

Now let's look at a multidimensional example in which an array of character strings is used as an argument for a *menu( )* function. This is also a multidimensional array:

```
#include <stdio.h>
main()
{
    static char *choices[] =
        {"A)dd an address",
         "E)dit an address",
         "D)isplay an address",
         0
        };
    static char title[40] = "Main Menu\n\n";
    void menu();

    menu(title,choices,3);
```

continued

```
}

void menu(title,selections,size)
char *title;
char *selections[];
int size;
{
    int i;
    printf(title);
    for (i=0; i<size; i++)
        printf("%s\n",*(selections+i));
    return;
}
```

The main program uses character arrays within another array or, more accurately, an array of pointers. This is declared as static and initialized to the menu choices. Another character array is used for the title that will be used for the menu.

The function is called as *menu(title,choices,3)*. The first two arguments are arrays. From the previous section, you should realize that in both cases you are passing the address of the first element of the array to the function. You are not passing the values of the array to the function. The function uses the address (pointer) to recover the actual data using:

```
printf("%s\n",*(selections+i));
```

Techniques for Using Arrays

1. The first element of the array is always of subscript 0. The last element will have a subscript of one less than the number of elements in the array.

2. Variables cannot be used in any expression to declare the size of the array.

3. Only static and externally declared arrays can be initialized. If you do not initialize an array, the program will execute, but will assume garbage values in the array.

4. QuickC does not check to see if the index exceeds the array bounds. The programmer must do this.

5. Remember that functions access the original array data (using pointers), not a copy of the data. A function can change the original array data.

6. In using functions with arrays, the function has no way of knowing the size of the array. As a safety precaution, always pass the size of an array to a function with the array. This is a wise step, even with character string functions.

7. In loops involving arrays, set the initial condition to 0, set the terminating condition as one less than the highest subscript and increment after using the index variable as:

```
for (index=0; index < MAXSIZE; index++)
     ...;
```

Using Pointers

The ability to use pointers is a very important feature of C that is not available in many other languages. It also gives the programmer the possibility of making some very dangerous mistakes. Let's look at an example. Try the following program with your QuickC and look at the output:

```
#include <stdio.h>
main()
{
    int *ptr;

    *ptr = 7;
    printf("The value is: %d.\n",*ptr);
}
```

The program will compile correctly and will probably even execute properly, giving you the expected output message:

```
The value is 7.
```

So what's wrong? Here, *ptr* is a memory location that is used to store the variable. You've declared the variable, but not any storage location for the address of the variable. C will use a random memory location to store the address of the variable. You could spend days trying to find out what happened in your program. The proper way to write this same program would be:

```
#include <stdio.h>
main()
{
    int no;

    no = 7;
    printf("The value is: %d",no);
}
```

The ability to use pointers in C is a very important feature of the language. When using arrays (including character strings) and data structures (Chapter 12), you can pass pointers to a function and do not need to pass the actual data. This saves a large amount of execution time and memory space. At the same time, however, it opens the potential of using the pointers improperly.

The next chapters will clarify this even more, as the issue becomes very important when working with character strings and structures.

Exercises

1. Use the example for the mean calculation to calculate the mean from several input numbers. Enter more than MAXSIZE entries. What does QuickC do?

2. Write a program to permit you to enter up to 20 integer values and display the maximum value entered.

3. Why was C designed to require the address of the array rather than the array values passed to a function?

4. Which of the following are valid:

   a. ptr = &i
   b. ptr = &++i
   c. ptr = &(i+1)

Answers

1. The result is unpredictable. With QuickC, the program may execute properly.

2.

```
#include <stdio.h>
#define MAXSIZE 20
#define MAXNEGINT 0100000
main()
{
     static int values[MAXSIZE];
     int index = 0, size, max = MAXNEGINT;
     char inputa[10];

     do {
         printf("Please enter a number: ");
         fgets(inputa,10,stdin);
         values[index] = atoi(inputa);
         }
```

continued

```
        while (values[index++] != 0);
        size = index - 1;
        for (index=0; index < size; index++)
            if (values[index]>max)
                max = values[index];
         printf("The maximum value is %d\n", max);
    }
```

Note

When using large constants, parameterize the constant to improve portability when changing machines or compilers.

3. For large arrays, to pass the value would require the function to have enough memory space for a copy of the array. In addition, the program would execute slowly as the entire array would have to be copied to the function array.

4. Only the first is valid.

11

Using Character Strings

Let's pause for a fun experiment. Let me challenge your knowledge of C with two little problems as an introduction to working with character strings. After the challenge, you'll get a discussion of the two methods you can use to store a string in C and an overview of the character string functions.

The Two Mysteries

Start up your QuickC and try your hand at solving both of the two problems of this section.

Problem 1

Now, Mr. Sherlock Holmes, try wrestling with the first problem:

```
#include <stdio.h>
main()
{
    char *msg;

    printf("What is your favorite flower? ");
    fgets(msg,10,stdin);
    printf("Your favorite flower is the %s\n",msg);
}
```

With QuickC, this program will compile and execute properly, but there is a very serious problem that lurks about. Here is how it executes— just as you would suspect:

```
What is your favorite flower: rose <Enter>
Your favorite flower is the rose.
```

What is wrong with the program?

The program itself is legal and compiles, as we said, correctly. The variable *msg* is a pointer to a character array. The problem is that no memory was allocated for the character string. The variable *msg* is a memory location that stores the address where the array starts. The input text will be stored beginning in whatever random address is stored in *msg*. This could be very dangerous if the address is used by some other part of the program or even DOS. In some compilers you may get a warning message, but with QuickC you will get nothing. This program will compile and may seem to execute correctly, but it contains this serious problem.

Here is the correct program:

```
#include <stdio.h>
main()
{
    char msg[20];

    printf("What is your favorite flower? ");
    fgets(msg,10,stdin);
    printf("Your favorite flower is the %s",msg);
}
```

Now you have assigned space for the text string (twenty characters) by declaring the array variable.

Problem 2

For the next challenge, try your hand at this program:

```
#include <stdio.h>
main()
{
    char msg[20];

    msg = "Hello out there!";
    printf("The computer's message is %s",msg);
}
```

This one won't even compile correctly. What's wrong? You have declared an array for the text and then it appears you tried to assign a text string to this array. When you try to compile it, however, you get the message:

```
2100 left operand must be lvalue
```

The problem is that the compiler thinks you are trying to assign the address of a character string to *msg*. Array names storage locations for the address that contains a pointer for the starting character of the array. They are constants that can't be modified or assigned a value. The correct form is:

```
#include <stdio.h>
main()
{
     char msg[20];

     strcpy(msg,"Hello out there!");
     printf("The computer's message is %s\n",msg);
}
```

or here is another solution:

```
#include <stdio.h>
main()
{
     char *msg;

     msg = "Hello out there!";
     printf("The computer's message is %s\n",msg);
}
```

Now let's look at how those character string pointers really work.

Character Strings and Pointers

A character string, as already mentioned, is a *char* array terminated with a null character ('\0'). You have already seen two ways of declaring a character string array. Let's look now at the two and how they differ.

The Array Form

The array form declares a *char* array of a fixed size to store the string:

```
static char msg[] = "rose";
```

Here, an array of five bytes is declared for the storage of the text. There will be four bytes for the text string and another for the null character ('-0'). After the declaration, C will recognize *msg* as storing the address of the first array element:

```
msg == &msg[0]
```

It is important to realize here that *msg* is a constant. It is fixed, and cannot be modified by the program. That is why, in the earlier problem, you got the message:

```
2100 left operand must be lvalue
```

In the program of the first problem you were trying to assign the address of a text string to *msg*, a constant:

```
msg = "Hello out there!";
```

With an array, you can't use any operation like this, ++*msg*, or *msg* = *msg+1* to find the next element of an array. The name of the array is a constant, and is a pointer to the first element of the array. To put it another way, the array size is fixed and stored at a memory location determined at compile time. The constant *msg* is a storage location for a pointer to the first element of the array.

The Pointer Form

You could also declare the array as:

```
static char *msg= "rose"
```

Again, C will store this as an array of five elements, just as before. In addition, however, C sets aside a sixth storage location for a variable *msg*. The pointer to the text string is now a variable, and can be modified by the program as desired. You can now use the increment or decrement operators on the variable to output the string:

```
while ( *(msg) != '\0')
    putchar( *(msg++);
```

Which to Use?

Both methods work in many applications. For example:

```
#include <stdio.h>
main()
{
```

continued

```
        static char array_msg[]="Hello out there!";
        char *ptr_msg = "Hello out there!";
        int index=0;

        for (index = 0; index < 17; index++)
            putchar( *(array_msg + index) );
        putchar('\n');
        for (index = 0; index < 17; index++)
            putchar( *(ptr_msg + index) );
        putchar('\n');
}
```

would display:

```
Hello out there!
Hello out there!
```

This little program uses both methods to store the same text string. The array pointer is a constant, but is never incremented or altered, so the program works as shown.

Now look at the following form:

```
while ( *(ptr_msg) != '\0')
    putchar( *(ptr_msg++) );
```

This will work. The following, however, will not work:

```
while ( *(array_msg) != '\0')
    putchar( *(array_msg++) );
```

Here, you are trying to increment a constant, which is not permitted.

In assigning one array to another, the same limitation holds. The following is valid:

```
ptr_msg = array_msg
```

The following is not valid:

```
array_msg = ptr_msg
```

as you cannot assign a value to a constant.

The ability to use pointers to process arrays gives C a very strong advantage over other languages that do not provide much pointer support. For example, look at this program:

```
#include <stdio.h>
main()
```

continued

```
{
      static char *msg = "Pointer copy test";
      static char *out_string;

      out_string = msg;
      printf("%s",out_string);
}
```

Your first impression might be that a copy of the string is made and then displayed. In reality, however, only the pointer is copied. The text string is never copied. If you have a program with a very large array, copying the one pointer to an entire array is much faster and more efficient than trying to copy all the elements of an array.

Initializing a Character-String Array

Remember that auto arrays cannot be initialized. If you wish to initialize a character-string array, it must be declared static or external.

```
static char msg1[] = "Hello";
static char msg2[] = {'H','e','l'.'l','o','\0'};
static char msg3[40] = "Hello";
static char *msgptr = "Hello";
```

In the first case, the array is declared and allocated six bytes (five plus the one for the null character), and initialized. The second case is identical to the first. In the third case, the array is declared and allocated 40 bytes. The text string is stored in the first 5 bytes. All 35 of the remaining bytes are initialized to null ('\0') characters. In all three cases, *msg1*, *msg2*, and *msg3* cannot be modified by the program.

The reason *msg1*, *msg2*, and *msg3* cannot be modified in the program is that they are constants and, to modify them, would be used as lvalues. An *lvalue* is a variable to the left of an assignment operator. Since a constant cannot be modified, an error message is generated which will say that the *lvalue* cannot be modified.

In the fourth case, an array is declared and the initialization assigns six spaces for it (five plus one for the null character). A seventh location is also reserved to store *msgptr*, which is a variable used as a pointer and can be modified by the program. The string length determines how much space will be reserved for the array.

Remember in declaring an array using the third method to allocate space for the largest string you expect to use *plus* the *null character*. For example, to use a variable *zip* to store five-character zip codes you would need six bytes:

```
char zip[5+1];
```

Using Character-String Arrays

In the last chapter you saw an example of an array of character strings:

```
#include <stdio.h>
main()
{
    static char *choices[]=
        {"A)dd an address",
         "E)dit an address",
         "D)isplay an address"
        };
    static char title[40] = "Main Menu\n\n";
    menu(title,choices,3);
}
menu(title,selections,size)
char *title;
char *selections[];
int size;
{
    int i;

    printf(title);
    for (i=0; i<size; i++)
        printf("%s\n",*(selections+i));
    return;
}
```

In this example selections is an array of three pointers to character strings. Each character string is an array of characters, so *selections* is really an array of three pointers to arrays. The first pointer, *selections[0]*, pointer to the beginning of the first string; that is, *selections[0]* contains the address of where the first string starts. The second pointer, *selections[1]*, points to the beginning of the second string.

```
*selections[0] == 'A'   *selections[1]=='E'
*selections[3] == 'D'
```

This gives an array with rows of varying length, and the length of each row is determined by the string to which it was initialized.

You could also initialize the same array as:

```
static char selections[3][40];
```

This would declare an array of three rows, each of 40 characters. The rows are all equal length. This takes more space than the former, but sometimes may be just what you need (the creation of fixed-length records for a file, for example).

Using String Functions

The QuickC library provides several functions for processing strings. You have already met the string input and output functions (Chapter 4) and the *strcmp()* function (Chapter 6). Now let's look at a few more: *strlen()*, *strcat()*, and *strcpy()*. In addition, we'll look at some variations of *strcmp()*.

Finding a String's Length

The *strlen()* function can be used to find the length of a string. One common use is to be sure the length of an input string does not exceed the array space allocated for it. As remarked earlier, C does not check this. If you wish it checked, it must be done by the programmer:

```
#include <stdio.h>
#define MAXLEN 10
main()
{
    static char name[MAXLEN];

    printf("Please enter name: ");
    fgets(name,10,stdin);
    if (strlen(name) > MAXLEN)
        *(name+MAXLEN) = '\0';
    puts(name);
}
```

In this example an input string is read, then the length compared with the maximum size of the array. If the string is too long, the last character in the space allocated for the array string is changed to a null character. The array here has 11 elements, as the first element will be zero. The maximum input string is ten characters plus the null character. The null character is not counted in the string length total.

Comparing Strings

In comparing strings, you must use caution or you can experience some interesting results. For example, try the following program:

```
#include <stdio.h>
#define MAXNAMES  4
#define MAXNAMECHARS  10
#define NULL 0
#define END ""
main()
{
    char *name_ptr[MAXNAMES];
    static char name_array [MAXNAMES][MAXNAMECHARS];
    int i, index=0;
    void sort();

    printf("Enter Name: ");
    while ( index < MAXNAMES &&
        fgets(name_array[index],10,stdin) != NULL &&
        name_array[index] != END )
        {
        name_ptr[index] = name_array[index];
        index++;
        printf("Enter Name: ");
        }
}
```

This routine reads a series of input names. The basic idea is that if the array size is exceeded, there is no input error, and no null input string (carriage return entered), the name is accepted and a request is made for another name. This will work fine except for the last condition. If you enter a carriage return only, the program continues to ask for another name. You can't terminate the program.

The error is in the test condition:

```
name_array[index] != END
```

END is a pointer. The pointer will never be equal to the value of *name_ array[index],* so the condition always succeeds.

Now try this with a *strcmp()* function:

```
#include <stdio.h>
#define MAXNAMES  4
#define MAXNAMECHARS  10
```

continued

```
#define NULL 0
#define END ""
main()
{
    char *name_ptr[MAXNAMES];
    static char name_array [MAXNAMES][MAXNAMECHARS];
    int i, index=0;
    void sort();

    printf("Enter Name: ");
    while ( index < MAXNAMES &&
        fgets(name_array[index],10,stdin) != NULL &&
        strcmp(name_array[index],END) != 0)
        {
        name_ptr[index] = name_array[index];
        index++;
        printf("Enter Name: ");
        }
}
```

This will work. Notice that part of the test for ending the input is now:

```
strcmp(name_array[index],END) != 0)
```

This compares the strings referenced by the two pointers. The *strcmp( )* function always takes two string pointers as arguments and returns a value of 0 if they are the same.

What if they are not the same? Here's an example of a string sorting function that uses the return value of *strcmp( )*:

```
/* BUBBLE sort routine */
/* sorts an array of character string arrays */
void sort(array,size)
char *array[];
int size;
{
    int i, j;
    char *temp;
    for (i = 0; i<size-1; i++)
        for (j=i+1; j<size; j++)
            if (strcmp(array[i],array[j]) > 0)
            {
            temp = array[j];
            array[j]=array[i];
```

continued

```
        array[i] = temp;
        }
}
```

This brings up an interesting point about *strcmp( )*: it compares strings, not arrays. Only the character string up to the null character is used in the test.

Now let's look at our original question. The return value for QuickC is the difference between the two ASCII values; that is, the following statement writes a –2:

```
printf("%d\n",strcmp("A","C"));
```

This is not true for all C compilers, but with all compilers the *strcmp( )* function returns a negative value with the previous statement. If the first string precedes the second alphabetically, you'll get a negative number. If the second precedes the first, you'll get a positive number. The actual ASCII values (see Appendix C) are used for comparison. An "A" is not equal to "a."

Tip

If you are comparing an input string with something and the input string might be in uppercase or lowercase, use a function to capitalize the input string before comparing.

Now what would you imagine as the output of:

```
printf("%d\n",strcmp("AA","AC")):
```

With QuickC, the output is the same as before, a –2. The *strcmp( )* checks the strings until the first mismatch, then returns the difference of the ASCII values at that pointer.

There are several variations of the compare function in the C library:

strcmp(string1,string2)	Compares two strings and returns 0 if strings are equal, a positive number if string1 > string2 and < 1 if string a negative number string2.
strcmpi(string1,string2)	(Case insensitive version of strcmp function. Uppercase and lowercase of the same character are considered equal.)
stricmp(string1,string2)	(Same as above — case insensitive version of strcmp function.)

`strncmp(string1,string2,n)`	Compares first n characters of string1 and string2, returning 0 if n characters are equal, a positive number if string1 > string2 and < 0 if string a negative number string2.
`strnicmp(string1,string2,n)`	(Case insensitive version of strncmp. Uppercase and lowercase of the same character are considered equal.)

As an example, the following compares *last_name* with name, displaying the message if both are equal:

```
char last_name[40], name[40];
if (0 == strcmp(last_name,name))
    printf("The names are equal.\n");
```

The following program looks at the first three characters of zip to see if they are equal to or greater than 972:

```
char zip[5]
if (strncmp(zip,"902",3) >= 0)
    printf("The first three digits are greater than 972.\n");
```

Now suppose you wanted this same program to test the last two characters for equality to 12. Then you would have:

```
char zip[5]
if (strncmp(&zip[3],"12",2) == 0)
    printf("The last two digits are equal to 12.\n");
```

In the previous examples the name of the array was used. When the name of an array is used in a function or another expression, it actually represents the zero element of the array. Here, we wish to reference the fourth element of the array. We use as an argument, then, a pointer to the fourth element. The & operator is used to show the address. The expression *&zip[0]* and *zip* are equivalent, but you should avoid the former.

Concatenating Strings

You can also concatenate strings using the *strcat()* function. Here's an example:

```
#include <stdio.h>
main()
{
     static char msg[10];
     static char add[80]="Your favorite flower is the ";

     printf("What is your favorite flower? ");
     fgets(msg,10,stdin);
     strcat(add,msg);
     puts(add);
}
```

The function has two arguments:

```
strcat(add,msg);
```

The function concatenates the second string to the first string, returning the concatenated string as a modified first string. The strings, not the arrays, are concatenated. As a result, the output is:

```
What is your favorite flower? rose <Enter>
Your favorite flower is the rose.
```

Even though the input array is 80 characters, the input string is suffixed only to
the character string, not the array.

Tip

C does not check to see if the concatenated string fits in the array. If
you don't allocate enough array space for the first argument, you can
experience *serious* problems.

Copying Strings

In an earlier section, you saw how you could copy the address of an array and
save the time of moving an entire array:

```
#include <stdio.h>
main()
{
     static char *msg = "Pointer copy test";
     static char *out_string;
```

continued

```
        out_string = msg;
        printf("%s",out_string);
}
```

Sometimes, however, you may wish to copy the entire array. Then you would use the *strcpy( )* function:

```
#include <stdio.h>
main()
{
        static char *msg = "Pointer copy test";
        static char out_string[40];

        strcpy(out_string,msg);
        printf("%s",out_string);
}
```

This program uses two character arrays, and the function copies the first string to the second. The first argument is the destination array.

Tip

C does not check to see if the destination array is large enough for the source. If you don't allocate enough array space for the first argument, you can experience *serious* problems.

An Example with String Functions

Here is an example of a program using string functions to read an input series of names, sort them, and then display the list:

```
#include <stdio.h>
#define MAXNAMES  4
#define MAXNAMECHARS  10
#define NULL 0
#define END ""
main()
{
        char *name_ptr[MAXNAMES];
        static char name_array [MAXNAMES][MAXNAMECHARS];
        int i, index=0;
        void sort();
```

continued

```
        printf("Enter Name: ");
        while ( index < MAXNAMES &&
                fgets(name_array[index],10,stdin) != NULL &&
                strcmp(name_array[index],END) != 0)
                {
                name_ptr[index] = name_array[index];
                index++;
                printf("Enter Name: ");
                }
        sort(name_ptr,index);
        printf("\n\n");
        for (i=0; i<index; i++)
                printf("%s\n",name_ptr[i]);
}


/* BUBBLE sort routine */
/* sorts an array of character string arrays */
void sort(array,size)
char *array[];
int size;
{
        int i, j;
        char *temp;
        for (i = 0; i<size-1; i++)
                for (j=i+1; j<size; j++)
                        if (strcmp(array[i],array[j])>0)
                        {
                        temp = array[j];
                        array[j]=array[;];
                        array[i] = temp;
                        }
}
```

Exercises

1. How many bytes are required to store "A"? 'A'?

2. What's wrong with this?

```
static char msg[]={'T','E','S','T'};
```

3. What is the output of the following?

```
#include <stdio.h>
main()
```

continued

```
{
        static char msg[] = "Hello out there!";
        char msgptr;

        msgptr = msg;
        puts(++msg);
        puts(msg);
        msg[3] = '\0';
        puts(msg);
}
```

4. What will be the output of this program?

```
#include <stdio.h>
main()
{
        static char msg[] = "Hello";
        char msgptr;

        msgptr = msg + strlen(msg);
        while (--msgptr >= msg)
                puts(msgptr);
}
```

Answers

1. Two, one.
2. There is no terminating null character in the string.
3.

```
Hello out there!
ello out there!
He
```

4.

```
o
lo
llo
ello
Hello
```

12

Using Data Structures

$\mathbf{A}$rrays permit you to store a list of data in memory and access it quickly—even multidimensional lists. Arrays do, however, have a serious limitation. Each element of the array for all dimensions must be of the same type. This poses a problem sometimes. Remember the sales program of the last chapter in which the salesperson number and sales were both stored in the array? It worked because the salesperson number and the sales amount were both float data. But suppose we wish to store the salesperson's name instead of the number? The array approach would not work, as you would be trying to store both strings (character arrays) and float data in the same array. You cannot mix element types in an array.

Data structures allow you to build your own data types, allowing you to mix data of different types in the same structure. This chapter will show you how this is done.

A Simple Data Structure

Let's begin with a simple example of a program using a structure, a program to enter and display an address:

```
#include <stdio.h>
#define PAD 2;
main()
{
    struct address_rec
        {
        char address_no[3+PAD];
        char name[40+PAD];
        char street[40+PAD];
        char city[20+PAD];
        char state[2+PAD];
```

continued

```
          char zip[5+PAD];
          };
     struct address_rec address;

     printf("Name: ");
     fgets(address.name,sizeof(address.name),stdin);
     printf("Address: ");
     fgets(address.street,sizeof(address.street),stdin);
     printf("City: ");
     fgets(address.city,sizeof(address.city),stdin);
     printf("State: ");
     fgets(address.state,sizeof(address.state),stdin);
     printf("Zip: ");
     fgets(address.zip,sizeof(address.zip),stdin);
     printf("Number: ");
     fgets(address.address_no,sizeof(address.address.no),stdin);
     printf("\n\n%s\n",address.address_no);
     printf("%s\n",address.name);
     printf("%s\n",address.street);
     printf("%s %s %s\n", address.city,
          address.state, address.zip);
}
```

If you try to execute this program, you would get something like the following:

```
Name: George Washington <Enter>
Address: 1600 Pennsylvania Ave <Enter>
City: Washington <Enter>
State: DC <Enter>
Zip: 30070 <Enter>
Number: 1 <Enter>


1
George Washington
1600 Pennsylvania Ave
Washington DC  30070
```

Now let's see how the program works.

The Structure Template

In this example we need a data structure to store the address that will consist of six parts: name, street, city, state, zip, and an address number. All the components are character strings. This structure is defined using the *struct* keyword:

```
struct address_rec
     {
     char address_no[3+PAD];
     char name[40+PAD];
     char street[40+PAD];
     char city[20+PAD];
     char state[2+PAD];
     char zip[5+PAD];
     };
```

This does not define or reserve any space for the variable. All you have done is define a template or format and assigned this template a tag called *address_rec*. The members of the template can be integers, floats, characters, arrays, or even other data structures. The definition ends with a semicolon.

In using character string arrays in the structure, be sure to include space for the carriage return and line feed characters. The zip code may be only five characters, but you will need additional character spaces for the pad making it an array of seven characters. The state name is two characters, but with the null pad it is an array of four characters.

Declaring a Structure Variable

Once you have defined this template, you can use it as a data type in the program just as you would in another data type:

```
struct address_rec address;
```

In this example the variable name is *address*. This variable is declared as of the type struct *address_rec*. At this point variable space is reserved for the variable *address*. The variable will take 122 bytes: 5 for *address_no*, 42 each for the name and street, 22 for the city, 5 for the state, and 7 for the zip. The name of the template is called a *tag*, and is not a variable.

You can use the same structure for several variables if you wish. It is a data type, just as any other data type:

```
struct address_rec input_address;
struct address_rec output_address;
```

Here, both *input_address* and *output_address* are declared of the *struct address _rec* type. Both variables will take 116 bytes of storage.

You can find the size of the structure with a simple program:

```
main()
{
```

continued

```
          struct address_rec
               {
               char address_no[3+PAD];
               char name[40+PAD];
               char street[40+PAD];
               char city[20+PAD];
               char state[2+PAD];
               char zip[5+PAD];
               };
          struct address_rec address;

          printf("%d",sizeof (address));
     }
```

You may wish to experiment with this, changing or eliminating various structure elements or types to see how it affects the structure size.

In this example both the template and variable are defined inside the function. You can also put the template outside the function:

```
#include <stdio.h>
struct address_rec
     {
     char address_no[3+PAD];
     char name[40+PAD];
     char street[40+PAD];
     char city[20+PAD];
     char state[2+PAD];
     char zip[5+PAD];
     };
main()
{
     struct address_rec address;
}
```

When the template is defined within the function, it can only be used to declare variables within that function. When the template is defined outside of the functions or main program, it can be used by the main program or any function.

It is also possible to define the structure and declare the variable at the same time:

```
#include <stdio.h>
#define PAD 2
main()
{
     struct
```

continued

```
        {
        char address_no[3+PAD];
        char name[40+PAD];
        char street[40+PAD];
        char city[20+PAD];
        char state[2+PAD];
        char zip[5+PAD];
        }  address;
}
```

Here, there is no structure name (*address_rec*). The variable name, *address*, is added at the end after the closing brace of the definition. This is acceptable if the structure will only be used for one variable, but is not advisable if the structure is used for multiple variables.

For multiple variables, you could add them with commas after the closing bracket:

```
#include <stdio.h>
#define PAD 2
main()
{
    struct
        {
        char address_no[3+PAD];
        char name[40+PAD];
        char street[40+PAD];
        char city[20+PAD];
        char state[2+PAD];
        char zip[5+PAD];
        }  input_address, output_address;
}
```

Tip

Although structures without tags (names) can be used in this way, using tags improves the readability of the program and is generally best.

Initializing Structured Variables

Whether a structured variable can be initialized follows the same rules as for an array variable. Structure variables can be initialized if the variable is external or static. Whether a variable is external or not depends upon where the variable is declared, not where the template is defined.

```
            main()
            {
                struct parameters
                        {
                        char company_name[40+PAD];  /* company name */
                        char default_drive;       /* default drive */
                        int access_level;        /* access level */
                        };
                static struct parameters address =
                        {
                        "ACME Manufacturing Company"
                        'D'
                        3
                        };
            }
```

In initializing a structure, it is not necessary that all components be of the same type. In the previous example, a character array, character, and *int* integer are all components of a single structure.

Access Structure Components

QuickC permits only four operations with a structure variable: you can access one of the members, you can assign one structure equal to another, you can use *sizeof(structure)* to get the size of the structure, or you can use the & operator to access the address of a structure. The first two are discussed in this section. The third and fourth operations are discussed later in the chapter under *Structures and Pointers*.

Once you have declared a structure variable, you can access the variable using the structure name, the *period operator*, and the component name. The period operator is also called a *dot* or *member operator*:

```
fgets(address.name,sizeof(address.name),stdin);
printf(address.name);
```

You can use *address.name* just as any other character string variable. If you have multiple variables of the same type, each is a separate variable:

```
#define ass_struct(a,b) movemem(&a, &b,   sizeof(b));

struct address_rec input_address;
struct address_rec output_address;
```

```
fgets(input_address,sizeof(input_address),stdin);
ass_struct(output_address,input_address)
printf(output_address);
```

This illustrates also another important aspect of data structures: you can assign a value of one structure to another. In this example the entire structure contents (and not just a pointer) are copied to the other structure.

Arrays of Structures

Our little address program is not very useful now; usually we will wish to enter multiple addresses. To do this, the program must be modified to permit storing an array of structures:

```
#include <stdio.h>
#define MAXADDR 5
#define PAD 2
main()
{
    struct address_rec
        {
        char address_no[3+PAD];
        char name[40+PAD];
        char street[40+PAD];
        char city[20+PAD];
        char state[2+PAD];
        char zip[5+PAD];
        };
    struct address_rec address[MAXADDR];
    int count = 0;
    int index;

    printf("Name: ");
    while (count<MAXADDR &&
        strlen(fgets(address[count].name,sizeof (address[count].
            name),stdin) != NULL )
        {
        printf("Address: ");
        fgets(address[count].street,sizeof(address[count],
            street),stdin);
        printf("City: ");
        fgets(address[count].city,sizeof(address[count].
            city),stdin);
```

continued

```
                    printf("State: ");
                    fgets(address[count].state,sizeof(address[count].
                        state),stdin );
                    printf("Zip: ");
                    fgets(address.zip[count],sizeof(address.
                        zip[count]),stdin);
                    printf("Number: ");
                    fgets(address.address_no[count++],5,stdin);
                    if (count<MAXADDR)
                        printf("Name: ");
                    }
            for (index=0; index<count; index++)
                {
                printf("\n\n%s\n",address[index].address_no);
                printf("%s\n",address[index].name);
                printf("%s\n",address[index].street);
                printf("%s %s %s\n",address[index].city,
                        address[index].state, address[index].zip);
                }
    }
```

This is a little more complex, but is really not difficult to understand. The template is defined exactly as before. The first clue to the difference is when the variable is defined:

```
struct address_rec address[MAXADDR];
```

At this point you are reserving variable space for an array of type *struct address_ rec*. The array has a maximum dimension of 5, which means the declaration will reserve 5 × 122 bytes for the *address[5]* variable or 610 bytes. As you can imagine, complex array structures can use a lot of memory if you are not careful.

Accessing members of the array means that you will have to use a subscript to identify the member. The subscript is after the structure name, not to the member of the structure:

```
gets(address[1].name);
```

If the component is an array, you can also use subscripts on the component name to identify the member of that array. For example:

```
printf(address[1].name[3]);
```

would print the fourth letter in the name of the second address.

The program mechanics of the example are quite simple. A *while* loop is used to enter the addresses until either the maximum number of addresses has been entered (5) or a null name has been entered (carriage return with no name entered). After all the addresses are entered, a *for* loop displays the list.

Nested Structures

You can also use structures as part of other structures, creating nested structures. For example, assume a job costing program in which you are tracking various jobs and the time and cost of each:

```
struct time
     {
     int days;
     int hours;
     int minutes;
     };
struct job_rec
     {
     int job_code
     char  desc[30]
     struct time billing_time
     };
struct job_rec job;
```

Now if you've worked with database management (such as with dBASE III) you've probably recognized something very interesting here. The address program of the earlier example defined a record and the fields of the record using a data structure (Figure 12.1). Now, however, the field itself becomes like a record within a record with its own subfields—something you can't do with dBASE III or other high-level languages (Figure 12.2).

Figure 12.1
Traditional Database Management Structure

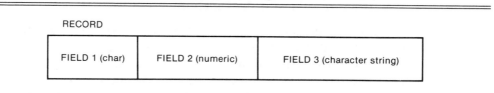

RECORD

| FIELD 1 (char) | FIELD 2 (numeric) | FIELD 3 (character string) |

Accessing members is done by using two period operators on the structures with substructures. For example, to assign the number of job hours as 8:

```
job.time.hours = 8;
```

Figure 12.2
Database Structures Permitted with QuickC

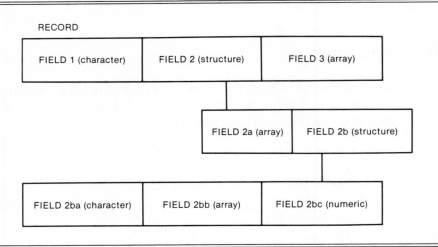

Pointers and Structures

QuickC permits the use of pointers with structures, just as with other data types. This provides three useful advantages:

1. As with arrays, pointers to structures are easier to manipulate than the structures themselves. You don't need to copy one structure to another; just use the assignment operator.

2. Pointers enable the creation and use of many interesting data structures, such as hierarchical record fields.

3. You can use structures with functions and pass the pointer to the structure to the function. This eliminates the time needed to copy the structure values to the function variables.

The ampersand operator (&) is used, as with arrays and other variables, to refer to the address of the pointer to the structure. As with arrays, this operator is used with the structure name as an argument in using a function with a structure. The asterisk (*) is used to indicate the data in an address. One new operator, the *indirect membership operator* (->) is also used to indicate the data of a member.

Let's see how these work:

```
#include <stdio.h>
#define PAD 2
```

continued

```
main()
{
     struct address_rec
            {
            char name[40+PAD];
            char street[40+PAD];
            char city[20+PAD];
            char state[2+PAD];
            char zip[5+PAD];
            };
     static struct address_rec address[2]=
            {       {"James Smith",
                "Box 34",
                "Portland",
                "OR",
                "97211" },
                {"Bill Roberts",
                "34 Fairlane Dr.",
                "Seattle",
                "WA",
                "98732"}
            };

     struct address_rec *one_address;
     one_address = &address[0];
     printf("The first address is %u\n",one_address);
     printf("Here is the address again: %u\n",&address[0]);
     printf("The first name is %s\n",one_address->name);
     one_address=&address[1];
     printf("The second address is %u\n",one_address);
     printf("Here is the address again: %u\n",&address[1]);
     printf("The second name is %s\n",one_address->name);
}
```

Here we have declared an address array as before, and then it is initialized. After the initialization a pointer is defined:

```
struct address_rec *one_address
```

The expression *one_address* is now defined as a pointer to the structure. The next statement assigns it the value of the address of the first address:

```
one_address = &address[0]
```

The next statement prints the value of the address that holds the pointer to the first address:

```
printf("The first pointer is %u\n",one_address)
```

Since *one_address* is also *&address[0]*, the next statement prints the same number.

The next statement introduces a new operator, the indirect membership operator:

```
printf("The first name is %s\n",one_address->name);
```

This prints the actual data value that is in the variable name that is a part of the address pointed to by *one_address*.

The address pointer is then set to the next address and the cycle repeated. The actual output would be similar to:

```
The first address is 3200
Here is the address again: 3200
The first name is James Smith
The second address is 3309
Here is the address again: 3309
The second name is Bill Roberts
```

Notice that the following are all equal:

```
address[0].name   (*one_address).name   one_address->name
```

if

```
one_address == &address[0]
```

Functions and Structures

Data structures can be used with functions just as you would use arrays. The address of the structure is passed to the function, and the function operates on the data using the address. As a general rule, you should not pass the structure itself to the function, as that would be too time consuming and require too much memory. This means that, as with arrays, you must use caution as a function can unintentionally modify the original data if the address is passed to the function.

As an example of using structures with functions, let's take a function that creates screen forms. The desired form is defined as a structure, and this is passed to the function and used to draw the screen:

```
#include <stdio.h>
struct data_frame
      {
      int row,col;
      char *msg;
      };
main()
{
      static struct data_frame main_menu[] =
           {
           10, 25, "MAIN MENU",
           13, 20, "A)dd an address",
           14, 20, "E)dit and address",
           15, 20, "D)isplay an address",
           0,  0,   NULL
           };
      int index;
      void display_form(struct data_frame *);
      display_form(main_menu);
}
void display_form(form)
struct data_frame form[];
{
      int index;
      void displayline(struct data_frame *);

      printf("\033[2J");
      for (index=0; form[index].msg != NULL; ++index)
           displayline(&form[index]);
}
void displayline(ptr_form)
struct data_frame *ptr_form;
{
      printf("\033[%d;%dH",ptr_form->row,ptr_form->col);
      fputs(ptr_form->msg,stderr);
}
```

This is used to write *msg* at coordinates *row, col*. The graphic aspects of this are
described in Chapter 14, but for now let's look at the indirect operation. First,
let's use this structure to initialize an array of these structures:

```
static struct data_frame main_menu[] =
     {
```

continued

```
10, 25, "MAIN MENU",
13, 20, "A)dd an address",
14, 20, "E)dit and address",
15, 20, "D)isplay an address",
0,  0,   NULL
};
```

In this example the NULL is an empty string used to indicate the end of the list of display lines.

The next statement declares the return value of the *display_form( )* function as *void*. It also defines the argument to be used with the function as a *structure data_form* pointer:

```
void display_form(struct data_form *);
```

Here the main program then does nothing but call the *display_form* function, passing a pointer to the form to be used.

The *display_form( )* function clears the screen, then accesses each line of the array for display. The pointer to the structure that contains the display message, row, and column for display is passed as:

```
displayline(&form[index])
```

The NULL is used to sense the end of the array. It is defined in the *stdio.h* file and is an integer with a value of zero.

The *displayline( )* function is used to display each line of the array. The first line in the function is:

```
printf("\033[%d;%dH",ptr_form->row,ptr_form->col);
```

This statement moves the cursor to row, col. For example, the following statement moves the cursor on an IBM screen to row 10, column 8:

```
printf("\33[%d;%dH",10,8);
```

The only difference here is that the membership indirection operator (->) is used to obtain the row and column from the structure passed to the function. The following are both equivalent:

```
ptr_form->row     (*ptr_form).row
```

In both cases the expression represents the actual value of row in the structure. The final function statement outputs the message at the cursor location.

Be very careful in using pointers. You can make some simple changes in the program and the program may still compile and execute properly. Even more strangely, you may find you can compile the program and execute it external to QuickC (using QCL), but if you compile it under the QuickC environment the computer locks up or does other unusual things. The problem is usually the improper use of pointers. Review the warnings at the end of Chapter 10 and recheck your program.

Tip

QuickC does not check completely for proper use of pointers. If you experience compiling problems, check for proper use of pointers. For better protection, turn on the QuickC pointer checking during compile time. This slows down execution some, but is a very good idea during debugging.

Applications for Data Structures

There are three basic reasons for using structures in a program: to permit the use of complex data forms, to permit the use of multiple data types in an array-like structure, and to improve readability.

Structures permit you to create complex data forms, and are particularly useful when data members need to be grouped as part of a larger unit of data. You have already seen that for database management, the data fields become the structure members and the record becomes the unit structure. Data structures can also be used to create binary trees for indexing in database management. Queues, heaps, hash tables, stacks, and graphs can all be represented with data structures. You can also create linked structures, building a network of data with items linked in complex interrelationships.

Structures also permit you to combine data of different types in a single structure. In this chapter, you saw how you could store a numeric value with character strings in an address structure, yet access each member as easily as if it were part of an array.

Structures also improve the readability of the program. In the array example of the last chapter *sales[2][1]* was the sales of the third salesperson. Using a data structure, this could become:

```
salesperson[2].sales
```

which is much more readable.

Finally, structures are the building blocks of complex data types, which form the foundation of object oriented programming. In such applications a structure is used to store all the attributes of the object, which is then used in the program as a single entity.

Unions

A *union* is a method in QuickC for storing different data types in the same memory space. They are used much in the same way as structures; that is, you create a tag or structure and then use this tag to declare variables.

As an example, you could create a union tag called *table* as:

```
union table {
        int number;
        long  address;
        char  code;
        };
```

You could then declare three variables as:

```
union table co_address;
union table code_string[10];
union table address_no;
```

QuickC allocates enough space to hold the largest value that will be stored.

You will find an application of this in Chapter 16 in which the computer's register values are set up to be accessed as 8-bit or 16-bit using a union.

Exercises

1. What would be the advantage of using a structure to store the attributes of various objects in an adventure game written in C?

2. Write a simple function that uses as input the number of the month and the day of the month to return the number of days in the year to that date. Use a structure that contains the month number, name of the month, and the number of days in the month.

Answers

1. The object could be treated as a single entity in the program. For example, the "object" could be passed to a function for an operation. As opposed to an array, you could use different data types for the attributes, including other structures.

2.

```
main()
{
        int no,day;
        int days();
```

continued

```
        char daya[3], noa[3];

        printf("Please enter month number: ");
        fgets(noa,12,stdin);
        printf("Please enter day of month: ");
        fgets(daya,3,stdin);
        no = atoi(noa);
        day = atoi(daya);
        printf("That day is the %sth day of the year.\n",
            days(no-1)+day);
}
int days(month_num)
int month_num;
{
        struct month
            {
                char name[10];
                int days;
                int month_no;
            };
        static struct month month_array[12] =
            {
            {"January",31,1},
            {"February",28,2},
            {"March",31,3},
            {"April",30,4},
            };
        int i,sum;
        for (i=0, sum=0; i <month_num; i++)
            sum += month_array[i].days;
        return(sum);
}
```

Note

You may also wish to add checks to be sure the month number is valid and the day of the month is valid.

13

Using Files and Other Input and Output

In the previous chapters, you have been using a variety of input and output functions without regard to the technical aspects of the internal workings of these functions. This chapter will take you into another level of creating input and output. You will see how to direct output to the printer, how to control keyboard echo on the display, buffer control, and how to use files.

Let's begin by looking at some very general aspects of input and output, then we'll apply these to some applications.

Using Buffers

Most of the input and output functions buffer the data. Essentially, this means the data is stored temporarily in a memory location until it is ready to be used (Figure 13.1). This temporary location is called a *buffer*. This is done automatically. You do not need to define or create this buffer.

Figure 13.1
Using a Buffer

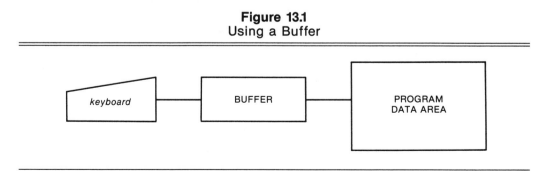

For example, for most applications you will want incoming keyboard characters saved in a buffer until an entire line has been entered. This permits you to backspace, correct any errors, and then continue to enter more. Once you hit the

⟨Enter⟩ key, the buffer contents are sent to the program and the buffer is cleared for the next line. The *getchar(), scanf()*, and *gets()* functions are all buffered input functions. This means that for each of these, no action is taken by the program until the ⟨Enter⟩ key is pressed. The *stdin* (keyboard) variable used by the *fgets()* function usually refers to buffered input, and the ⟨Enter⟩ key and ⟨Control-Z⟩ are handled in a special way in this type of buffered input.

Sometimes you may wish unbuffered input. For example, after a menu is displayed you want the program to wait for the user to enter an option. The user should press one key (no carriage return), after which the option is initiated. The action should be immediate without the need for the pressing of the ⟨Enter⟩ key. In this case you wish direct input without buffering. To do this, use the *getche()* function:

```
printf("Option: ");
option = getche();
```

Another use for unbuffered input is to wait for a user response after an error has been detected:

```
printf("Answer must be 'Y' or 'N'\n");
printf("Press any key to continue\n");
getche();
```

Any command to the program generally should be entered as unbuffered input, as you would want immediate action.

Echoing

During most entries you will want the keyboard entry to echo on the screen immediately after a key is pressed. All of the I/O functions you have used up to this time provide this immediate echo, whether they were buffered (as *fgets()*) or unbuffered (as *getche()*). Sometimes, however, you may not wish the keyboard input echoed.

If the user is entering a password, you do not wish this echoed to the screen as it is typed by the user. For single character input when you do not wish an echo, use the *getch()* function. For example, to enter a password you could use:

```
printf("Please enter password: ");
for (i=0; i<strlen(password+1); i++)
    {
    reply[i]=getch();
    putchar('*');
    }
strcat(reply,"\0");
```

continued

```
if (strcmp(reply,password) != 0)
    {
    printf("Illegal password.\n");
    printf("Press any key to continue.\n");
    getche();
    exit(0);
    }
```

The *getch( )* function is very similar to the *getche( )*, except that the input character is not echoed. The program loads the keyboard entry to a reply buffer, then compares it to the password previously stored in password.

Files

Data stored in the computer memory is volatile; that is, it is lost as soon as you turn the computer off. To save something for later sessions, files are used. Files are named sections of storage on a floppy disk, hard disk, tape, or other storage device. QuickC uses many files such as your source program file, library files, and include files. In some cases, however, you may wish to use files in your program to store data.

For example, if you write a program to process addresses, you would wish to store the addresses in a file so that you can use them in subsequent sessions.

Data is physically stored on the disk in bytes, sectors, and tracks (Figure 13.2). Each of these are of a fixed length on a given machine. Programs, however, view data in logical records. Records may be of varying lengths or of fixed lengths. The records, in turn, are composed of one or more fields (Figure 13.3). For example, assume you have a collection of addresses you wish to store in a file. Each address in the file is a record. The last name, first name, street address, city, state, and zip code are all separate fields in the record.

It is the file buffer that permits the transfer between physical and logical storage. For example, the buffer size for file transfers is defined in the *stdio.h* file as 512 bytes. In writing addresses (records) to this buffer the transfers from the program to the buffer continue until the buffer becomes full. At that time the C I/O system automatically transfers all 512 bytes to the disk, clears the buffer, and then begins again wherever it left off in the current record.

Types of File Transfer

File transfer functions can generally be grouped into four groups, depending upon how they transfer data. For the moment, we'll use as examples the I/O functions with which you are familiar:

Figure 13.2
Physical File Storage

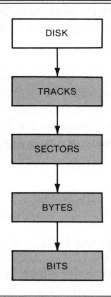

Figure 13.3
Logical File Storage

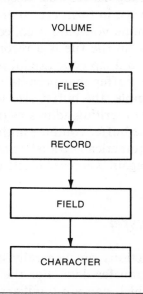

Character I/O: data is transferred a character at a time (examples include *putchar( )* and *getchar( )*).

String (I/O): data is transferred as a character array. The string may be formatted with some functions, with others it is not formatted. (Examples of unformatted string I/O functions include *gets( )* and *puts( )*.) (Examples of formatted string I/O functions include *scanf( )* and *printf( )*.)

Record I/O: data is transferred as a fixed length character string. (There are no examples of this used yet; it will be introduced in this chapter.)

High-Level Versus Low-Level Access

The file read and write functions can generally be grouped into two mutually exclusive groups: high-level and low-level. The high-level functions support buffered transfer, are generally portable with different C compilers, are easiest to use, and provide more internal error checking. The low-level functions provide more direct access of the data and require less memory, but support less error checking and contain no buffering. Table 13.1 shows a relative comparison of the two groups of functions. For most file operations, you will want to use high-level data transfers.

Later in the chapter, you will be introduced to low-level functions such as *open( )*, *close( )*, *write( )*, and *read( )*. These are *low-level functions* for nonbuffered transfers. They are less portable with various versions of C, but are useful in some applications.

Buffered File Transfers

This section will introduce the most common file transfer functions—those used for buffered file transfers. These are all known as high-level functions, and are portable to all C languages; that is, if a program is written using any of these, the call is not likely to need to be changed to compile under another C implementation.

Opening a File

Before a file can be used, it must be opened. This creates a buffer for any file input or output and sets up other necessary control variables (Figure 13.4).

Figure 13.4
Buffered File Data Transfers in a Computer

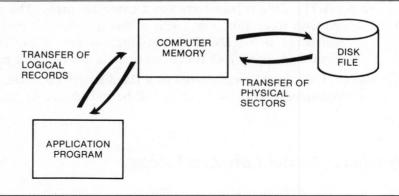

To open a file, you need to use a data structure that is defined in *stdio.h*:

```
#define  FILE     struct _iobuf
extern FILE
    {
    char *_ptr; /* current buffer pointer */
    int   _cnt; /* current byte count */
    char *_base; /* base addr. of I/O buffer */
    char  _flag; /* control flags */
    char  _file; /* file number */
    _NEAR _CDECL _iob[];
    }
```

You can then open a file by defining a pointer to this structure and using the *fopen( )* function to open the file. In its simplest form, this becomes:

```
#include <stdio.h>
main()
{
    FILE *param_file;
    param_file=fopen("ADDRESS.DAT","r");
    :
    :
```

This defines *param_file* as a pointer to a structure for the file ADDRESS.DAT. The *fopen( )* function has a general form:

```
fopen(<file_name>,<access_type>)
```

where access type is:

r = read only. The file must exist.

r+ = read and write. The file must exist.

w = write only. Any current file is deleted.

a = append to current file. Create if it does not exist.

The actual list for available types is much longer, but this will do for our present purposes. The function returns a pointer to the open file. If an error is detected, a NULL is returned.

> **Tip**
>
> Always check for an error return from *fopen( )*. This prevents you trying to read a file that does not exist. For example:

```c
#include <stdio.h>
main()
{
    FILE *param_file=NULL;
    static char file_name[] = "PARAM.DAT";

    if (NULL== (param_file=fopen(file_name,"r")))
        {
        printf("Error opening file!\n");
        printf("Press any key to continue.\n");
        getche();
        exit(0);
        }
}
```

Closing a File

Once you are through with a file, you should always close it. For an output file, this writes any data still in the buffer to the file. For any file, it releases the buffer space for another file. The general form of the file close function is:

```c
fclose(<file_pointer>)
```

Notice that the file pointer is the argument, not the file name. In its simplest form, the close statement becomes:

```c
fclose(param_file);
```

> **Note**
>
> Failure to close a file that is used for writing can cause a loss of data.

> **Tip**
>
> It's possible to check to be sure the file is closed properly. The function returns a value of zero if the file closes properly, and /1 if an error occurred:

```
if (fclose(param_file) != NULL)
    {
    printf("Error on closing.\n");
    printf("Press any key to continue.\n");
    getche();
    exit(0);
    }
```

Reading and Writing Data

The functions for reading and writing data are similar to those for inputting and outputting data you have already used. Let's look at the file I/O functions by pairs.

The *fprintf()* and *fscanf()* Functions

These two functions work like the *printf()* and *scanf()* functions, permitting the input and output of formatted data with a file. The difference is the inclusion of an extra argument for the file pointer. The general form for each is:

```
fprintf(<file_pointer>,<format_string>,<string_pointer>)
```

```
fscanf(<file_pointer>,<format_string>,<string_pointer>)
```

Since both functions are processing arrays, pointers must be used to the arrays. Here is an example of a program to create a PARAM.DAT file of three input character strings:

```
#include <stdio.h>
#include <string.h>
#define PAD 2
main()
```

continued

```
{
    FILE *param_file=NULL;
    static char file_name[] = "PARAM.DAT";
    char reply[80];
    static char ctitle[60+PAD];
    static char pass[2+PAD];
    static char password[40+PAD]="\n";
    int z, i

    puts("Enter Company Name: ");
    fgets(ctitle,sizeof(ctitle),stdin);
    puts("PASSWORD CONTROL ON? (Y/N): ");
    fgets(pass,sizeof(pass),stdin);
    if (stricmp(pass,"Y\n") == 0)
        {
        puts("PASSWORD: ");
        fgets(password,sizeof(password),stdin);
        }
    if (NULL== (param_file=fopen(file_name,"w")))
        {
        printf("Error opening file!\n");
        printf("Press any key to continue.\n");
        getche();
        exit(0);
        }
    fprintf(param_file,"%s",pass);
    fprintf(param_file,"%s",password);
    fprintf(param_file,"%s",ctitle);
    if (fclose(param_file) != NULL)
        {
        printf("Error on closing.\n");
        printf("Press any key to continue.\n");
        getche();
        exit(0);
        }
}
```

Numeric data is automatically converted to ASCII on writing. For example, if you used *fprintf( )* to write the short integer number 254 to a file, it would read it from memory as two bytes, but write it to the file as three characters, or three bytes. On reading data, the *scanf( )* function does just the reverse, converting the file ASCII data to numeric values if that is the format in *fscanf( )*.

In using *scanf( )* to read a file, the return value will be EOF(–1) if the end of the file is reached. This should always be checked:

```
z = fscanf(param_file,"%s",name);
if (z == EOF)
    {
    printf("The end of the file was reached.\n");
    exit(0);
    }
```

The *fputs()* and *fgets()* Functions

These two functions are similar to *puts()* and *gets()*, except that an extra file pointer argument is added. These have the general form:

```
fputs(<string_pointer>,<file_pointer>)

fgets(<string_pointer>,<no_of_characters>,<file_pointer>)
```

Notice an important difference from the *fprintf()* and *fscanf()* functions: the file pointer is the last argument here, not the first. The function returns a string pointed to by *string_pointer*, and reads characters until either of the following conditions is met:

- A new-line character is read
- The end of the file is encountered.
- *no_of_characters*-1 is read.

You can use this, then, to read either sequential record fields in a file of variable length separated by new-line characters or to read fixed-length record fields of *no_of_characters-1*.

We could read the file written in the previous section using:

```
#include <stdio.h>
#include <string.h>
main()
{
    FILE *param_file=NULL;

    static char file_name[] = "PARAM.DAT";
    static char ctitle[60+1];
    static char pass[1+1];
    static char password[40+1]="\n";

    if (NULL !=  (param_file=fopen(file_name,"r")))
        {
        fgets(pass,80,param_file);
        printf("%s",pass);
        fgets(password,80,param_file);
```

continued

```
            fgets(ctitle,sizeof (ctitle),param_file);
            printf("%s",password);
            printf("%s",ctitle);
      if (fclose(param_file) != NULL)
            {
            printf("Error on closing.\n");
            printf("Press any key to continue.\n");
            getche();
            exit(0);
            }
      else  {
            printf("Error on opening.\n");
            printf("Press any key to continue.\n");
            }
      }
}
```

The *fputf( )* function, like *fprintf( )*, does not copy the new-line character or a null to the output device. The *fgets( )* function replaces any new-line characters read from the file with a null character.

As with *fscanf( )*, you should always check the return value of *fgets( )*. If an error or end-of-file is reached, the return value will be NULL.

In this book, we have used *fgets( )* as the preferred input function. The reason for this is that *fgets( )*, unlike *gets( )*, monitors the length of the input line and ensures there is no buffer overflow. The *gets( )* function, if reading an input character string that is too long, can overflow allocated stack space and destroy local variables. There is a trade-off, however. For the QuickC *fgets( )* function, the buffer must be padded by two bytes. The input stream is read up to and including the new-line character (carriage return and line feed). For QuickC, then, the input string is padded by two bytes, as both a carriage return and line feed are read. The last byte is converted to a null.

The *getc( )* and *putc( )* Functions

There are also file versions of the single character I/O functions *getchar( )* and *putchar( )*. These functions work like their counterparts except that the file pointer is included. For example, to read one character from the PARAM.DAT file previously opened you could use:

```
ch = getc(param_file);
```

and to output:

```
putc(ch, param_file);
```

in fact, if you remember from earlier in this chapter the *getchar( )* and *putchar( )* functions are defined in terms of these:

```
#define getchar() getc(stdin)
#define putchar(c) putc((c),stdout)
```

Always check the return value. If the end-of-file is reached, an EOF will be returned:

```
#include <stdio.h>
main()
{
    FILE *param_file=NULL;

    static char file_name[] = "PARAM.DAT";
    static char ctitle[60+1];
    static char pass[1+1];
    static char password[40+1]="\n";

int ch; /* note ch is declared as int */

  if (NULL !=  (param_file=fopen(file_name,"r")))
      {
      fgets(pass,80,param_file);
      while (ch = getc(param_file) != EOF)
              printf("%c",ch);
      fclose(param_file);
      }
    else
      puts("Error on opening");
}
```

In QuickC, the EOF value is –1.

Random Access

QuickC also permits you to randomly access the file, moving quickly to a specific record. Suppose for example, you have a file of addresses and each address takes 130 bytes exactly. If Betty Adams is the fifty-first address in the file, you could use the *fseek( )* function to move directly to the first byte of the address. You would take the length of each address, multiply it by 51, then move directly to that byte in the file using *fseek( )*. This saves the time of having to read all those first 50 addresses.

The general form of the *fseek( )* function is:

```
fseek(<file_pointer>, <offset>, <mode>)
```

Let's look at each of these arguments. The *file_pointer* argument is familiar, but what about the other two?

The *offset* argument tells the function how far to move in the file. It must be a *long* value, and can be positive or negative. The *mode* argument tells where to measure the offset from and has the following values:

Mode	Measure From
0	start of file
1	current position in file
2	end of file

For our file, to find the fifty-first address we would use:

```
fseek(param_file, (long) (51-1) * sizeof address, 0);
```

Note

The offset must be a *long* value.

The file pointer points to the byte in the file where the next access will occur. The *fseek( )* function moves this pointer.

Tip

Whenever possible, use a mode value of zero. This ensures an absolute reference point for your positioning. The mode value of 1 should be avoided unless absolutely necessary, as the current file position may not be what you expect.

The *sprintf()* Function

There is one other buffered I/O function that is useful for creating records, the *sprintf( )* function. This function does not do any output or input, but does permit the creation of a formatted text string. The output is to a buffer you create, which can then be displayed, printed, or written to a file. Here is a simple program using the function:

```
#include <stdio.h>
#define DELIM '~'
```

continued

```
#define EOR '\n'
main()
{
     char name[40+1];
     char password[20+1];
     int len_record;
     char pass_rec[80+1];
   char access_level[9+1];

     printf("Please enter user's first name: ");
     gets(name);
     printf("Please enter password for this user: ");
     gets(password);
     printf("Please enter access level permitted: ");
     gets(access_level);
     len_record=sprintf(pass_rec,"%s%c%s%c%s%c",name,
             DELIM,password,DELIM,access_level,EOR);
     printf("%s %d",pass_rec,len_record);
}
```

Here is a sample session with this program:

```
Please enter the user's first name: bob  〈Enter〉
Please enter the password for this user: able  〈Enter〉
Please enter the access level permitted: 2 〈Enter〉

bob~able~2
11
```

The function creates a composite record from several fields. In this case *pass_
rec* is created from *name, password*, and *access_level*. The fields can be a combination of various data types. Since the fields will be concatenated, it is up to the user to add any necessary delimiter (DELIM, or ~ in this case) to separate the fields. The string will be terminated with null characters, but you may choose to add some type of end-of-record character to mark the end. The function returns the number of characters in the record.

The QuickC library does not provide any internal function to recover a specific field from records created with *sprintf()*, but you can write your own function to do just that:

```
/* routine to extract field from record */
recfield(dest_string,sourc_string,field)
char dest_string[];
char sourc_string[];
int field;
```

continued

```
{
    int dest,source;
    /* get to start of field */
    for (source = 0; --field && sourc_string[source] != '\0';)
        {
        while (sourc_string[source] != '\0' &&
            sourc_string[source] != DELIM)
            ++source;
        if (sourc_string[source] == DELIM)
            ++source;
        }
    /* copy from source to destination */
    for (dest = 0; sourc_string[source] !='\0' &&
        sourc_string[source] != DELIM;
        ++source, ++dest)
        dest_string[dest] = sourc_string[source];
    dest_string[dest] = '\0';
    return;
}
```

This function extracts the field number *field* from *sourc_string* and returns it with a null terminator as *dest_string*. The first field will be 1.

Binary Transfers

In some cases you may wish to save data in a file in binary form. In a nonbinary mode (the default), carriage-return-line-feed configurations are translated to a single line-feed input, and line-feed characters are translated to carriage-return-line-feed combinations on the output. With nonbinary files, a ⟨Control-Z⟩ is used to mark the end of the file. When reading the file, reading terminates with the ⟨Control-Z⟩. In a binary file, the ⟨Control-Z⟩ could be a part of the data, and reading continues until the physical end of the file.

To use buffered binary transfers, append a *"b"* to the access type when opening the file. For example, to open a binary file for reading and writing use:

```
fopen(file_name,"rb+")
```

> **Note**
>
> Avoid trying to edit a binary file with a text editor. The results are unpredictable.

Low-Level I/O

In some cases you may wish to use low-level file transfers. Low-level are unbuffered data transfers, permit more direct control of the data transfer, and can be more efficient than with the use of high-level functions. In this case most of the buffering and error checking is done in the program itself, rather than in the library function.

As an example, assume a mailing list file using random-file access. The file is opened in binary mode. Here is the program to create and list the file:

```
#include <stdio.h>
#include <fcntl.h>
#define ERROR_MSG(x) printf("%s\7\n", x); exit(1)
#define QUERY(msg,reply) puts(msg); fgets(reply, 80, stdin)
#define TRUE 1
#define FALSE 0

main()
{
    int fh_address;
  int cmd;
    char *msg, *x, buffer[20];
    char reply[80];
    long address_no;
    struct address_rec
        {
        long num;
        int flag;
        char last[25+1];
        char first[25+1];
        char street[40+1];
        char city[20+1];
        char state[2+1];
        char zip[5+!];
        };
    struct  address_rec address;

    /* open the file in binary mode */
    if (-1==(fh_address=open("address.dat",O_RDWR | O_CREAT |
O_BINARY)))
            ERROR_MSG("No file: address.dat");
    while (TRUE)
    {
    QUERY("Add or List? ",reply);                          continued
```

```
cmd=reply[0];
if (cmd !='a' && cmd !='l')
      {
      close(fh_address);
      return(0);
      }
QUERY("Number: ",reply);
address_no = atol(reply);
printf("%d",address_no*sizeof (address));
lseek(fh_address, (long) address_no * sizeof (address),0);
if (cmd== 'a')
      {           QUERY("Last name: ",address.last);
      QUERY("First name: ",address.first);
      QUERY("Address: ",address.street);
      QUERY("City: ", address.city);
      QUERY("State: ",address.state);
      QUERY("Zip: ",address.zip);
      write(fh_address,&address,sizeof address);
      }
else if (cmd='l')
      {
      read(fh_address,&address, sizeof (address));
            {
            puts(address.last);
            puts(address.first);
            puts(address.street);
            puts(address.city);
            puts(address.state);
            puts(address.zip);
            }
      }
}
return(0);
}
```

Notice that the file is opened with *open()*. The record is located with *lseek()*. Records are read with *read()* and written with *write()*. The file is closed with *close()*. The argument definitions vary somewhat from the buffered access versions and can vary with the C implementation. Notice here that the *open()* function uses the file name, not the pointer to the file. This program will work using QuickC.

To open a file in binary mode the access code uses a masked template with bits set using previously defined codes. The bits are defined by O_RDWR, O_CREATE and O_BINARY. The bits are ORed together. These definitions are defined in *fcntl.h*, so this file must be included. One of these bits sets the access for binary mode.

Here is an example of using unbuffered functions with a program buffer to create a password file:

```
/* Low-level I/O Example */
#include <stdio.h>
#include <string.h>
#include <fcntl.h>
#define DELIM '~'
main()
{
    int param_file;
    static char file_name[] = "PARAM.DAT";
    char reply[80];
    char ctitle[60+1];
    char pass[1+1];
    static char password[40+1]="\n";
    char param_record[80];
    int cmd;
    int z, i, len_record;

    puts("Create or List Parameter File?");
    fgets(reply,80,stdin);
    cmd = reply[0];
    if (cmd != 'c' && cmd != 'l')
        return(0);
        if (cmd=='c')
            {
            printf("Create option\n");
            puts("Enter Company Name: ");
            gets(ctitle);
            puts("PASSWORD CONTROL ON? (Y/N): ");
            gets(pass);
            if (stricmp(pass,"Y") == 0 )
                {
                puts("PASSWORD: ");
                gets(password);
                }
            if(-1==(param_file=open("PARAM.DAT",
                O_RDWR | O_CREAT | O_BINARY)))
                {
                puts("Error on opening file.\n");
                puts("Press any key to continue\n");
```

continued

```
                    getche();
                    exit(0);
                    }
            len_record = sprintf(param_record,"%s%c%s%c%s",
                    ctitle,DELIM,pass,DELIM,password);
            if ((z  = write(param_file,param_record,80))==(-1))
                    {
                    puts("Error in writing to file.\n");
                    puts("Press any key to continue\n");
                    getche();
                    exit(0);
                    }
            if (close(param_file) == (-1))
                    {
                    printf("Error on closing.\n");
                    puts("Press any key to continue\n");
                    getche();
                    exit(0);
                    }
        }
}
else if (cmd=='l')
    {
    if(-1==(param_file=open("PARAM.DAT",O_RDONLY | O_BINARY)))
                    {
                    puts("Error on opening file.\n");
                    puts("Press any key to continue\n");
                    getche();
                    exit(0);
                    }
    if (z = read(param_file,param_record,80) == (-1))
                    {
                    puts("Error in reading file\n");
                    puts("Press any key to continue\n");
                    getche();
                    exit(0);
                    }
        recfield(ctitle,param_record,1);
        puts(ctitle);
        recfield(pass,param_record,2);
        puts(pass);
        recfield(password,param_record,3);
        if (close(param_file) == (-1))
                {
            puts("Error on closing.\n");
```

continued

```
                        puts("Press any key to continue\n");
                        getche();
                        exit(0);
                        }
                if (strcmp(pass,"Y") == 0 )
                    {
                    printf("Please enter password: ");
                    for (i=0; i<strlen(password); i++)
                        {
                        reply[i]=getch();
                        putchar('*');
                        }
                    if (strcmp(reply,password) != 0)
                        {
                        printf("\nIllegal password\n");
                        printf("Press any key to continue\n");
                        getche();
                        }
                    }
                }

        }
```

The listing for the *recfield()* function was given earlier in this chapter. In this example input data is concatenated with the *sprintf()* function to a record, which is then written with a *write()* function. The record is then read with the *read()* function and the fields removed.

Note

Avoid mixing buffered and unbuffered I/O functions with the same open file.

Printing: Using Standard Devices

If you will examine the *stdio.h* file that came with QuickC, you will find the *getchar()* and *putchar(c)* functions defined as macros:

```
#define getchar() getc(stdin)
#define putchar(c) putc((c),stdout)
```

Notice from this that the *getchar( )* and *putchar(c)* functions are defined in terms of the *getc( )* and *putc( )* functions that reference *stdin* and *stdout* arguments. These arguments are defined in the same file to point to the keyboard and display, respectively. Notice in this same file several other standard devices are defined:

stdin	Keyboard
stderr	Output device for error messages
stdaux	Auxiliary port
stdprn	Printer port

You might imagine, then, that you could define your own output printing function as:

```
/* Printing routine  */
#include <stdio.h>
#define prnchar(c) putc((c),stdprn)

main()
{
    int character;
    character = getchar();
    prnchar(character);
}
```

This new *prnchar( )* function works identically to *putchar( )*, except that the output would go to the printer. The program receives one input character from the keyboard and then prints the one character.

As you will see, this concept of standard devices gives the C language tremendous versatility. In BASIC, to change output from a display to a printer you would need to change all the respective *print* statements to *lprint*. In C, it is only necessary to change a single *#define* at the beginning of the program. You could test a program output on the display and then, when it is close to what you wish, switch it to the printer. You could also have the user queried for the desired output device, then select the proper function using an *if . . . else* structure.

As we shall see later, there are similar variations of the *puts( )* and *printf( )* functions that permit us to direct output to the printer. For example, you could output a string to the printer as:

```
fputs("This is a test.\n\r",stdprn);
```

Before looking at these, however, let's see how the QuickC language processes file input and output.

General Design Rules

This chapter introduced you to the most common file I/O functions, but there are more you will find in your library manual that you can use, such as *fwrite( )* and *fread( )*. All of these are useful, but try to be consistent with your program as mixing buffered functions can add unnecessary length to your program.

As you gain experience, you will find you will want to write your own I/O functions. Most of the standard library functions have limited abilities. For example, here are some ideas for sample functions you might wish to write:

1. A function to accept as input a Y, y, n, or N (without a carriage return) and return an error code if any other value is entered.

2. A function to accept input against a defined template that is passed to the function.

3. A function to accept input between two specified values inclusively, with the range passed as arguments to the function. Any value outside of the range results in the function returning an error value.

The *getchar( )* and *putchar( )* functions permit a lot of flexibility in the design of such functions.

Table 13.1
C Routines for File Operations

Operation	Low-Level Routine	Buffered Routine (High-Level)
Open a file	open	fopen
Close a file	close	fclose fcloseall
Read from a file	read	fread fgets fgetc fgetchar fscanf
Write to a file	write	fwrite fputs fputc fputchar fputf
Reposition file pointer	lseek	fseek rewind
Get file pointer position	tell	ftell

Exercises

1. What are the advantages of the high-level I/O functions over low-level functions?

2. What include file is necessary for all high-level file functions?

3. What include files are necessary for most low-level file functions?

4. Rewrite the low-level example in this chapter to use high-level functions. What is the difference in the size of the executable file?

Answers

1. The high-level functions are generally more reliable, checking for error conditions than low-level functions ignore. They are also more portable to other C implmentations. There are more of them than of the low-level functions, and are easier to use.

2. stdio.h

3. fcntl.h, io.h, types.h, and stat.h

4. Using high-level functions the program becomes:

```c
#include <stdio.h>
#include <string.h>
#include <fcntl.h>
#define DELIM '~'
main()
{
    FILE *in, *out;
    int param_file;
    static char file_name[] = "PARAM.DAT";
    char reply[80];
    char ctitle[61];
    char pass[2];
    static char password[41]="\n";
    char param_record[80];
    int cmd;
    int z, i, len_record;
    long labels;
    char label_string[5], address_file[9];

    puts("Create or List Parameter File?");
    fgets(reply,80,stdin);
    cmd = reply[0];
    if (cmd != 'c' && cmd != 'l')
        return(0);
        if (cmd=='c')
            {
            printf("Create option\n");
            puts("Enter Company Name: ");
            gets(ctitle);
            puts("PASSWORD CONTROL ON? (Y/N): ");
            gets(pass);
            if (strcmp(pass,"Y") == 0 )
                {
                puts("PASSWORD: ");
```

continued

213

```
                                    gets(password);
                                    }
                            puts("Enter Address File Name:");
                            gets(address_file);
                            puts("Enter Number lines per label: ");
                            gets(label_string);
                            if( (out=fopen("PARAM.DAT","rb+"))==NULL)
                                    {
                                    puts("Error on opening file.\n");
                                    puts("Press any key to continue\n");
                                    getche();
                                    exit(0);
                                    }
                            len_record =
sprintf(param_record,"%s%c%s%c%s%c%s%c%s",
ctitle,DELIM,pass,DELIM,password,
DELIM,address_file,DELIM,label_string);
                            fwrite(param_record, 180, 1, out);
                            fclose(out);
                            }
        else if (cmd='l')
                {
                if ( (in = fopen("PARAM.DAT","rb"))==NULL)
                                {
                                puts("Error on opening file.\n");
                                puts("Press any key to continue\n");
                                getche();
                                exit(0);
                                }
                fread(param_record,180, 1, in);
                recfield(ctitle,param_record,1);
                puts(ctitle);
                recfield(pass,param_record,2);
                puts(pass);
                recfield(password,param_record,3);
                puts(password);
                recfield(address_file,param_record,4);
                puts(address_file);
                recfield(label_string,param_record,5);
                labels= atol(label_string);
                printf("%d\n",labels);
                fclose(in);
                if (strcmp(pass,"Y") == 0 )
                        {
```

continued

```
            printf("Please enter password: ");
            for (i=0; i<strlen(password); i++)
                {
                reply[i]=getch();
                putchar('*');
                }
            reply[i]='\0';
            printf("%s %s\n",password,reply);
            if (strcmp(reply,password) != 0)
                {
                printf("\nIllegal password\n");
                printf("Press any key to continue\n");
                getche();
                }
            else
                {
                puts("legal!\n");
                getche();
                }
            }
        }
    }
```

Assuming all other considerations are the same (such minimizing error-checking on the first program), this program will take about 1200 more bytes for the executable.

14

Using Graphics

There are three basic methods of doing graphics with QuickC (Table 14.1). The first is by using the ANSI driver, and is very portable to other C languages and hardware. The second method uses a special QuickC graphics library. Although not as portable, this method provides fast and extensive graphic support. The third method is by using the BIOS services. The first two methods are relatively simple and are described in this chapter (Table 14.1). A brief overview of the third method is described.

Table 14.1
The Three Graphic Support Methods

ANSI Driver	QuickC Functions	BIOS Services
Very portable	Limited portability	Very portable
Slow	Fast	Slow
Limited features	Extensive features	Extensive features
Easy to use	Easy to use	Complex

Using Graphics with the ANSI Driver

One method of creating graphics is to use ANSI output commands. This is a screen-control standard defined by the American National Standards Institute and is supported by an IBM (or Microsoft) driver supplied with DOS called ANSI.SYS. To use this method, the ANSI driver must be installed as a part of DOS by adding the following line in the CONFIG.SYS file:

```
device=ANSI.SYS
```

Once this is installed and the system booted with this new CONFIG.SYS file, you have effectively added a new option to your computer. The driver permits sending commands to the display to clear it, control the cursor, and do other useful features.

This driver is also supported by IBM-compatible computers as well as some computers that are not IBM-compatible, but the installation instructions may differ. Once installed, however, you can use any of the graphic techniques of this section, and you can use them with almost any C language, including QuickC.

How the Driver Works

The ANSI driver is essentially an extension of DOS that sits in memory and intercepts any output to the screen. In monitoring the screen output, it is looking for special codes that identify commands for the ANSI driver. Once it finds one of these character groups, it removes them from the output character string and then acts on the command.

The commands are identified by a special two-byte prefix code. The first byte is an escape character; the second is a left bracket. Following these are some bytes that identify the command itself. For example:

```
printf("\033[2J");
```

will clear the screen. The \033 prefix is the escape character. The left bracket follows, and finally the 2J that identifies the command (clear screen).

This same technique permits cursor control. For example, to move the cursor to row 10 and column 15 you could use:

```
printf("\033[%d;%dH",10,15);
```

To use these commands, the easiest method is to add the commands as an include file to your program. Figure 14.1 shows an example of such an include file. Using this, you could execute the previous example as:

```
MOV_CURSOR(10,15);
```

You could also execute any of these commands directly, as in the first example of this book in which a program to calculate a monthly payment for a load clears the screen before starting.

Pros and Cons

Using the ANSI driver offers the advantage of portability with hardware and C languages, and is a good alternative if you only need to do simple graphics. It

Figure 14.1
Graphic *#include* File for an ANSI Graphics Driver

```
#define CLR_SCREEN puts("\033[2J") /* clear screen */
#define CLR_LINE puts("\033[K")   /* clear to end of line */
#define CUR_MOVE(r,c) printf("\033[%d;%dH",r,c) /* move to r, c */
#define CUR_UP(x) printf("\033[%dA",x) /* move cursor up x rows */
#define CUR_DOWN(x) printf("\033[%dB",x) /* move cursor down x rows */
#define CUR_RIGHT(x) printf("\033[dC",x) /* move cursor right x spaces */
#define CUR_LEFT(x) printf("\033[dD",x) /* move cursor left x spaces */
#define CUR_SAVE puts("\033[s") /* save cursor position
#define CUR_RESTORE puts("\033[u") /* restore cursor position */
```

does have, however, some disadvantages. It is a slow method of generating graphics, frustratingly slow for most programs. For a quick clearing of the screen it is fine, but for trying to draw figures on a slower-type PC this method is not recommended. It also requires the installation of the ANSI driver. Without the driver installed, the command codes will display on the screen and the cursor will do nothing. Finally, graphic support is limited to that supplied by the ANSI driver, which is relatively limited.

The Extended Graphic Set

IBM also provides an extension to the standard ASCII codes that can be used for output. The computer represents symbols for display (characters) as numeric values in memory. The American Standard Code for Information Interchange (ASCII) defines what numbers are used for what characters. IBM extended this definition to include a wide variety of graphic characters. This extension is listed in Appendix C. For example, to print the upper-left corner of a double-line box you could use:

```
puttchar('╔');
```

The ASCII code for this graphics is 201. To enter it from the keyboard when creating your source program, put the keyboard in numeric *mode*, hold down the Alt key, and type 201. Release the Alt key, and the graphic should be displayed in your program listing.

These graphics may not print on your printer when used. They may not work with some C output routines. You may also discover that your editor will not support the entry of the Alt characters. The internal QuickC editor does support the entry of Alt characters.

An Example

Now let's look at a simple example showing how these codes are used:

```c
/* procedure to draw a frame */
#include <stdio.h>
#define CUR_MOV(row,col) printf("\033[%d;%dH",row, col)
#define CLR_SCREEN printf("\033[2J")
main()
{
      int lc,rc,tr,br,i;
      char *msg;

      msg = "MAILING LIST PROGRAM" ;

      /* find the coordinates for the frame */
      lc = ((80 - strlen(msg))/2 )-3;
      rc = 80 - lc;
      tr = 8;
      br = 12;

      /* clear screen */
      CLR_SCREEN;
      /* output frame, then add message */
      frame(lc,rc,tr,br);
      CUR_MOV(tr+2,lc+4);
      printf("%s\n\n\n\n",msg);
      printf("Press any key to continue");
      getche();
}

frame(leftcol,rightcol,toprow,bottomrow)
int leftcol,rightcol;
int toprow,bottomrow;

{
      int vline, hline;

      /* Display four corners */
      CUR_MOV(toprow,leftcol);
      putchar('╔');       /* ASCII 201 */
      CUR_MOV(toprow,rightcol);
      putchar('╗');       /* ASCII 187 */
      CUR_MOV(bottomrow,leftcol);
```

continued

```
putchar('╚');     /*  ASCII 200 */
CUR_MOV(bottomrow,rightcol);
putchar('╝');     /*  ASCII 188 */

/* Display vertical edges */
for (vline=toprow+1;vline<=bottomrow-1;++vline)
    {
    CUR_MOV(vline,leftcol);
    putchar('║');     /* ASCII 186 */
    CUR_MOV(vline,rightcol);
    putchar('║');
    }

/* Display horizontal edges */
for (hline=leftcol+1;hline<=rightcol-1;++hline)
    {
    CUR_MOV(toprow,hline);
    putchar('═');     /* ASCII 205 */
    CUR_MOV(bottomrow,hline);
    putchar('═');     /* ASCII 205 */
    }
}
```

This is a simple example that clears the screen, then puts a double-line frame around a message. You could use these routines in any program, and they are very portable. You should try these to get a feeling of the speed of this type of graphic output on your computer.

Using the QuickC Graphic Functions

QuickC supports the ANSI graphic output previously described, but also includes a collection of graphic mode routines for doing everything from a simple clearing of the screen to animation. These are fast and efficient, and are the preferred method of graphic mode operations with QuickC unless language portability is necessary. In addition, using the QuickC graphic functions means your program will work with whatever graphic video mode the user is using. You don't have to worry whether your user has EGA or a CGA adapter; your program automatically adjusts to whatever adapter is being used if the mode is supported by the QuickC compiler.

The Library

To permit your program to use graphics, you must take two precautions. You must have an include statement for the *graphics.h* file in your program, and the compiler must also have access to the graphics library. These methods of accessible library are discussed in Appendix A.

The Graphics Program Structure

To use the graphic functions with a QuickC program, there is a basic program structure that must be followed. Figure 14.2 shows this structure. There are basically three steps:

1. Set up for graphics operation.
2. Execute the body of your program.
3. Restore the terminal to its default *mode*.

This means you need to write two functions to add to your program. The first, *setup()*, sets up your program. The second, *cleanup()*, restores the terminal:

```
main()
{
    setup();
    <main program body>
    :
    cleanup();
}
```

Note

These functions are not internal to QuickC. You must write them yourself, but once written can be a part of any graphics program you write.

Now let's look at each of these.

The *setup()* Function

The *setup()* function must do two things: It sets which video *mode* to use for the graphics and then gets the data for that mode and stores it to a data structure for program access. The data for the desired mode is in a global data structure and accessible from your program as external variables. In some cases, *setup()* may set other default conditions, such as a fill color, origin, or whether the cursor is displayed or not.

Figure 14.2
The Structure of a QuickC Graphics Program

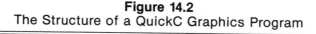

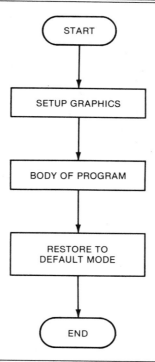

In its simplest form, you could write a *setup( )* function as:

```
#include <graph.h>
struct videoconfig config;
void      setup()
{
    extern struct videoconfig config;
    _setvideomode(_ERESCOLOR);
    _getvideoconfig(&config);
}
```

Both *_setvideomode( )* and *_getvideoconfig* are functions internal to the QuickC graphics library. This routine sets the screen to high-resolution color (EGA) *mode* and then puts the data about this mode for the program to a data structure named *config*.

If you haven't yet, take the time to print the *graph.h* file with QuickC and look at the data in it. You'll see the various arguments for *_setvideomode( )* defined:

```
/* arguments to _setvideomode() */
#define _DEFAULTMODE    -1    /* restore screen to original mode */
#define _TEXTBW40 0           /* 40 x 25 text, 16 grey */
#define _TEXTC40 1            /* 40 x 25 text, 16/8 color */
#define _TEXTBW80 2           /* 80 x 25 text, 16 grey */
#define _TEXTC80 3            /* 80 x 25 text, 16/8 color */
#define _MRES4COLOR     4     /* 320 x 200, 4 color */
#define _MRESNOCOLOR    5     /* 320 x 200, 4 grey */
#define _HRESBW         6     /* 640 x 200, BW */
#define _TEXTMONO 7          /* 80 x 25 text, BW */
#define _MRES16COLOR    13    /* 320 x 200, 16 color */
#define _HRES16COLOR    14    /* 640 x 200, 16 color */
#define _ERESNOCOLOR    15    /* 640 x 350, BW */
#define _ERESCOLOR      16    /* 640 x 350, 4 or 16 color */
#define _VRES2COLOR     17    /* 640 x 480, BW */
#define _VRES16COLOR    18    /* 640 x 480, 16 color */
#define _MRES256COLOR   19    /* 320 x 200, 256 color */
```

You will also find the data structure *videoconfig* defined:

```
short far _setvideomode(short);
struct videoconfig
    {
    short numxpixels; /* number of pixels on X axis */
    short numypixels; /* number of pixels on Y axis */
    short numtextcols;      /* number of text columns available */
    short numtextrows;      /* number of text rows available */
    short numcolors;  /* number of actual colors */
    short bitsperpixel;     /* number of bits per pixel */
    short numvideopages;    /* number of available video pages */
    short mode;             /* current video mode */
    short adapter           /* active display adapter */
    short monitor           /* active display monitor */
    short memory            /* adapter video memory (K) */
    };
```

This means once you set a mode, the number of x and y pixels as well as the number of rows and columns for that mode are available to your program as external variables.

Now let's improve our *setup( )* program by adding some default settings and permitting the function to be used with several modes:

```
#include <graph.h>
#include <stdio.h>
struct videoconfig config;
void    setup()
```

continued

```
{

    extern struct videoconfig config;

    int set_mode(void);

    if (!set_mode())
        {
        printf("This video mode not supported.\n");
        exit(0);
        }
    _getvideoconfig(&config);
    _setcolor(5);
    _setlogorg(config.numxpixels / 2 - 1,
        config.numypixels / 2 - 1);

}
int set_mode()
{
    if(_setvideomode(_ERESCOLOR))
        return(_ERESCOLOR);
    if (_setvideomode(_HRES16COLOR))
        return(_HRES16COLOR);
    if (_setvideomode(_HRESBW))
        return(_HRESBW);
    else
        return(0);
}
```

This permits the program to scan, starting from the EGA mode, to find a mode that the executing hardware will support. If no mode is found, the program exits with the message that "This video mode is not supported." You can add to this *set_mode( )* list as many options as you wish (including VGA), but the order is important. The scan should start at the highest resolutions (with color) first. Create a good copy of *setup( )* and use it with all your programs.

This *setup( )* routine also has two other statements that you may wish to use. The first, *_setcolor( )*, sets the default fill color for closed objects such as rectangles and ellipses. The purpose of the second statement, *_setlogorg( )*, will be discussed in another section entitled "Physical and Logical Coordinate Systems."

The *cleanup( )* Function

The *cleanup( )* function has as its primary purpose the resetting of the video to the default mode. The function is very simple:

```
#include <graph.h>
struct videoconfig config;
void cleanup()
{
    _clearscreen(0);
    _setvideomode(_DEFAULTMODE);
}
```

This clears the screen and resets the video to the mode it was in before the program started.

Writing Text

You can also use graphic routines to write text to the display. Use two internal QuickC functions, _settextposition() and _outtext(). The first function positions the cursor; the second writes the text at the cursor position. For example, to output a message on the last line of the screen you could use:

```
extern videoconfig config;
    :
_settextposition(config.numtextrows,1);
_outtext("Press <CR> to continue...");
```

You can also write your own function to output text at a specified position:

```
#include <graph.h>
#include <stdio.h>
int set_mode(void);
struct videoconfig config;
main()
{
    extern struct videoconfig config;

    void setup(void), cleanup(void);
    void graphout(char[],int,int);

    char msg[80];

    setup();
    graphout("Press any key to continue",config.numtextrows,1);
    getche();
    cleanup();

}
```

continued

```
void graphout(msg,row,col)
char *msg[];
int row,col;
{
     extern struct videoconfig config;
     static char buffer[0]= '\0';

     _settextposition(row,col);   /* set cursor position */
     strcpy(buffer,msg);
     _outtext(buffer);            /* output the text */
}
```

The _settextposition( ) function arguments refer to the actual row and column on the display, not to any pixel location values. You can, however, make this function mode independent by using the variables of the *config* structure and the technique of this example.

Notice also that the use of the _outtext( ) routine does not affect the use of any input routines. Input routines, which relate to the keyboard, are not affected by the use of any graphic routines.

The Coordinate System

Most of the QuickC graphic functions for drawing lines and figures use pixel values as arguments. A pixel is the smallest available display unit on a screen. A typical EGA system uses a display of 640 pixels in each horizontal line and 350 pixels in each vertical line.

For example, if you wish to draw a line you must move the cursor to a starting pixel position (vertical, horizontal pixel value) using one function and then draw the line to a second pixel value pair. Both of these QuickC functions use pixel values. Each point on the screen is identified by a unique set of coordinates. QuickC supports two coordinate systems, a physical and logical. Both coordinate systems use the same number of pixels. For example, for the EGA display mode previously referenced with a 640 × 350 display, you have 640 pixels available in the horizontal dimension and 350 in the vertical.

The Physical Coordinate System

When the graphics mode is entered the system assumes the origin is in the upper-left corner of the screen, and the coordinate values increase going down or to the right; that is, there are no negative coordinate values. This is the default coordinate system and is referred to as the *physical coordinate system*.

The statement:

```
_moveto(174,319);
```

moves the cursor to pixel row 174 and pixel column 319, the center of an EGA display. You can make this statement generic for any type of display supported by using:

```
struct videoconfig.config;
_moveto(config.numypixels/2-1,config.numxpixels/2-1);
```

Tip

In using graphic functions, use the *config* variables as much as possible to keep your program independent of the display mode.

The Logical Coordinate System

You can change the origin of your coordinate system to anywhere on the screen using the _*setlogorg( )* function. You can then, for example, set the origin at the middle of the screen and have both positive and negative coordinate values. Here is an example in which the *setup( )* function has been modified to set the logical origin to the middle of the screen. As before, the program draws a line from the middle of the screen to the lower right:

```
#include <graph.h>
#include <stdio.h>
int set_mode(void);
struct videoconfig config;
main()
{
    extern struct videoconfig config;
    int color;
    void setup(void), cleanup(void);

    setup();
    _moveto(0,0);
    _lineto(config.numxpixels/2 -1,config.numypixels/2 -1);
    getche();
    cleanup();

}
void setup()
{
    extern struct videoconfig config;

    int set_mode(void)
```

continued

```
        int xorigin, yorigin;

        if (!set_mode())
            {
            printf("This video mode not supported.\n");
            exit(0);
            }
        _getvideoconfig(&config);
        xorigin = config.numxpixels/2 - 1;
        yorigin = config.numypixels/2-1;
        _setlogorg(xorigin,yorigin);
}
int set_mode()
{
        if(_setvideomode(_ERESCOLOR))
            return(_ERESCOLOR);
        if (_setvideomode(_HRES16COLOR))
            return(_HRES16COLOR);
        if (_setvideomode(_HRESBW))
            return(_HRESBW);
        else
            return(0);
}
void cleanup()
{
        extern struct videoconfig config;
        _settextposition(config.numtextrows, 1);
        _outtext("Hit <CR> to continue...");
        getchar();
        _clearscreen(0);
        _setvideomode(_DEFAULTMODE);
}
```

Setting the Color

The colors of shapes, pixels, and lines drawn with the graphic functions are set
with the _setcolor() function. For example:

```
_setcolor(1);
_moveto(0,0);
_lineto(config.numxpixels/2 -1,config.numypixels/2 -1);
```

on the EGA screen draws the line as dark blue. Table 14.2 shows the actual color codes for the EGA display.

Table 14.2
EGA Color Codes

No	Color	No	Color	No	Color	No	Color
0	black	4	red	8	dark gray	12	light red
1	dark blue	5	magenta	9	light blue	13	light magenta
2	green	6	brown	10	light green	14	yellow
3	cyan	7	light gray	11	light cyan	15	bright white

Tip

Use the *setcolor( )* function in your *setup( )*; function to set a default color for your graphics. If not set, the default color will be bright white.

An example of setting colors for shapes is shown under *Drawing Shapes*.

Using the *_settextcolor( )* function, you can set the colors for any text displayed with the *_outtext( )* function:

```
_settextcolor(1);
_outtext("This will be in dark blue.");
```

Controlling the Cursor Display

Use QuickC's internal *_displaycursor( )* function to turn the display cursor on or off in the graphics mode. In the default graphics mode, the cursor will be off:

```
_settextposition(15,1);
_outtext("Continue? ");
_settextposition(15,11);
_displaycursor(_GCURSORON);
in = getche();
_displaycursor(_GCURSOROFF);
```

The _GCURSORON and _GCURSOROFF argument values are defined in *graphic.h*.

Drawing Lines

The previous examples show how a line is drawn with QuickC. The *_moveto()* function is used to move the cursor to the starting position, then the *_lineto()* function is used to draw the actual line.

The type of line is determined by the *_setlinestyle()* function. The general form is:

```
_setlinestyle(<mask>)
```

where *mask* is a 16-bit template used to determine the pixel pattern of the line. The default mask is 0xFFFF, which displays a solid line. To set up to draw a dashed line, for example, the mask would be 0xAAAA and the statement becomes:

```
_setlinestyle(0xAAAA);
```

Drawing Shapes

You can also use graphic functions to create graphic objects. The following is a list of the available functions for drawing shapes and the corresponding shape draw:

Function	Shape
_rectangle()	rectangle
_ellipse()	ellipse
_arc()	arc
_pie()	pie

As an example, let's write a program to draw a rectangle. The general form of the *_rectangle* function is:

```
_rectangle(<control>,x1,y1,x2,y2)
```

where:

control	= the fill flag
x1,y1	= upper-left corner in pixel coordinates
x2,y2	= lower-right corner in pixel coordinates

For the control, you can use either of the following, which are defined in *graph.h*:

_GFILLINTERIOR	Fill rectangle with current color from last *_setcolor()*.
_GBORDER	Do not fill rectangle

The rectangle is drawn with the current line style.

As an example, let's draw a rectangle that covers the center fourth of the screen in dark green:

```
#include <graph.h>
#include <stdio.h>
int set_mode(void);
struct videoconfig config;
main()
{
    extern struct videoconfig config;

    void setup(void), cleanup(void);

    setup();
     /* set color to green */
    _setcolor(2);
    xorigin = config.numxpixels/2 - 1;
    yorigin = config.numypixels/2-1;
    /* set logical coordinates */
    _setlogorg(xorigin,yorigin);
    /* draw rectangle and fill */
    _rectangle(_GFILLINTERIOR,-xorigin/2,
         -yorigin/2,xorigin/2, yorigin/2);

    _settextposition(config.numtextrows,1);
    getche();
    cleanup();
}
```

If the first argument of _rectangle( ) is changed to _GBORDER, the rectangle will have a solid green border with an interior that is the same as the background.

To draw rectangles in various colors, the entire program becomes:

```
#include <graph.h>
#include <stdio.h>
#define TRUE 1
int set_mode(void);
struct videoconfig config;
main()
{
    extern struct videoconfig config;

    void setup(void), cleanup(void);
```

continued

```
        int no;
        char noa[9];

        setup();
        do    {
            _clearscreen(0);
            _settextposition(1,1);
            _outtext("Please enter a color number: ");
            fgets(noa,9,stdin);
            no = atoi(noa);
            _setcolor(no);
            _settextcolor(no);
            x = config.numxpixels / 2 - 1;
            y = config.numypixels / 2 - 1;
            _rectangle(_GFILLINTERIOR,-x/2,-y/2,x/2, y/2);
            _settextposition(config.numtextrows,1);
            _outtext("Press any key to continue");
            getche();
            } while (no > 0);
        cleanup();
}
void setup()
{
        extern struct videoconfig config;
        int set_mode();

        if (!set_mode())
            {
            printf("This video mode not supported.\n");
            exit(0);
            }
        _getvideoconfig(&config);
        _setcolor(5);
        _setlogorg(config.numxpixels / 2 - 1,
            config.numypixels / 2 - 1);
}
int set_mode()
{
        if (_setvideomode(_VRESCOLOR))
            return(_VRESCOLOR);
        if(_setvideomode(_ERESCOLOR))
            return(_ERESCOLOR);
        if (_setvideomode(_HRES16COLOR))
            return(_HRES16COLOR);
```

continued

```
        if (_setvideomode(_HRESBW))
                return(_HRESBW);
        else
                return(0);
}
void cleanup()
{
        extern struct videoconfig config;
        _settextposition(config.numtextrows, 1);
        _outtext("Hit <CR> to continue...");
        getchar();
        _clearscreen(0);
        _setvideomode(_DEFAULTMODE);
}
```

The Third Method of Creating Graphics

The third method of creating graphics involves the use of the *int86()* function, which is beyond the scope of this book. This function permits you to load values directly to registers and then activate a software interrupt. Like any method involving the BIOS services, it is slow, but is faster than using ANSI.SYS. It provides far more flexibility than with the use of the ANSI driver.

Note

Portability implies the program can be compiled with a wide base of C compilers for execution on many operating systems. A QuickC program, once compiled, should run on any PC-compatible computer.

Exercises

1. Why should you use the videoconfig variables (such as *numtextrow*) in your program as much as possible instead of your own variables?

2. Write your own *setup()* and *cleanup()* programs as shown in this chapter and check them using a display of a simple rectangle with a fill color.

Answers

1. This permits keeping your program independent of the type of mode of the screen and the hardware of the user.

III

Developing Programs
with QuickC

A large computer program is just as complex as a bridge, building, or automobile. Designing a large computer program is just as difficult as designing the same bridge, building, or automobile. You would not purposely begin the construction of anything that is complex without carefully planning things in advance. Writing a computer program without carefully planning it ahead of time would be like sending a construction crew to construct a building without first giving them a plan from which to work.

One common feature of any complex program is that, once completed, it seldom works exactly as you planned. There are always hidden problems that remain increasingly difficult to resolve. Most major computer manufacturers will freely admit to hidden problems in their operating systems that can never be resolved in spite of a large user base and the best intentions of the manufacturer. If the program was well-designed from the beginning, finding any problems requires a minimum of time and is simple. If the program was poorly designed from the beginning, finding elusive problems can be costly and time-consuming.

In this section, we'll look at some of the basic issues of designing and testing programs. The basic issues of this section apply to any programming language, but QuickC will be used for illustration purposes. We'll take a small mailing list program and follow it through the design and programming. Although this system is relatively simple, it is purposely kept that way to illustrate the principles involved. The principles described in this part apply to any complex system such as a general ledger, job-costing system, inventory control system, or other application.

15

Introduction to Structured Programming

Several years ago I received a request to develop a job-costing system for a well-known company that prepared media advertising for many companies. They had a program that had been developed by someone with a little programming experience using a very popular high-level language, but it didn't work and didn't do what they needed. They wanted me to get everything working.

My first request was for the plans for the system they were currently using. What were the goals? What did the programs they had do? How did the programs relate to each other? What was the database structure? There were no plans. They suggested I list the programs and work backward, doing what is known to programmers as "reverse engineering." The original goals had never been clearly defined, however. Working backward to study a program that didn't meet the needs would have not solved the problem.

The final result was to begin again, defining what really needed to be done in clear objective goals, then carefully working through the design, and then writing the program. A lot of cost and time could have been saved had this structured design been done the first time.

This chapter will look at two alternatives to resolving this type of problem: structured design and rapid prototyping. The chapter will also introduce the principles of structured design as applied to a mailing list program.

The Five Steps

Any *system* is a set of components that acts as a whole. In the context of designing a software system, we could say a system is an integrated collection of programs and data that acts as a unit. The purpose is to process information. The output is generally reports, labels, or display screens. In other cases the system may be called upon to do a specific action, such as activating traffic signals, sounding an alarm, or activating a robot for the assembly of a product. The input to the system is normally data supplied by the user, but could also be data from sensors or another computer. Systems use feedback to ensure that the goals are met; that is, part of the output is fed back to the input and becomes a part of the input data.

The process of developing a system can be seen as five steps: analysis, design, programming, implementation, and maintenance (Figure 15.1). This figure seems to imply that the development is a linear process in time, beginning with the analysis and concluding with the implementation. In reality, this is true to only a limited extent. Although the idealistic goal is to complete each step before moving to the next, in most applications there is a considerable amount of backtracking and redesign. The development process itself is a systematic process, and feedback is constantly used to ensure that the development goals are being met.

Figure 15.1
Developing a System

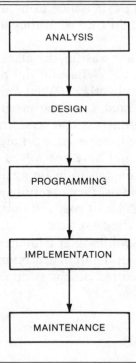

For each phase, there are many tools and techniques available. For many applications, the most cost-effective approach is that of structured development.

Structured Development

The word *structured* here is a general term that can be applied to any of the five phases. Structured development implies the following two aspects:

1. Modularity—the system involves a collection of smaller modules. The automobile is really a collection of smaller systems or modules: the cooling system, the electrical system, the drive system, and the braking system. Engineers view all these very complex systems as a collection of modules, which are in turn collections of small modules. Each module has less complexity than the whole. For example, the ignition system is a part of the electrical system. When repairing a car, the first objective is to identify the smaller system (or module) that is causing the problem. This localizes the problem and reduces diagnostic time.

2. Hierarchical—this implies that there is an order or relationship between the modules. The order is "top-down." In the design, for example, we start at the top with the design of the main program, or control program. What is the objective here? From this we can define what modules or programs will be needed at the next level to support the main objective. Once this is done, we can define the modules and functions at the next level. What should be the objective of each of these? This continues until we reach the lowest level of the program (Figure 15.2). No matter how complex the system, this generally leads to a solution. For example, in starting we know what the main module is supposed to do. That's defined by our overall global objectives. This can then be "chunked" out to small objectives, which are less complex. Eventually we can get down to very small modules that are easy to design and develop.

Structured techniques can be applied to each of the four steps.

Structured Analysis

The objective during this step is to study the problem in detail before beginning the design. The analysis should yield a goal as well as subgoals for the individual modules. The goals should be documentable in clear, objective terms so that the system performance later can be measured against these goals. From this, specifications can be created and a cost analysis made. There should also be feedback at this level to ensure that the specifications are accurate.

The analysis cycle may involve surveys. Generally, two types of surveys are involved: management and user.

The management survey should involve the people who will be using the data from the program. What type of data do they need to make decisions? What type of data do they already have? Too much data is as bad as too little. Are

Figure 15.2
Modular Design

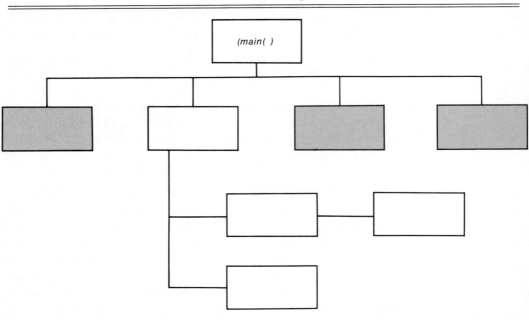

graphics or charts needed? What type? What financial resources and time frames are available for solving the problem? What hardware and software resources are already available? If reports or charts are currently being used, these should be studied for missing data or data that is not necessary.

The user survey involves those who will be entering the data to the computer, using the program directly, and capturing the output for the management. What type of software interface do they need for maximum productivity? Many aspects of this will be covered in later chapters of this section, but this is a good chance to identify problems currently in how the data is obtained, entered, and processed. For example, in one company a receptionist answered the phone and, in addition, had the job of entering data to the computer between phone calls and welcoming visitors. Such a three-way job description could seriously impair the accuracy of the data being entered as well as frustrate the user. It would have been better to rotate the responsibility, having someone else at the front desk for the hour or so a day it took the user to enter the day's data.

The Specifications

In our example here, the analysis is for the design of the mailing list processing system. The general specifications from the analysis phase is shown in Figure 15.3. The sheet should also include specifications for submodules and, if possible, the low level modules below this.

Figure 15.3
The Specification Sheet

MAILING LIST PROGRAM SPECIFICATIONS

OBJECTIVES

The design of a mailing list program for the processing of an organization's membership for reports and mailing labels.

GENERAL OVERVIEW

The program should permit the management of an address list of 500-1000 names. The addresses are all US with single-line street address lines. This will be used to print the annual membership directory and for printing mailing labels for newsletters. This system will replace the current service bureau processing.

COST ANALYSIS

Currently the address list is processed by a local service corporation that charges $25 to process 500 labels, or 5 cents a label for each monthly mailing. Using the computer resources that are already in-house, the system should permit us to reduce this to 1 cent a label. We would also have much better control over the updating of the list, eliminating many duplicate mailings and bad addresses.

The development cost could be shared by three other local organizations that are interested in a similar program and perhaps marketed to other local organizations that are part of our national charter.

MODULE LISTING

```
Add - Add an address to the mailing list
Edit - Edit or change an existing address
Delete - Delete an address from the mailing list
Display - Display a mailing list address
List     - Print or display mailing list output
        Directory - print entire directory
        Labels - print mailing labels
Miscellaneous - Displays file status, edits parameter file
```

ADDRESS DATABASE

The database consists a single address file with records of seven fields:

Description	Type	Size
[Membership number]	numeric	1-1000
Last name	character	25
First name	character	25
Street Address	character	40
City	character	20
State	character	2
Zip	character	5

Figure 15.3 (Cont.)

The first name should be stored in a separate field from the last name to permit use with a form letter module that might be added later. All entries except the State and Zip might contain spaces, periods, or other special characters. Prefixes (Mr., Mrs., etc.) should be permitted as a part of the first name and suffixes (Ph. D, etc) permitted as part of the last name.

The database construction may be updated in the future to include a comment or other fields. The system should be designed with this in mind.

MODULE SPECIFICATIONS

General

All modules should reflect a common user interface to help the user as much as possible. Error conditions should be trapped as much as possible and a message displayed for a user action.

Two files are used. A parameter file is used to control the company name (displayed on each screen), the address file currently in use (displayed on each screen), and the number of lines for the mailing label. These can be edited from a parameter edit program. The file also contains a flag on whether a password access is used and the current password code (one-level). These cannot be changed from within the program. The second file is the address file, which supports the address database. It contains a header with the number of records in the file.

Main Menu

This is the main program initiated when the system is started. It should verify access with a password, then display the main menu. The user selects the desired option, which then calls the appropriate program. No carriage return should be necessary with the option entry. The options should be coded by function (A=Add, for example), and not by numbers (1 = Add). Option entry in upper and lower case should be permitted. All illegal options should be identified and the appropriate message displayed. The message should remain on the screen until the user presses a key.

Add

This module adds a name to the mailing list. The program is a two-screen input program. The first screen displays a request for the membership number. If there is no name on file for that number, a form is then displayed for the entire address to be entered. If there is a name on file for that number, the user is notified and a request is made for another number. If a blank number is entered, the program returns to the main menu.

Within each field during entry simple editing (backspace and overtyping) should be permitted.

After the entire address is entered, address verification by the user should be permitted before the address is saved. If the address is accepted, it is saved. If rejected, the user can edit the address before saving.

Edit

This module edits or changes an existing address. It should function as a two-screen program, like the Add. The first requests the membership number to edit, then verifies the name is on file. The current address is then displayed for editing. The user may accept the address, then choose whether to write the address to the file or not. If the address is rejected, it is displayed again for editing.

Delete

This option deletes an address from the mailing list. The first screen requests the membership number, and the address is retrieved and displayed. An option to delete is then displayed.

Figure 15.3 (Cont.)

<u>Display</u>

This option display a mailing list address. Like the Add, Edit, and Delete modules it uses two screens. The first screen requests the membership number. If an address is found for that number, the address is displayed with a second screen. If no address is found, an error message is displayed.

<u>Report</u> - Menu for label or directory printing.

Directory - This option prints the direction in a one-up paged form.

Labels - This option print mailing labels at a specified number of lines per label.

<u>Miscellaneous</u> - displays status and edit parameter file.

Status- This displays the current status of the address file, showing the number of records in the file and the number of non-deleted addresses in the file.

Parameter - This permits editing of the company name, the address file name, and the number of lines per label. The password access control cannot be changed from this program.

GENERAL ERROR RECOVERY DESIGN STRATEGIES

Illegal data entry should be trapped as much as feasible and identified with an error message to the user. Illegal menu options, membership numbers out of range, etc, should all be trapped for error messages.

The last line of the screen should be used for all error messages. They should be in plain english. The message should contain the request to "Press any key to continue", and remain on the screen until the user presses a key. The bell should also sound.

Specifications are the starting point for the design and programming. You may wish to backtrack and modify them later, but they should be specific and detailed. You cannot hold the programmers accountable for something that isn't in the specifications. For example, you might start with a single line for the street address. Later (during programming) you discover some new members coming in that need two lines for the street address. Then you'll have to backtrack to square one, then make a decision on whether the cost involved justifies the need to modify the specification. In making the original specifications, you could save some time by putting in a note that it should be easy to change the field specifications at a later time. You would also need to specify what this "later time" means (before or after you start adding addresses to the file?). Adding this note, however, could increase the design cost.

The Data Flow Diagram

The next step is the creation of the data flow diagram. This data flow diagram (DFD) is a graph of related functions and files showing the interfaces between all the system components. This is called a bubble diagram by some developers, as each component is represented by a bubble. The diagram shows only how the data flows, and does not illustrate the control of this data.

If there is an existing system, you could start by drawing a diagram of this current system. This is important, even if the old system (Figure 15.4) did not use a computer. At this initial state, the diagram may include names and departments. Between the bubbles will be lines representing reports, forms, and other forms of current data communication.

Figure 15.4
The Physical Analysis Diagram for the Old System

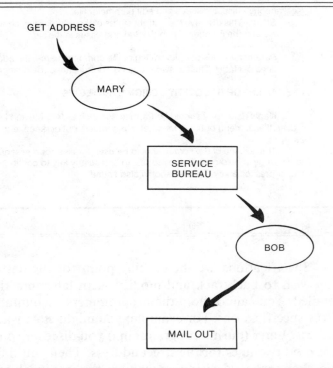

This diagram is then converted to a logical diagram. The bubbles will now contain verb phrases ("Enter address"). Between the bubbles the lines will contain the objective of that phase ("Mailing labels"). An example is shown in Figure 15.5.

The key question with both diagrams is always how detailed to make them. A single bubble can be expanded to several in a more detailed diagram (Figure 15.6). For most practical applications in QuickC, make the diagrams as detailed as possible. Overview diagrams may also be done that are less detailed, but show the overall flow better.

Figure 15.5
A Logical Diagram for the New System

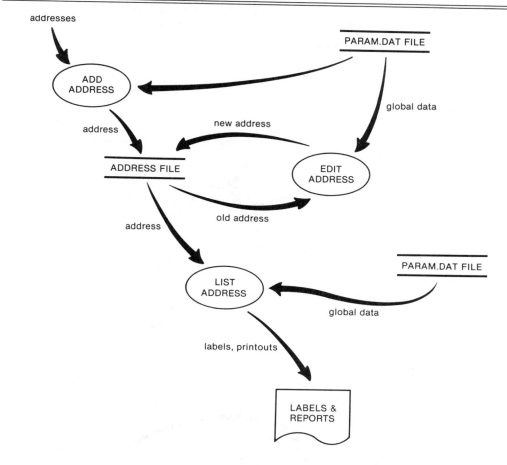

The Data Dictionary

The DFD is a very valuable communications tool for the programmer, the managers, and the users of the system. A parallel document, the data dictionary, is a set of definitions for data flows, data elements, files, databases, and processes on the DFD. It is the glossary for the DFD.

For more information on structured analysis, the reader should see *Structured Analysis and System Specification*, by Tom De Marco (Prentice-Hall, Inc., 1979).

Figure 15.6
A Detailed Diagram for the Add Module

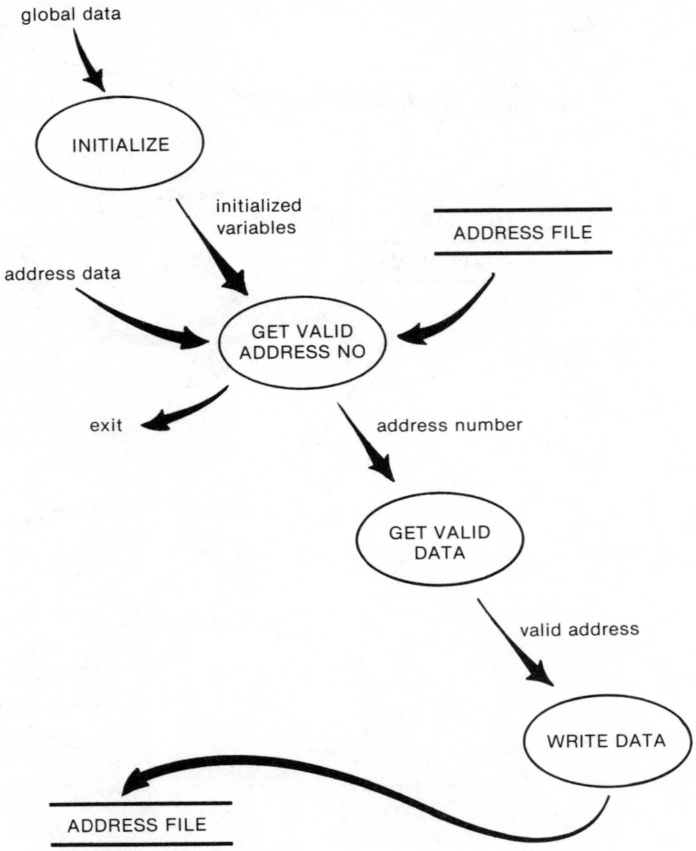

Structured Design

The purpose of the design step is to transform the specifications and data flow diagram into a plan for implementing the proposal. *Structured design* implies conquering the complexity of the system by partitioning and hierarchical organization.

Structured design uses two tools to accomplish its purpose: the structure chart and pseudocode.

The Structure Chart

The *structure chart* is a graphic tool that shows the partitioning of the system in modules. It is created from the DFD. The modules are rectangles in this diagram, and the lines between the modules show the flow of data.

Each rectangle in the structure chart solves one well-defined piece of the problem. It can be specified separately with its inputs and outputs. Each box has a single function. Each box should be as independent as possible.

Figure 15.7 shows the partial structure chart for the mailing list program. Notice the structure chart has a hierarchy, which can be of several levels.

Figure 15.7
Partial Structure Chart

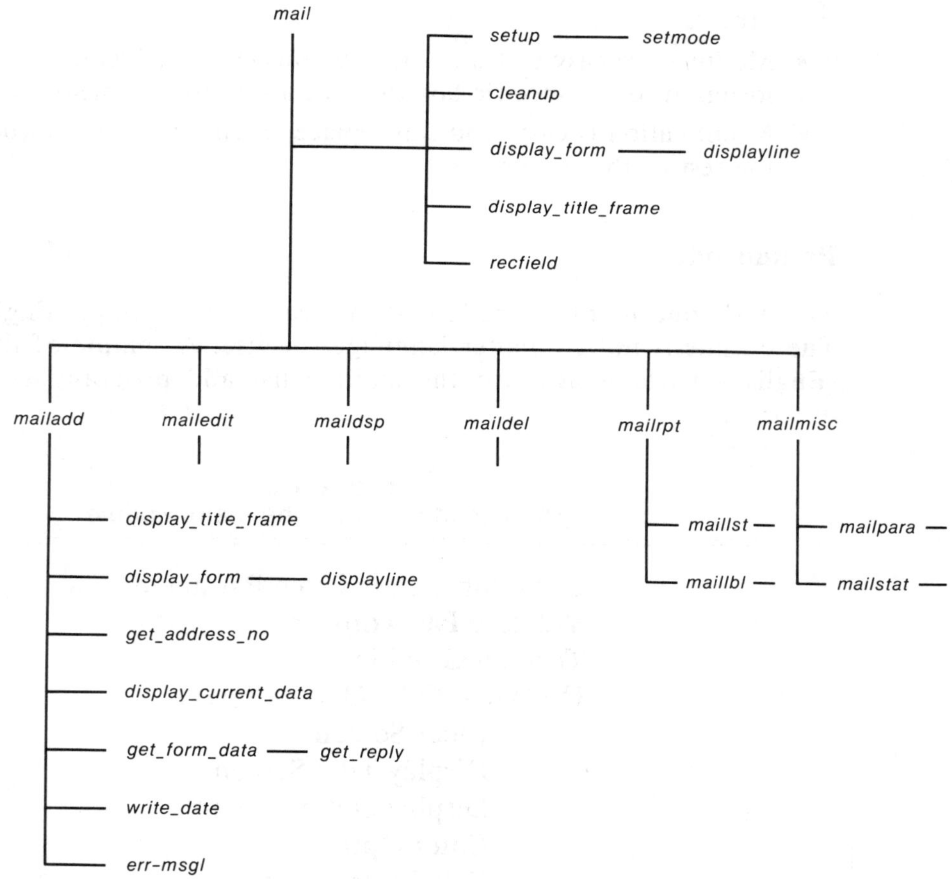

At the top level is a single module, the main menu module. This, in turn, can call any of five main modules:

ADD—adds an address

EDIT—edits an address

DISPLAY—displays an address

LIST—lists addresses

MISCELLANEOUS—indexes, controls parameters

Notice even at this level each module has a single well-defined function. Some of these modules have another level. For example, the LIST module can call either of two modules: one for listing labels, another for listing the directory.

This modular concept has several advantages:

- Modules are easy to construct. Each can be specified independent of the others.
- Modules are easy to test. If the system has a problem, it is easily localized to the specific box that is causing the problem.
- Modification is easy. You can replace an entire module without changing the rest of the system.

Pseudocode

The basic outline of the code is then created using simple English sentences. The outline is not computer language specific. A sample of the pseudocode (English-like language) for the mailing list add program is shown in Figure 15.8.

Figure 15.8
The Pseudocode for the Main Module

Get Global Data From Parameter File
Validate Password
Turn on Graphics
Do While OPTION < > QUIT
    Clear Screen
    Display Title Screen
    Display Option Menu
    Enter Option
    Call Option Module
Enddo
Return Screen to Default

Structured Programming

By now you've already had some experience with programming from Part II, but what exactly is structured programming? Again, this is simply following the rules of modularization that have already been described. As a general rule you will work top-down, writing the menu program first and then the next level modules. In some cases, however, you may write low-level modules, in essence working bottom-up. As a basic summary of this step:

- The programs, modules, and functions are designed as independent entities. Each is specified and written as an independent unit.

- The modules have a hierarchical relationship to each other.

- Each module performs a single function.

- Each module has a single entry point and a single exit point. You cannot "Goto" any particular point in the module, nor can you branch to another point based on a variable value.

- Common modules are stored as functions and used by multiple programs.

- Decision control is done with *if . . . else, while, and do . . . while.* You cannot use *gotos*.

- Indentation can be used with all decision controls.

- Data is passed to functions as arguments. Data is returned using arguments or return values. The use of global variables should be kept to a minimum.

- Modules should be documented.

- Data structures should be supported to permit the user to group like data in hierarchical relationships. Function arguments should be kept to a minimum and structures or arrays used to pass like data to a function as a single argument.

Whatever language is used for structured programming, it will need to support all these features. QuickC is specifically designed for structured programming and supports all these features. The remaining chapters of this section develop the structured programs for the mailing list example.

Structured Implementation

Structured Implementation refers to implementing programs a module at a time. For example, once the main menu program and add module are ready, the users could begin adding addresses while the remainder of the programs are being written.

At a more general level, structured implementation is often not as important as another aspect of implementation—parallel testing. For any complex system, both the new system and the old system should be used until there is a high degree of security about the new system. For example, if you are using a new computer program to implement a general ledger system, the older manual system or old computer program should be used with the new program for several periods. The reports should be compared for errors or discrepancies. This should be done even if the new program is a well-proven commercial product.

Structured Maintenance

Structured maintenance refers to the use of top-down techniques to resolve problems in the system. If your automobile is not working properly, the mechnaic begins by localizing the problem to the cooling system, fuel delivery system, electrical system, or another system. The meachanic works in a top-down fashion, from the general to the specific.

In the same way, software diagnostic procedures work top-down, from the general to the specific. The primary goal is to isolate the function involved as quickly as possible.

Documentation

Documentation is not something that is done when all the rest is done and there's time and money left. Documentation should be done at each step, and is the "baton" in the relay race that is passed to those working on the next step. If you have to backtrack to a previous step, update the documentation and then move forward again.

Rapid Prototyping

In some cases it is difficult, or impossible, to define the modules explicitly from the start and to work through the complete design before programming.

An example of this might be a diagnostic medical system. In this case, the goal might be specific with a defined small group of diseases as conclusions and another collection of symptoms as the input data. The relationship of the symptoms to the conclusions, however, may not be clearly known or the research knowledge is changing frequently. Then the structured approach would not meet the needs, and another alternative would be necessary.

One frequently used alternative is what is known as rapid prototyping or "step-wise" refinement. Here, a small system is created that does a limited part of what the user desires. The user begins with this, then makes suggestions for refinement. These suggestions are then implemented. Gradually, the system becomes more complex and useful. Program code that becomes repetitive is broken off as modules, and new statements are added that permit the addition of new features.

Modal Versus Modeless Programs

One important question that should be approached on design is whether the program is modal or modeless in design.

In a *modal* program, there is a certain linear flow to the modules that must be observed. A good example is a general ledger program. You start by creating a batch, then posting the batch, printing the ledger reports, and finally closing the period and printing the final reports. There is a linear time flow to the modules; that is, you have to use them in a certain order. The mailing list program of this section is designed as a modal program. In a modal program, the order of the menu items is important, as it reflects the way the user should use the modules.

In a *modeless* program, there is no overall order required in using the modules. A spreadsheet program is essential modeless, and so is the popular PageMaker® program by Aldus. The menu is displayed, and the user is constantly moving about with different menu options at different times. There is no "forward" or "backward" on the menu. Microsoft Windows is particularly good for developing modeless programs, but can also be used with modal programs. QuickC cannot be used with Microsoft Windows.

Preliminary System Design Goals

The system should give the user positive feelings. It should be easy to use (while perhaps supporting complex functions), predictable (it shouldn't work one way one day and another way another day), fast (keep up with the user), and reliable (the results should always be correct).

The designer should also keep in mind the environment in which the system will be used. Here are some general environment definitions:

Home/Entertainment

Business/Office

Industrial/Military/Commercial

Life-critical

Exploratory/Expert/AI

Scientific/Engineering

The environment and the experience of the user determine the vocabulary of the screens, the level of functionality to be supported, how reliable the program must be, how safe the program must be from invalid entries, the program complexity (size, cost, development time), and the help level that must be supported. In summary, the developer must always keep the user in mind in developing the program.

There may also be personal or physical constraints on the program design. A person with one hand may have less trouble using a mouse than a keyboard. A mouse interface may be required. Displays that use color can be difficult for a color-blind person to use if the colors are set to the wrong values. If you are writing a program for commercial distribution, all this must be taken into account.

One of the best starting points is to examine similar products that can be identified as well-designed. The type of application is not as important for this study as the method in which the product is designed and the user interface. The basic menu structure of Lotus 1-2-3®, for example, has been copied into other products, such as the Paradox database manager.

16

Developing with QuickC

Before beginning the design, let's take a short diversion to the actual mechanics of developing the system with QuickC. The system will involve a large number of programs that are interrelated. They will need to be compiled, linked, executed, and debugged. There must be a planned strategy in this process. This chapter will review the basic aspects of the mechanics of this development.

Compiling and Linking

The basic strategy is to compile the collection of source modules to the same number OBJ files, then link them with a linker to one final EXE file.

QuickC contains two compilers that can be used for development. You can use either or both in your development: the QuickC environment or the QCL program.

The QuickC Environment

The QuickC environment is the fastest and easiest to use. You start it as:

```
C:\QC  \lQCLIB  <Enter>
```

This method uses the internal editor, and normally compiles to a memory EXE image that can be executed immediately. The problem here is that each source program also uses functions in other source programs. Compiling any of the source programs in this chapter this way will give you many unresolved external error messages.

One method of resolving this is to use the Run Compile menu to compile each source to an OBJ file (Figure 16.1). Work at this level until the compiled code has no errors, then exit the QuickC environment and use an external linker to link object modules to an EXE file. This has the disadvantage, however, in not being able to use the internal QuickC debugger. You could, however, use CodeView.

Figure 16.1
The Run Compile Dialog Box

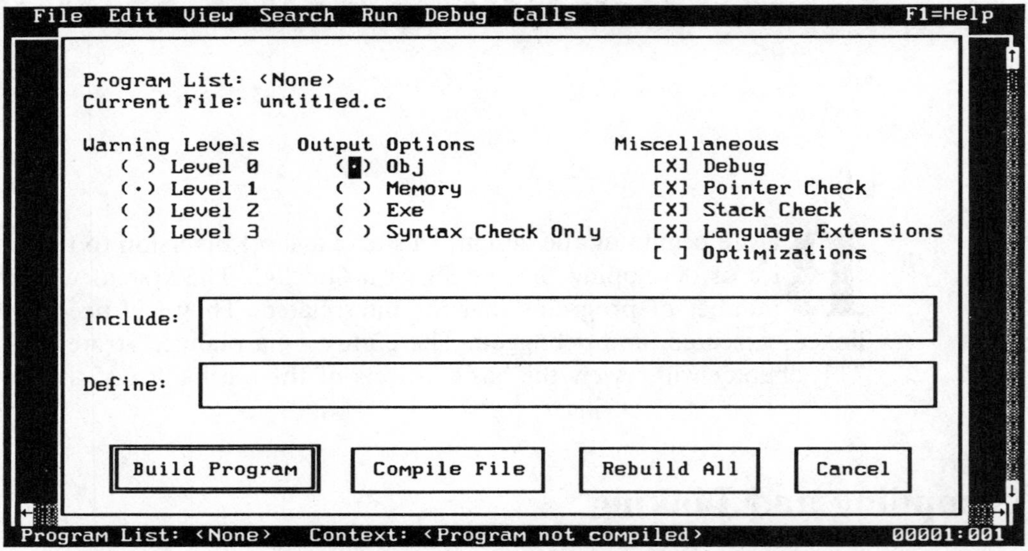

```
 File   Edit   View   Search   Run   Debug   Calls                    F1=Help

    Program List: <None>
    Current File: untitled.c

    Warning Levels    Output Options           Miscellaneous
       ( ) Level 0     (■) Obj                   [X] Debug
       (·) Level 1     ( ) Memory                [X] Pointer Check
       ( ) Level 2     ( ) Exe                   [X] Stack Check
       ( ) Level 3     ( ) Syntax Check Only     [X] Language Extensions
                                                 [ ] Optimizations


    Include: [                                                    ]

    Define:  [                                                    ]


     [ Build Program ]   [ Compile File ]   [ Rebuild All ]   [ Cancel ]

 Program List: <None>    Context: <Program not compiled>        00001:001
```

Another method is to create a program list with the names of the external modules using the File Set Program List command (Figure 16.2). This creates a MAKE file, which permits you to compile and link all the modules involved from within the QuickC environment (Figure 16.2) using Run Compile.

Another method that can be used to test any of the individual program modules in a system is to create a temporary stand-alone program module. This can then be compiled, linked, and executed in the QuickC environment with no program list. This also permits easy debugging. For debugging the MAILADD program of Chapter 19, for example, you could do the following:

1. Use the File DOS SHELL command in QuickC to create a new test program from MAILADD.C.

2. Load to the QuickC environment for editing and change the program name to *main( )*.

```
void main()
```

3. Add program lines to initialize the global variables that would normally be from the parameter file:

Figure 16.2
The Set Program List Dialog Box

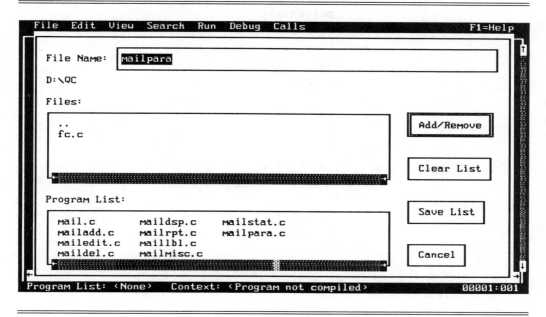

```
 File  Edit  View  Search  Run  Debug  Calls                    F1=Help

   File Name:  mailpara

   D:\QC

   Files:

      ..
      fc.c                                          Add/Remove


                                                    Clear List


   Program List:                                    Save List

      mail.c       maildsp.c     mailstat.c
      mailadd.c    mailrpt.c     mailpara.c
      mailedit.c   maillbl.c                         Cancel
      maildel.c    mailmisc.c

 Program List: <None>    Context: <Program not compiled>        00001:001
```

```
extern ctitle[]="OREGON PROFESSIONAL MICROSYSTEMS";
extern address_file[]="ADDRESS.DAT";
    ⋮
```

4. Add a call to *setup()* at the beginning and a call to *cleanup()* at the end.

5. Declare calls to *setup()* and *cleanup()* as void.

6. Merge in functions from other programs that are needed, such as *setup()*, *cleanup()*, *display_form()*, and so forth using File Merge.

You should then be able to compile, execute, and debug the program in the QuickC environment. Keep track of your corrections and transfer these later to MAILADD.C.

Another method to eliminate the need for a program list during testing is to comment out calls that are not currently used. For example, to test the main menu program of Chapter 18 you could comment out all the module calls:

```
option=getche();
_displaycursor(_GCURSOROFF);
if (islower(option))
     option = _toupper(option);
switch(option)
{
```

continued

```
/*
        case 'A' :
                mailadd();
                break;
        case 'E' :
                mailedit();
                break;
        case 'S' :
                maildsp();
                break;
        case 'D' :
                maildel();
                break;
        case 'R' :
                mailrpt();
                break;
        case 'M' :
                mailmisc();
                break;
/*
        case 'Q' :
                cleanup();
                exit(0);
        default :
                _settextposition(config.numtextrows,1);
                _outtext("Illegal input - press <CR> to continue");
                option=getche();
    }
```

This program should compile without a program list and can be executed directly.

The QCL Compiler

Another method of constructing a system is to use the external QCL compiler with a linker, just as with any other C compiler. This gives you better library access than with the QuickC environment, and is the preferred approach if you are having trouble with unresolved external library references. Use the /c option to compile a module to an object code, then link:

```
C:\QCL /c MAIL.C      <Enter>
C:\QCL /c MAILADD.C   <Enter>
C:\LINK mail+mailadd+mailedit+maildel+maildsp+maillst
```

```
+mailmisc+mailpara+mailstat+mailrpt+maillbl,mail,mail;
<Enter>
```

You can use the QuickC editor to create the program or your own editor. This may seem like reverting to the stone age when you've worked with the QuickC environment awhile, but remember that the QCL compiler is very fast and the library access is comprehensive.

Debugging

No matter how carefully you design and write your program, you can expect the eventual errors to plague your development and cost you valuable time. QuickC provides several internal debugging support techniques. This section will loop at several of these, plus provide an introduction for strategies beyond QuickC's internal debugging techniques.

Internal QuickC Debugging

QuickC provides three methods of internal debugging support: compiler options, tracing with breakpoints, and watch expressions. Let's look at each of these. All these methods use commands that are compatible with Microsoft's CodeView debugger that has been available for the Microsoft C Version 4.0 and Microsoft Macroassembler.

As an exercise on using these techniques, enter the following program, compile it, and be sure it works:

```
#include <stdio.h>
struct record
      {
      char first[20];
      char last[20];
      };
struct record name;
main()
{

      extern struct record name;
      void outname();

      printf("What is your first name? ");
      fgets(name.first,sizeof(name.first),stdin);
      printf("What is your last name? ");
```
continued

257

```
        fgets(name.last,sizeof(name.last),stdin);
        outname(&name);
}
void outname(name_ptr)
struct record *name_ptr;
{
        printf("Hello %s %s\n",name_ptr->first,name_ptr->last);
}
```

Now introduce an error by changing the last line of the main program to:

```
outname(name);
```

Compile it again. It will compile correctly, but it will not display your name after you enter it. Let's see how QuickC's debugging techniques can help us find the error.

Compiler Options

Click the Compile dialog box. The box will show a list of options on the far right (Figure 16.1). Here is a review of each of these:

Debug: Check this if you wish to use any of the debug options on the Debug menu or to use CodeView with your program for debugging. Compiling with this option introduces special code that is used for debugging purposes.

Pointer Check: This will force the compiler to generate code that verifies that pointer values address program data before the pointers are used. This offers dome protection against common pointer errors. You should turn on this during debugging, then turn it off for the final compile.

Stack Check: This will force QuickC to verify that your program has enough stack space at run time and returns a diagnostic message if not.

Language Extensions: This will permit the compiler to accept certain extensions to the ANSI C standard that have been defined by Microsoft. Using this option makes the program less portable and extends the keyword list, but adds several features that may be important in some applications (such as the use of near and far pointers).

Optimizations: This optimizes your program, but may make a larger program.

Note

QuickC is not an optimizing compiler, and this option on the menu is misleading. It does create 80286 code, which won't run on the older 8086 and 8088 processors.

For development, you will want the Debug, Pointer Check, and Stack Check turned on. Optimizations should be turned off. Debug and Pointer Check options will significantly slow the speed of the program's execution, so when creating your final program you will want to compile with these off.

Both options can also be switched on and off from the program using the *#pragma* compiler directive. For example, to turn both options on in the program from a defined point in the source code enter:

```
#pragma check_pointer(on)
#pragma check_stack(on)
```

In the same way, you could turn both off with:

```
#pragma check_pointer(off)
#pragma check_stack(off)
```

Try compiling your sample program (with its error) with Pointer Check and Stack Check. There will be no diagnostic messages, as the pointers correctly reference data and the stack is quite small.

Tracing

You can also trace your program execution. This is useful to see if a function is really being entered or to locate infinite loops that are hanging up the program. To trace the program execution:

1. Use the Compile menu to switch Debug on.
2. Press F8 to execute the first instruction.

You can now trace the execution using the F8 or F10 keys. F8 will show each instruction, stopping on each before it is executed. F10 is similar, except that the trace will skip around function calls. Using F10 is useful if you've already debugged your functions and you are only tracing the main program.

Try your program now with both the F8 and F10 debug keys. With the F8 key, each line is marked as the execution is traced. With F10, the function call is traced around.

Setting Breakpoints

Breakpoints are points in the program where the execution can be paused. Once the program is paused, the user may examine variables, single-step forward, jump to another location, execute to the next breakpoint, or execute unconditionally to the end of the program.

Traces can get cumbersome in large programs. Breakpoints eliminate the need to trace the entire program, permitting traces to be started and stopped from defined points in the program.

For example, a breakpoint can be put in a function. If the function is never reached, the breakpoint is never reached. Conversely, if a program is caught in a continuous loop in a function, a breakpoint inside the function will pause the program at each loop iteration, enabling the user to see what is happening.

When a breakpoint is reached, the program pauses. The operator can check variables using watch expressions (see next section), start a trace from that point using F8 or F10, or initiate execution again to the next breakpoint using F5.

Breakpoints with QuickC are easy to set. First, be sure your Compile Debug option is on. To set a breakpoint, put the cursor in the line at which you wish to pause and press F9 (or use Debug Toggle Breakpoint). You can set multiple breakpoints if you wish.

To clear a breakpoint, put the cursor on the line to clear and use F9 or Debug Toggle Breakpoint again. You can also use Debug Clear Breakpoints to clear all breakpoints.

With QuickC, lines with breakpoints are shown in color. Also, when the program is executing, the line where the execution is paused is shown in another distinguishing color.

For quick breakpointing, click the cursor to the line for pausing and use the F7 key to execute to the marked line. Another method of quick breakpointing is to click the right mouse button on the line to breakpoint. Execution will begin immediately and pause on the breakpointed line.

Here is a summary of the breakpoint function key commands:

Execute to the next statement	F8
Execute to next statement, skipping function calls	F10
Execute to current cursor position	F7 or right mouse button
Execute to next breakpoint	F5
Set or clear breakpoint	F9
Toggle output screen	F4

The F4 command is useful for examining the output screen at any time, toggling between the editor display of the source code and the output screen.

Try breakpoints now with your program that contains the error. Put a breakpoint in the function and try to determine if the function is being called.

Watch Expressions

Creating watch expressions enables you to examine variables at breakpoints in the program or during a trace. To set a watch expression, click the Debug menu and choose Add Watch. Enter the name of the variable or expression you wish to watch. You can add multiple expressions.

Add the watch expressions *name_ptr->first* and *name.first* (Figure 16.3). Put a breakpoint at the beginning of the function and initiate an execution. Figure 16.4 shows the screen at the breakpoint. Your first name should be displayed as the expression value.

Figure 16.3
Setting a Watch Value

Figure 16.4
Using Watch Expressions

```
 File  Edit  View  Search  Run  Debug  Calls                    F1=Help
name_ptr->first: "\0\0\0\0\0\0\0\0\0\0\0\0\0\0\0\0\0\0\0\0"
name.first: "Carl\0\0\0\0\0\0\0\0\0\0\0\0\0\0\0\0"
                         D:\C\debug.c
        char last[20];
        };
struct record name;
main()
{

        extern struct record name;
        void outname();

        printf("What is your first name? ");
        scanf("%s",name.first);
        printf("What is your last name? ");
        scanf("%s",name.last);
        outname(name);
}
void outname(name_ptr)
struct record *name_ptr;
{
        printf("Hello %s %s\n",name_ptr->first,name_ptr->last);

Program List: <None>   Context: debug.c:outname          00022:001
```

You can use any valid C expression as a watch expression. You can use variables, structures, or arrays. Add the structure name as a third watch expression and execute the program again.

You can also format the displayed expression value. Table 16.1 shows the permissible format codes.

Table 16.1
Format Specifiers for Watch Variables

Format Character	Output Format
d	Signed decimal integer
i	Signed decimal integer
u	Unsigned decimal integer
o	Unsigned octal integer
X	Hexadecimal integer (uppercase)
x	Hexadecimal integer (lowercase)
f	Signed floating point
e	Floating point, scientific notation
g	Floating point, signed or scientific, whichever is more compact
c	Single character
s	String

Note

These codes are quite similar to the *printf()* formatting codes.

External QuickC Debugging Tools

If you need more debugging support than provided with QuickC's internal debugger, you'll find several options available: CodeView, SYMDEB, preprocessors, and hardware debuggers.

CodeView

Although QuickC does not include Microsoft's popular CodeView, if you've purchased one of their products that does include CodeView (such as Macro Assembler 5.0 or the C Compiler Version 5.00 or later), you'll find that the CodeView that comes with this product will work with QuickC.

CodeView has many similarities to the internal QuickC debugger, but does have some extended features beyond the internal debugger:

- CodeView supports many languages: Assembly, C, BASIC, FORTRAN, or Pascal. You can create program modules with any of these languages, link them, and then use CodeView to debug the final system.
- CodeView supports 80386 instructions.
- Expanded memory and Microsoft Windows are both supported.
- Overlaid modules are supported.
- CodeView includes 8087 emulator support.
- New commands are included, as well as watchpoints and tracepoints.
- CodeView supports overlaid code and library modules.
- CodeView supports the use of a second monitor. Debugging commands and displaying can be done from a separate terminal while the program executes and displays its own output on the normal monitor.

There are also a few limitations of CodeView with respect to QuickC's internal debugger. CodeView, as yet, does not support structure pointers and other expressions that can be supported as watch expressions in the QuickC debugger. In addition, the following restrictions apply to both the QuickC debugger and CodeView:

- Include files cannot be debugged.
- The executable file must be in an EXE form.
- The program being debugged cannot alter the DOS environment.
- Programs being debugged cannot redirect input and output.

The Symbolic Debugger

Several Microsoft products also include a SYMDEB (symbolic debugger). Although more limited than CodeView, it does permit debugging using symbolic information in the executable file. To use the debugger, you first create a separate symbol file using:

```
MAPSYM DEBUG.MAP  〈Enter〉
```

This creates a DEBUG.SYM file. QuickC requires a version of MAPSYM 3.10 or later.

You can then start the debugger using:

```
SYMDEB DEBUG.SYM DEBUG.EXE   〈Enter〉
```

Preprocessors

Preprocessors are tools that permit checking of the C source code before the compiling is attempted. The simplest ones check for unbalanced brackets, comment markers, and parentheses. These are normally available free through public domain libraries and user groups. The better commercial products check for the type of pointer errors discussed in Chapter 11 and other problems that the compiler can't process. Even a simple (and free) preprocessor is often a valuable asset.

Hardware Debuggers

Professional C programmers generally use some type of hardware debugger. These monitor the program execution, permitting the user to actually "view" the program as it executes. One example is the Periscope product.

QuickC Memory Models

The processor family used by the IBM PC/XT/AT and PS/2 compatibles (8088, 8086, 80286 and 80386 microprocessors) use a segmented memory architecture in which the memory is allocated to the program in 64K segments. Most C implementations allow you to control the memory allocation to be sure adequate memory is allocated for execution. QuickC includes this support.

The minimum of memory required for execution of a C program in this processor environment is two segments, or 128K. One segment is used for the program code, the second for the data. This specification for memory allocation is referred to as the C *small model*.

You will need to use an alternative memory model if either of the following is true:

- You are compiling a program with the internal QuickC environment that has more than 64K of static data.

- A program compiled external to the QuickC environment has more than 64K of code or 64K of data.

Here, you must use one of the alternative memory models. The alternative models use a *far addressing* technique in which the segment and offset values are passed in addressing.

The C language supports five memory models (Table 16.2). The models are named *small, medium, compact, large*, and *huge*. QuickC supports all these but the huge model. From this, you can see that the memory model required for a particular application is determined by the number of code and data segments required. From the previous paragraph and this table, you can also see that the QuickC environment supports the medium model, and the external compiler defaults to small model.

Table 16.2
C Memory Models

Model	Compiler Option	Code Segments	Data Segments	Segments/ Data Item
small	/AS*	1	1	1
medium	/AM**	many	1	1
compact	/AC	1	many	1
large	/AL	many	many	1
huge***	/AH	many	many	many

   *   Default for QCL compiler
  **   QuickC environment mode
*** Not supported by QuickC

With the external QCL compiler, you can use the /A option to support the medium, compact, or large models. For example, to compile a program externally that uses the medium model so that it is compatible with the QuickC environment, you would use the /AM option.

With the QuickC environment, compiling is limited to the medium model. You can, however, use the *near* and *far* keywords with the environment to override the default addressing convention and use more than two segments for your program. These keywords are not a standard part of the C language, and are useful only for systems with a segmented architecture similar to the 8086 processors. As examples:

```
int far item; /* integer declaration */
char far parts[1000]; /* array declaration */
int far prompt();   /* function forward declaration */
```

Global Variable Management

Preprocessor directives are commands to the C preprocessor (which is an automatic part of a C compiling). You have already met two of these: the *#include*, which permits you to include external files at compile time, and the *#define* directive, which permits you to define substitutions for compiling.

Another important directive is the *#if . . . #endif* directive, which permits you to include code at compile time based on a specified condition. Let's see how this directive can be used to improve global variable management.

The use of global variables in a program introduce the need for control on the part of the programmer. A variable can be declared one way and then externally referenced as another type:

```
/* error example */
short counter;
main()
{
    extern int counter;
    :
```

To minimize this you should declare all globals in the include file and label them as such. Even this, however, is often not quite sufficient.

Now suppose we create an include file for the globals as:

```
GLOBAL      int      counter;
GLOBAL      char     buffer[100]; /* array - no initialization */
GLOBAL      char     string[]    /* this is a char string */
#ifdef INIT /* blocks initialization except in globals.c */
= "This is a dummy message"  /* initialization string    */
#endif
;                          /* note that the semicolon is here    */
GLOBAL     int    filecount /* an int to be initialized       */
#ifdef INIT
= 200                      /* here is the initialization       */
#endif
;


/* ==============    C o m m e n t ====================== */
/* GLOBAL is always defined in THE BODY OF THE PROGRAM
   In only one place it is defined as blank. Everywhere
   else it is defined as "extern". That piece of code
    contains the actual declarations and in that piece of
    code only, "INIT" should be defined.
   That way the initializations only occur one place.
*/
```

Now, in the program, we use:

```
/*    GLOBALS.C   Copyright 1987   Michael Maurice   */
/*    All rights reserved                            */

#include <stdio.h>
#include "config.h" /* configuration declarations     */
#include "std.h"  /* a file of standard typedefs      */

#undef GLOBAL          /* be sure no define for GLOBAL */
```

```
#define GLOBAL          /* create a define that is blank    */
#define INIT            /* turns on initialization of globals */
#include "globals.h"    /* where the globals are     */

/* ====================================================== */
This is what the declarations in globals.h will look like here
*/
     int   counter;
     char  buffer[100]
     char  string[]

= "This is a dummy message"

;

     int   filecount

= 200

;


/* ====================================================== */
/* This is what globals.h will look like in other code. */
extern      int   counter;
extern      char  buffer[100]
extern      char  string[]

;


extern      int   filecount   /* the semicolon is 4 lines down */
;
```

Note the carriage returns before the semicolon. This white space is not seen by the compiler.

This method gives us the protection needed for the global variables.

17

Managing Databases with QuickC

Many application programs designed with QuickC involve the creation of a *database*. A database is a single collection of data to which a user has access through a system of programs. A *database management system* is a system of programs that gives a user access to a collection of data. Typical examples include order entry systems, job costing systems, inventory control, or a simple mailing list processor.

As an example, this chapter will look at a design for a mailing list database. The basic principles are the same for any application.

Designing the Database

One of the first phases of your system design is the design of the database. The general design process looks like this:

1. What output information is needed to make decisions? What type of reports are needed? Who will be reading them? Obtain some samples of the desired output reports if possible, or manually create some dummy reports with a word processor or spreadsheet.

2. What input information do I need for these reports? Does it currently exist, or must some process be implemented for getting it? Which information is static (constant) and which is dynamic (changing)? How frequently does the dynamic information change? How is it entered to the computer?

Once you have a picture of the information flow, you can begin to design the database that will hold the information.

The Database

The database is composed of one or more files. Each file is composed of records, with each record representing one or more items. In an inventory system, for example, each record might represent a single part in the inventory. Within this record are fields, with each field representing something about the item.

For our mailing list database, each record represents one member (Figure 17.1). Records and fields are of fixed length, making it possible to use a direct access to locate each address. The fields are as follows:

Name	Description
[num]	[Membership number]
flag	Flag to control deletions
last	Last name
first	First name
street	Street address
city	City
state	State
zip	Zip

Each field is given a unique name. For C, the field name should be in lowercase alphanumerics and contain no spaces or special characters except the underscore. In this program, *flag* is used to indicate the state of the membership address (whether or not it has been deleted). In our example the membership number is the same as the record number, so there is no need to store the membership number in the record.

The next step is to decide the data type for each field. The type for each depends upon how the field will be used in the program. You can use some level of conversion, but typing each field correctly will minimize this conversion. Here, the membership number is *long*, the flag is *int*, and the remaining fields are all character arrays:

Name	Type	Description
flag	int	Flag to control deletions
last	char[]	Last name
first	char[]	First name
street	char[]	Street address
city	char[]	City
state	char[]	State
zip	char[]	Zip

Figure 17.1
The Mailing List Database

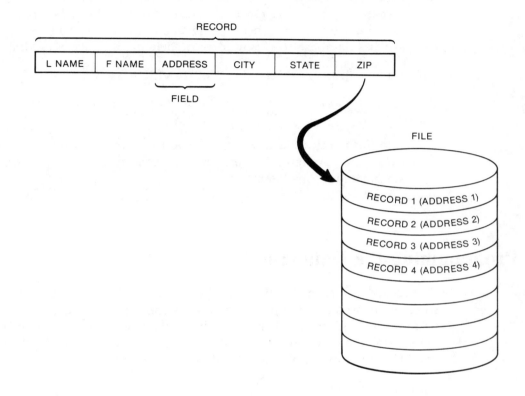

The next step is to assign a size of width for each character array field. As the fields and records are fixed length, each field width must be large enough for the field to contain the largest value that will be stored. The larger the fields, however, the more space the records will take on the disk. Assume the following widths for the fields:

Field	Width
first	25
last	25
street	40
city	20
state	2
zip	5

Note

It is very important to define the names, type and width specifically before programming. Once you begin adding addresses, changing any of these will require either writing a conversion program to convert the existing database to a new form or deleting all current addresses and reentering them.

Tip

Add a dummy field if you think the user may wish to add a field or fields later. Assign it a name *dummy* and enough space to cover any planned additions later.

Programming the Database

The record for each database file is defined with a structure in QuickC. The structure is used as a template for address entry, file storage, and reporting. The structure should be stored in an include file external to the main program and made available to all programs. The field sizes are defined using the define directive. There is the sample include file for the mailing list:

```
#define MAXLAST 25
#define MAXFIRST 25
#define MAXSTREET 40
#define MAXCITY 20
#define MAXSTATE 2
#define MAXZIP 5
#define PAD 2
struct address_rec
    {
    char last[MAXLAST+PAD];
    char first[MAXFIRST+PAD];
    char street[MAXSTREET+PAD];
    char city[MAXCITY+PAD];
    char state[MAXSTATE+PAD];
    char zip[MAXZIP+PAD];
    };
struct address_rec address;
```

The structure is defined using widths two more than needed for the field. This gives a total size of 129 bytes. You can verify this with the simple program:

```
#include "mail.h"
main()
{
    printf("%d",sizeof (address));
}
```

Header Design

Use the first record (Record 0) in the database as a header record, putting any data here that you wish to apply to the entire database. Typical data in the header record includes the number of records in the file and last update. You could also put the field descriptions and size in the header, reading these when the file is open and using them to control the forms that are displayed. It is not necessary that the header record have the same size and structure as the other records. In this example program, only the number of records in the file is saved in the header, and the header has the same structure as the other records in the file.

Indexing a Database

Using an index to locate a particular record in a database is like trying to use the index of a book to find information in a book. With a book, you look up a word of interest in the index and it gives you the page number for the information. You then turn to that page and locate the desired information.

With an index to a database, you look up the *keyword* using an index file, and the record number for that item is returned. This record number is then used to calculate the position of the record in the database file and *fseek( )* or *lseek( )* used to retrieve the record. The indexes to the various files are stored as separate files on the disk from the database files.

If the index is small, the entire index can be stored in memory as an array. When the program is started, the index file is opened, read to an array in memory, and then used as needed. If the index is large, an "index to the index" is stored in memory. This is then used to retrieve the desired record from the index file, which is then used to retrieve the database record. Actual indexes, then, are hierarchical structures that must be updated as the database is updated; that is, each time you add, edit, or delete a record all the corresponding indexes must be updated.

For index design purposes, you must decide how the database will be accessed. For example, on the mailing list file, would you access by membership number only? by last name? by last name plus first name? by zip code? The field by which you access the database is known as the *key* field. A field is a *primary key* if its value is unique in the database. In the address file, for example, the primary field is the membership number. A key is a *secondary key* if the field values are nonunique; that is, duplicates are allowed. The last name and zip code fields in our mailing list program are secondary keys.

In designing a database, you will generally want one primary key and perhaps one or more secondary keys.

The programming of indexing systems is beyond the scope of this book, and indeed is not really important for most programmers. For most purposes you can purchase any of the various indexing tools that are available as commercial products. This gives you a pretested function library that can be used to support your indexing.

For our purposes here, we will assume the membership number as the primary key, using it also as the record number for access on adding, editing, or displaying the address. There are no secondary keys. For printing and reporting in the desired order, an index array will be built in memory and used. This will keep the basic design simple, and the system can be enhanced later with a commercial indexing product. (A few calculations will ensure that the array for the 1000 addresses used here will fit in memory with the program. Simply take the length of the elements and multiply by the maximum number of addresses.)

Basic Database Design Considerations

Here are some basic principles to keep in mind in designing databases:

1. Keep the number of fields to a minimum. If fields might be added later, add a dummy field for the present.
2. Plan before programming. Redesign will mean the loss of existing data or the need to write a conversion program.
3. Keep in mind how the files will be accessed. For example, if a secondary key is used to update a database, the program will have to take into consideration that duplicates may exist.

Designing Multi-File Databases

Here are the basic rules for design of multi-file databases:

One-to-One Relationships

If two elements are related on a one-to-one relationship, put each in the same file, or files, that are linked on a primary key (see Figure 17.2). For example, if you wish to add a comment field for the addresses, you could put the comment in a separate file that also uses the membership number.

Figure 17.2
One-to-One Relationship

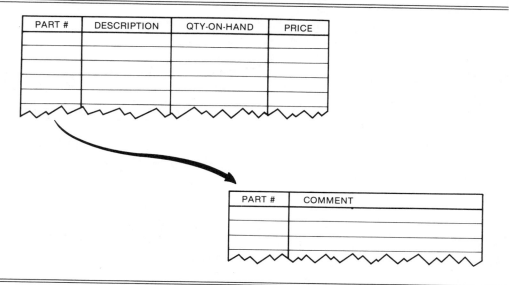

One-to-Many Relationships

If two elements are related in a one-to-many relationship, create a separate file for each, putting the primary key of the "one" in the file of the "many" (Figure 17.3). In a mail order system, for example, an address may be stored in a separate file where it is linked to several orders by a customer number. In the same way, a single order number in an order file may be linked to several line-item records in another file.

Many-to-Many Relationships

If two elements are related in a many-to-many relationship, build a third file using each of the other files that contains the keys of each (Figure 17.4). For example, again assume the last example, except that the same parts are used in several different models. Again create a model file and a part file, but also create a bill-of-material file with the model number as one field and the part number as a second.

Figure 17.3
One-to-Many Relationship

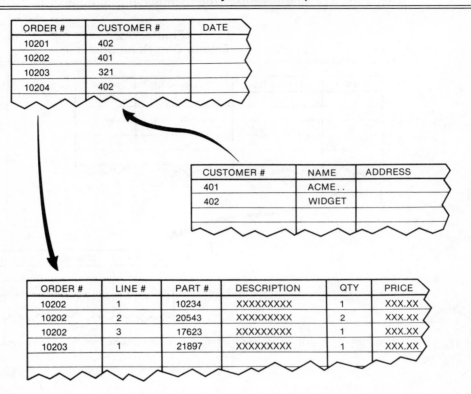

Design Considerations for Multi-File Databases

Here are some basic design considerations for databases with multiple files:

1. Minimize data redundancy. Repeat fields in files only as necessary, linking the files on key fields. In an invoice system, for example, you might store the addresses in a separate file and use only a customer number code in the invoice file. This permits using the same address in several invoices, minimizing redundancy.

2. Don't put a field in a record if only a few records will use the field. Create a second file with a common field. For example, to add a comment field to the address database with only a few addresses using it, create a new file with two fields: the membership number and the comment. (Here, you would need to use an index for the membership

number. The record number could not be used as the membership number in the comment file.)

Figure 17.4
Many-to-Many Relationship

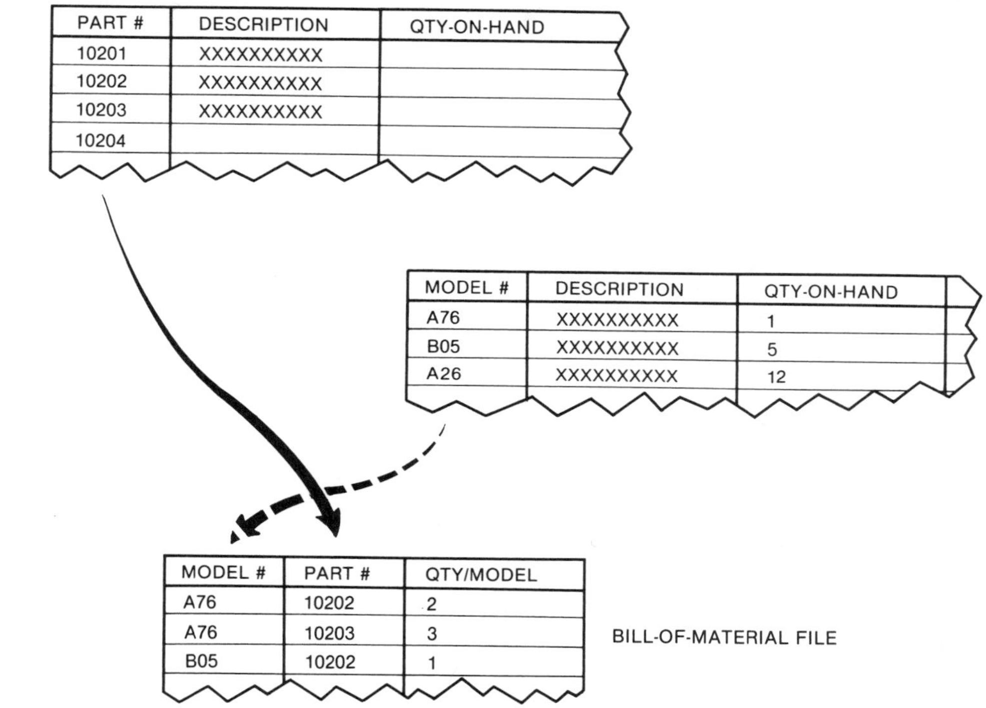

PART #	DESCRIPTION	QTY-ON-HAND
10201	XXXXXXXXXX	
10202	XXXXXXXXXX	
10203	XXXXXXXXXX	
10204		

MODEL #	DESCRIPTION	QTY-ON-HAND
A76	XXXXXXXXXX	1
B05	XXXXXXXXXX	5
A26	XXXXXXXXXX	12

MODEL #	PART #	QTY/MODEL
A76	10202	2
A76	10203	3
B05	10202	1

BILL-OF-MATERIAL FILE

3. Avoid complexity and make sure the system can keep up with the user. Nothing is more frustrating than for a user to have to wait while a program sequentially scans a file for data or works through several files to get what is needed. Be sure the system can keep up with the user. Create a prototype and test the execution speed if necessary before programming.

18

High-Level Design: Menus

Once you have completed the database design, the next step is to partition the programming for your system into functional blocks. You can then begin the programming of the high-level modules, which are generally menus. This chapter will introduce you to the design of menus and screens.

The Program Chart

A system of programs can generally be partitioned into functional blocks. The blocks form a hierarchy, with a single high-level function, a collection of middle-level functions, and eventually the lower-level functions.

> **Note**
>
> Be careful to distinguish the low-level functions we are talking about here from the low-level QuickC library functions. When this section refers to a low-level function, it refers to a function you write that is used by one or more higher-level programs. It is generally composed of multiple QuickC statements, which may contain QuickC library functions of a high- or low-level nature.

The highest-level program is normally a menu program. The user starts the system using only the name of this menu program. The main menu then calls middle-level programs (or other menus) to accomplish the desired purpose.

For the mailing list program, the program chart is shown in Figure 18.1. The main menu program is used to initiate each of the primary functions on the system proposal. Complex programs can have many levels of menus.

Figure 18.1
The Mailing List Program Chart

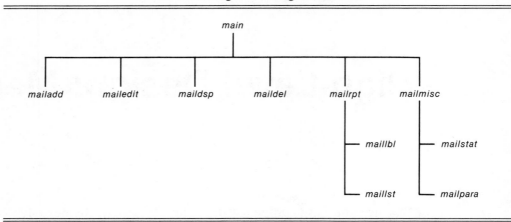

Primary Menu Design Goals

The menu is important as it defines the basic type of user interface that is supported. A good interface gives the user positive feelings of competence and security. The computer and the program should become invisible, enabling the user to concentrate on the solution of the problem. Two basic menu issues to resolve are the topology of the program structure and the type of menu to use.

Program Topologies

The topology of the program refers to the basic geometric order of the program modules, which should also reflect the general flow of using the various modules. Figure 18.2 shows some example topologies.

The single menu style is the simplest, and is the basic form for the example in this book. A single menu calls up each of the functions. This will only work if the number of functions is approximately seven or less (see next section).

The hierarchical, or tree, topology is the basic form when the number of functions is more than can be processed from a single menu. It assumes functions can be logically partitioned into subfunctions. The main menu calls up the function, from which a subfunction is chosen. For example, a main menu might have a report option, from which a report menu is used to select the type of report. Spreadsheets generally use this type of topology.

The linear topology is used if the program is modal, and the user moves

Figure 18.2
Menu Topologies

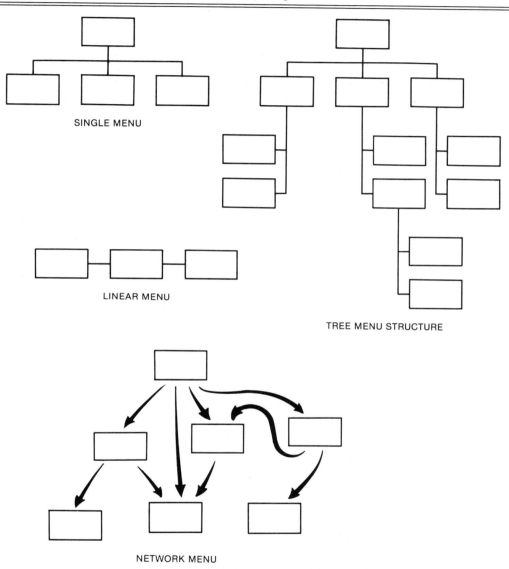

SINGLE MENU

LINEAR MENU

TREE MENU STRUCTURE

NETWORK MENU

from one program state to another. Then one program calls the next, which in turn calls the next. A good example is a general ledger program. First the batch is created, then the posting is done, and finally a closing is done.

Network topologies are useful if the program is modeless and the user is constantly moving between menus. Word processors and desktop publishing programs are generally of this type.

Menu Types

Programs use various types of menus, which often relate to the topology. The basic types are the multiple items, pop-up/pull-down menus, and permanent.

The multiple item menu displays a screen with a list of choices, from which the user selects a single option (Figure 18.3). It is often used with the simple and tree topologies, but also works well with the linear topology. It is losing favor today to other methods, but is easy to implement and can be very effective. It is the method used in this part for the mailing list program.

Figure 18.3
The Multiple Item Menu

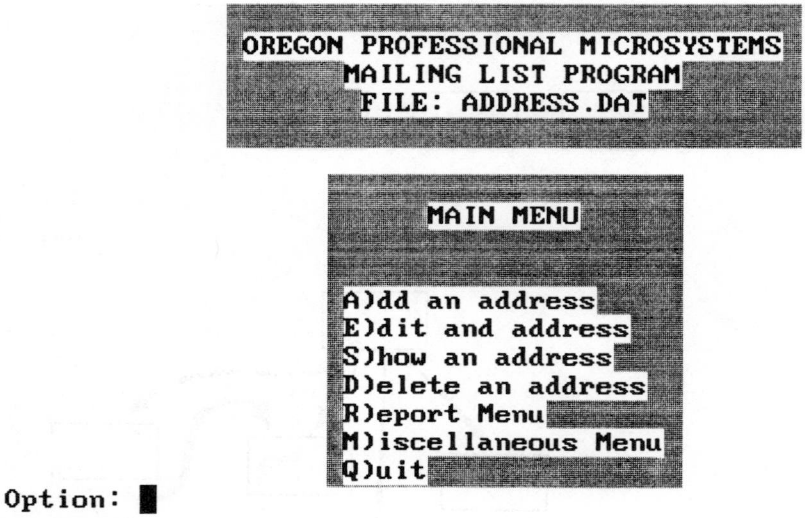

```
OREGON PROFESSIONAL MICROSYSTEMS
        MAILING LIST PROGRAM
          FILE: ADDRESS.DAT


                MAIN MENU


        A)dd an address
        E)dit and address
        S)how an address
        D)elete an address
        R)eport Menu
        M)iscellaneous Menu
        Q)uit

Option: █
```

The permanent menu is a menu panel that remains on screen the entire time the program is executing or is available at any time using a defined keystroke combination. Examples include the menus of Microsoft Word and Lotus 1-2-3 (Figure 18.4). The use of the menu is generally activated by a designated key (such as the forward slash with Lotus 1-2-3).

Pop-up menus or pull-down menus are menus that are pulled down by a mouse from a menu bar near the top of the screen. One example, of course, is the QuickC product itself (Figure 18.5). Other examples include Borland International's Turbo language products and Microsoft Windows. You can purchase the functions to create such menus commercially. (As this is written, one of the best products for creating such menus, Microsoft Windows, is not supported by QuickC.)

Figure 18.4
The Permanent Menu

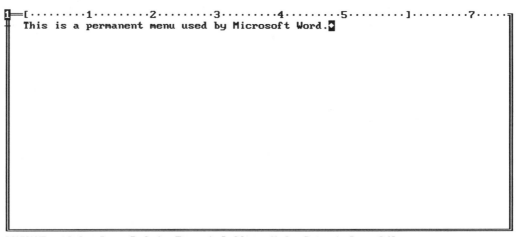

```
==[·········1·········2·········3·········4·········5·····]·········7·····
  This is a permanent menu used by Microsoft Word.
```

```
COMMAND: Alpha Copy Delete Format Gallery Help Insert Jump Library
         Options Print Quit Replace Search Transfer Undo Window
Edit document or press Esc to use menu
Page 1    {}                              ?            Microsoft Word:
```

Figure 18.5
Pull-down Menus

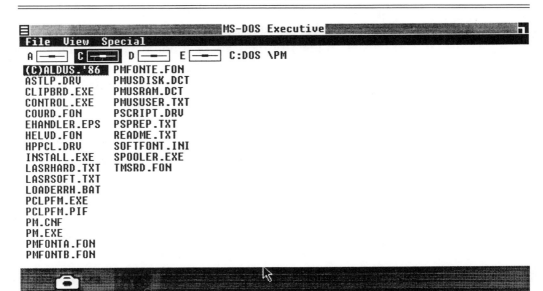

```
≡══════════════════════MS-DOS Executive══════════════════════
 File  View  Special
 A ═──═  C ═──═  D ═──═  E ═──═  C:DOS \PM
 (C)ALDUS.'86  PMFONTE.FON
 ASTLP.DRV     PMUSDISK.DCT
 CLIPBRD.EXE   PMUSRAM.DCT
 CONTROL.EXE   PMUSUSER.TXT
 COURD.FON     PSCRIPT.DRV
 EHANDLER.EPS  PSPREP.TXT
 HELVD.FON     README.TXT
 HPPCL.DRV     SOFTFONT.INI
 INSTALL.EXE   SPOOLER.EXE
 LASRHARD.TXT  TMSRD.FON
 LASRSOFT.TXT
 LOADERRH.BAT
 PCLPFM.EXE
 PCLPFM.PIF
 PM.CNF
 PM.EXE
 PMFONTA.FON
 PMFONTB.FON
```

Principles of Screen Design

For the purposes of this section, we'll stay with the simple multiple selection menu with some level of tree topology. Before starting, however, let's look at some very basic aspects of screen design. These principles apply to the design of any screen, whether a menu screen or not.

The screen is the basic output interface to the user. For this reason, the screen determines how the user perceives the system. If the program is a master-piece of design but with screens full of technical jargon and complex directions, the user will perceive the program as poorly designed, regardless of what lies beneath those screens. If the screens are well designed, the user will believe that what lies beneath those screens is also well-designed. It's somewhat like buying a car. If the car is clean and looks good, the potential purchaser will assume the motor has been cared for with the same detail.

Any information displayed on the screen should be centered both horizon-tally and vertically; that is, the screen should appear balanced. The design of the text, colors, and graphics should lead the eyes of the user to what is most impor-tant. For example, putting a multiple selection menu in a box or colored rectan-gle draws the eyes of the user to the contents of the box and away from the edges of the screen. Strong, vivid colors draw the eyes away from light or pastel colors.

Good screen design applies to any program. In the system described in this part, for example, the functions are called from the menu display multiple screens. Each screen represents a different mode, or state, of the function.

Here are some basic rules of screen design:

1. Keep the screen as simple as possible. Avoid complexity. Use multiple screens, if necessary, to keep the screen simple. Don't display what the user isn't using at the time.

2. Use screens to identify the state or mode of a particular program.

3. Use a heading, with space between the heading and the rest of the screen. Typical heading information should include company name, program name, date, and program function that is active.

4. Keep the screen balanced. Center headings.

5. Use plenty of blank space on the screen to improve legibility. Don't try to put too much on a screen. Only display what is needed.

6. Use color as appropriate if the user's system supports color.

7. Design the screen so that the text, color, and graphics draw the eyes to the most important information.

8. Use simple words. Use *basic* instead of *elementary, get* instead of *appropriate*, and *delete* instead of *eliminate*.

9. Avoid technical words and use a vocabulary with which the user is familiar. For example, if an accountant is using a general ledger system, the menu should use accounting terms.

10. Use precise and specific words. Use active instead of passive tense.

11. If any linear flow exists, the screen should reflect this. Add and Edit options, for example, should be before a Report option. Don't try to correct a bad menu order using highlighting or color. Reorder the menu.

12. The screen should be viewed as a paragraph and express a single idea. There should be no more than one idea on a screen.

13. Use colors, reverse, and highlighting to call attention to important information (such as error messages).

14. Use the last line of the screen to display error messages. Use some programming method to hold it until it is read.

15. Avoid sound effects and cute remarks. These become irritating after a while.

16. Use graphics to enhance the readability of the screen.

17. Give the user a chance to abort a bad selection. For example, if the menu is designed so that an option is entered with no carriage return, the program immediately goes to the function designated by any key touched. This may be fine for some programs, but for a print or processing program this can inadvertently start the wrong action. In this case, you should provide some query at the beginning of the program for the user to verify the entry to the option.

18. Consider the possibility of alternative input devices. Mice are good for selecting between choices or moving the cursor to a point for text entry. Keyboards are best for data and text entry.

The Main Menu

The main menu controls the execution of the entire system, and is the only program called by name by the user. The basic structure of the menu program is first written in pseudocode. This code is a narrative-type description of what each part of the program will do:

```
<initialize>
<setup for graphics>
DO WHILE TRUE
     <display title screen>
     <display menu options>
     <get option>
     IF FUNCTIONAL OPTION
         <do option>
     IF EXIT
         <cleanup, then exit>
```

continued

```
        ELSE
            <error routine>
    ENDDO
```

The complete program is then rewritten as shown in Listing 18.1, which is saved as *mail.c.*

Listing 18.1
The Main Menu Program

```
/* MAILING LIST MAINTENANCE PROGRAM */
/* 11/18/87 */
#include <stdio.h>
#include <graph.h>
#include <conio.h>
#include <ctype.h>
#include "mail.h"
/* the following are in mail.h file                    */
/* char ctitle[] = "OREGON PROFESSIONAL MICROSYSTEMS"; */
/* char address_file = "ADDRESS.DAT";                  */
/* ****                                                */
main()
{
    /* external references */
    extern struct videoconfig config;
    extern char ctitle[];

    /* locals */
    COUNT option;
    COUNT param_file;
    char reply[80];
    char param_record[80];
    COUNT z, i;
    static struct data_frame main_menu[]=
        { MENUSTART, MENULEFT+5, "MAIN MENU",
          MENUSTART+3, MENULEFT, "A)dd an address",
          MENUSTART+4, MENULEFT, "E)dit and address",
          MENUSTART+5, MENULEFT, "S)how an address",
          MENUSTART+6, MENULEFT, "D)elete an address",
          MENUSTART+7, MENULEFT, "R)eport Menu",
          MENUSTART+8, MENULEFT, "M)iscellaneous Menu",
          MENUSTART+9, 30, "Q)uit",
          0, 0,    NULL
          };
```

continued

```
/* turn on graphics */
setup();
/* display menu & get option */
while (TRUE) {
    _clearscreen(0);
    /* display screen */
    display_title_frame(ctitle, RED);
    display_form(main_menu,BLUE);
    /* get input option */
    _settextposition(20,10);
    _displaycursor(_GCURSORON);
    _outtext("Option: ");
    option=getche();
    _displaycursor(_GCURSOROFF);
    if (islower(option))
        option = _toupper(option);
    switch(option)
    {
        case 'A' :
            mailadd();
            break;
        case 'E' :
            mailedit();
            break;
        case 'S' :
            maildsp();
            break;
        case 'D' :
            maildel();
            break;
        case 'R' :
            mailrpt();
            break;
        case 'M' :
            mailmisc();
            break;
        case 'Q' :
            cleanup();
            exit(0);
        default :
            _settextposition(config.numtextrows,1);
            _outtext("Illegal input - press <CR> to continue");
            option=getche();
    }
```

continued

```
        }
        cleanup();
}
/* DO SETUP FOR GRAPHICS MODE */
void   setup()
{
        extern struct videoconfig config;

        COUNT set_mode();

        if (!set_mode())
               {
               printf("This video mode not supported.\n");
               exit(0);
               }
        _getvideoconfig(&config);
        _setlogorg(config.numxpixels / 2 - 1,
               config.numypixels / 2 - 1);

}
COUNT set_mode()
{
       if(_setvideomode(_ERESCOLOR))
              return(_ERESCOLOR);
       if (_setvideomode(_HRES16COLOR))
              return(_HRES16COLOR);
       if (_setvideomode(_HRESBW))
              return(_HRESBW);
       else
              return(0);
}
/* RESTORE VIDEO MODE */
void cleanup()
{
        extern struct videoconfig config;

        _clearscreen(0);
        _setvideomode(_DEFAULTMODE);
}


/* DISPLAY A FORM ON THE SCREEN */
void display_form(form, color)
struct data_frame form[];
COUNT color;
```

continued

```
{
        extern struct videoconfig config;

        COUNT index;
        COUNT z, maxlen=1;
        COUNT leftcol=80;
        COUNT lastrow=0;
        COUNT xorigin, yorigin, width, height;

        _setcolor(color);
        /* find the longest message line & leftmost point */
        for (index=0; form[index].msg != NULL; ++index)
                {
                z = strlen(form[index].msg);
                if (z>maxlen)
                        maxlen = z;
                if (form[index].col<leftcol)
                        leftcol=form[index].col;
                if (form[index].row>lastrow)
                        lastrow = form[index].row;
                }
        /* set origin of display from first row and column */
        yorigin = (form[0].row-2) * config.numypixels / config.numtextrows;
        xorigin = (COUNT) (((long) (leftcol-2)) * (long) config.numxpixels /
                (long) config.numtextcols);
        _setlogorg(xorigin,yorigin);
        /* convert frame to pixel size and output */
        width = (COUNT) (((long) (maxlen+2)) * (long) config.numxpixels /
                (long) config.numtextcols);
        height = (lastrow+2-form[0].row) * config.numypixels /
                config.numtextrows;
        _rectangle(_GFILLINTERIOR,0,0,width,height);
        /* output all text lines */
        for (index=0; form[index].msg != NULL; ++index)
                displayline(&form[index]);
}
/* DISPLAY A LINE IN THE FORM */
void displayline(ptr_form)
struct data_frame *ptr_form;
{
        _settextposition(ptr_form->row,ptr_form->col);
        _outtext(ptr_form->msg);
}
```

The functional hierarchy of this program is shown in Figure 18.6. The map shows the conventional graphic *setup( )* and *cleanup( )* routines, as well as a *display _form( )* function to display a screen frame defined by the structure *data_frame*.

Figure 18.6
The Functional Hierarchy of the MAIL.C Program

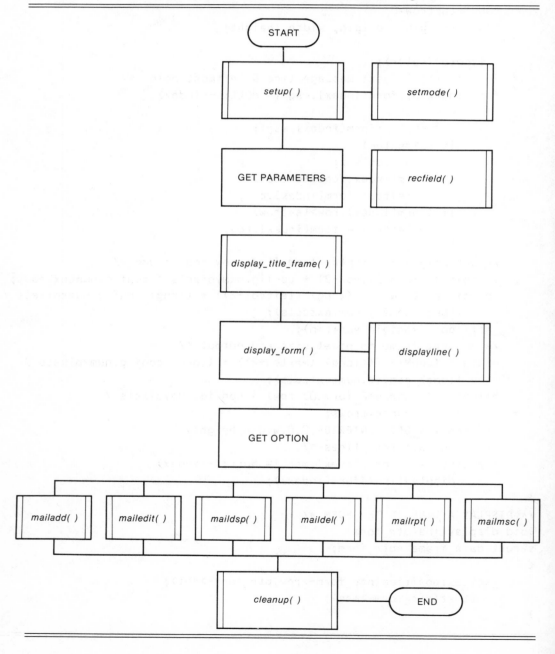

The program initializes and sets up for the graphic mode, then enters an "eternal loop," that is, a loop with no condition to exit. There is an exit, however, defined by the Quit option on the menu. The loop displays a single screen with two forms: the *title* form and the *main_menu* form. A request is then made for the option, which is used to call the desired function. If the Quit option is selected, the program does a graphic cleanup and then exits. Figure 18.7 shows the screen display.

Figure 18.7
The Menu Program Display

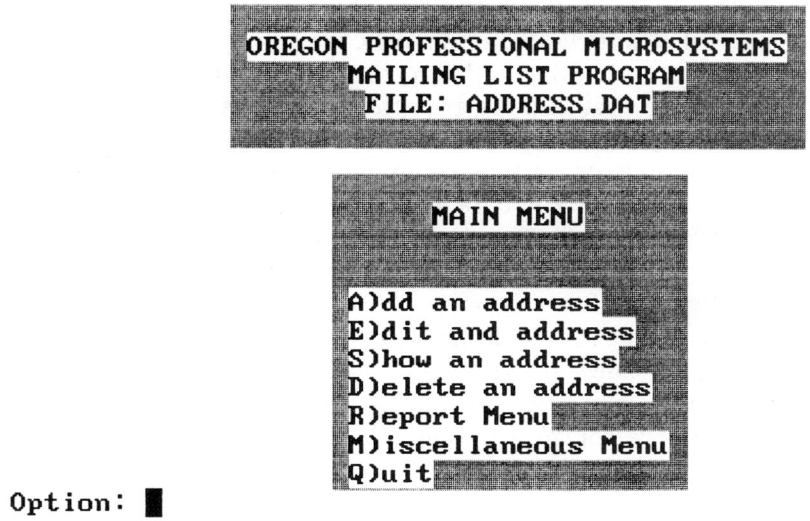

The screen displays are all done from two functions:

`display_title_frame(title, color)`	Displays the title frame at the top of the screen with title and in a rectangular frame color. (Function is defined in the menu program.)
`display_form(form,color)`	Displays an input form defined by pointer form in a rectangle of color. The size of the rectangle is automatically calculated from the size of the form.

The basic structure for *display_form()'s* form argument is an array of lines. Each line is defined as *row, col*, and **msg*. The *row* and *col* arguments define the starting point for the line, and *msg* defines the line of text. The line is terminated when *msg* is found to be NULL.

Adding Global Data

For most programs you will wish to add global data that can be used in the various functions that will be called from the main program. Examples typically include the company name, passwords, and perhaps a default disk or directory drive for the data. This file also should include the prototypes for the functions that will be used, with all arguments and returned values declared.

Global data is put in the *mail.h* file and compiled into the program. Examples of this include data forms common to several programs, *true* and *false* values, and other values shared between programs.

Data that changes after the program is compiled is called dynamic data, and is stored in a parameter file. This file is then read when the menu program is first started and the data is put in an externally declared data variable.

Parameter file data is of two types. The first is data that is available to the user for changes. This could include the company name, the default disk drive, or a printer type code. This data is edited from a parameter file editor program that is called from the main menu. The second type is data that cannot be altered by the user. This includes whether password control is used and the password. These variables are set using a special external program that creates and lists the parameter file (see Chapter 13 for this program). Listing 18.2 shows the final include file for all programs of the next few chapters.

Listing 18.2
The MAIL.H Include File

```
/* DEFINITIONS */
#define TRUE 1
#define FALSE 0
#define DELIM '~'
#define ERROR -1
#define STARTROW 12
#define FLAG 3
#define CRLF "\n\r"
#define MENUSTART 10
#define MENULEFT  30
#define PAD 1

/* MODES */
#define ADD 1
#define EDIT 2
```

continued

```
#define DISPLAY 3
#define DELETE 4

/* COLORS */
#define BLUE 1
#define GREEN 2
#define RED 4

/* FIELD DEFINITIONS */
#define MAXLAST 25
#define MAXFIRST 25
#define MAXSTREET 40
#define MAXCITY 20
#define MAXSTATE 2
#define MAXZIP 5
#define MAXADDRESSES 500

/* STRUCTURES */
struct videoconfig config;
struct data_frame
      {
      int row,col;
      char *msg;
      } ;
struct address_rec
      {
      char aflag[5];
      char last[MAXLAST+PAD];
      char first[MAXFIRST+PAD];
      char street[MAXSTREET+PAD];
      char city[MAXCITY+PAD];
      char state[MAXSTATE+PAD];
      char zip[MAXZIP+PAD];
      };
struct address_rec address,new_address,header;

/* TYPEDEFS */
typedef int COUNT;

/* GLOBALS */
char ctitle[61],address_file[13],label_string[rk ]5];
char pass[2];
char passwrd[41];
char address_filex[8];
```

continued

```
                 FILE *in, *out;

                 /* FUNCTION PROTOTYPES */
                 COUNT set_mode(void);
                 void display_form(struct data_frame *,COUNT);
                 void setup(void), cleanup(void);
                 COUNT err_msg1(char[]);
                 void err_msg(char[],int);
                 void display_title_frame(char[], COUNT);
                 void display_current_data( long * );
                 void get_form_data(void);
                 void write_data(long *, long *);
                 void displayline(struct data_frame *);
                 void display_address_no(char[], COUNT);
                 void read_data(long *);
                 COUNT count_file(char[]);
                 void mailpara(void);
                 void mailstat(void);
                 void maillbl(void);
                 void maillst(void);
                 void page_header(COUNT);
                 void sorterz(COUNT);
                 void sortera(COUNT);
                 COUNT load_sorterz(void);
                 COUNT load_sortera(void);
                 COUNT get_address_no(int,long *, long *);
                 void get_reply(COUNT,COUNT,char[],COUNT);
```

Listing 18.3 shows the mailing list program modified to use a parameter file. This permits a company name and address file name to be displayed on the screens and adds a password access.

The program reads the parameter file before entering the main loop and loads the variable values to global variables. If password access is being used (as determined by the parameter file flag), the password is requested and compared with the parameter file password. If the passwords do not match, the program exits.

Listing 18.3
The Main Menu with Parameter File Access

```
/* MAILING LIST MAINTENANCE PROGRAM */
/* 11/18/87 */
#include <stdio.h>
#include <graph.h>
```

continued

```
#include <conio.h>
#include <ctype.h>
#include "mail.h"
main()
{
     /* external references */
     extern struct videoconfig config;
     extern char ctitle[], address_file[], label_string[];
     extern char passwrd[];
     extern char pass[];
     extern char address_filex[];

     /* locals */
     COUNT option;
     COUNT param_file;
     char reply[80];
     char param_record[80];
     COUNT z, i;
     static struct data_frame main_menu[]=
          { MENUSTART, MENULEFT+5, "MAIN MENU",
            MENUSTART+3, MENULEFT, "A)dd an address",
            MENUSTART+4, MENULEFT, "E)dit and address",
            MENUSTART+5, MENULEFT, "S)how an address",
            MENUSTART+6, MENULEFT, "D)elete an address",
            MENUSTART+7, MENULEFT, "R)eport Menu",
            MENUSTART+8, MENULEFT, "M)iscellaneous Menu",
            MENUSTART+9, 30, "Q)uit",
            0,  0,   NULL
            };

     /* open and read parameter file */
     if( (in = fopen("PARAM.DAT","rb")) == NULL)
          err_msg("No PARA.DAT File.\n",1);
     if (z = fread(param_record, 180, 1, in) != 1)
          err_msg("Error in reading file\n",2);
     /* pull off parameter file variables and close */
     recfield(ctitle,param_record,1);
     recfield(pass,param_record,2);
     recfield(passwrd,param_record,3);
     recfield(address_filex,param_record,4);
     recfield(label_string,param_record,5);
     strcpy(address_file,address_filex);
     strcat(address_file,".DAT");
     fclose(in);                                        continued
```

```
/* do we have a password? */
if (stricmp(pass,"Y") == 0 )
     {
     printf("Please enter password: ");
     for (i=0; i<strlen(passwrd); i++)
          {
          reply[i]=getch();
          putchar('*');
          }
     reply[i]='\0';
     if (strcmp(reply,passwrd) != 0)
          err_msg("\nIllegal password\n",3);
     }
else    {
     if (stricmp(pass,"N") != 0   != 0)
          err_msg("\nBad parameter file\n",4);
     }
/* turn on graphics */
setup();
/* display menu & get option */
while (TRUE) {
     _clearscreen(0);
     /* display screen */
     display_title_frame(ctitle, RED);
     display_form(main_menu,BLUE);
     /* get input option */
     _settextposition(20,10);
     _displaycursor(_GCURSORON);
     _outtext("Option: ");
     option=getche();
     _displaycursor(_GCURSOROFF);
     if (islower(option))
          option = _toupper(option);
     switch(option)
     {
          case 'A' :
               mailadd();
               break;
          case 'E' :
               mailedit();
               break;
          case 'S' :
               maildsp();
               break;
```

continued

```
                case 'D' :
                        maildel();
                        break;
                case 'R' :
                        mailrpt();
                        break;
                case 'M' :
                        mailmisc();
                        break;
                case 'Q' :
                        cleanup();
                        exit(0);
                default :
                        _settextposition(config.numtextrows,1);
                        _outtext("Illegal input - press <CR> to continue");
                        option=getche();
            }
        }
    cleanup();
}
/* DO SETUP FOR GRAPHICS MODE */
void  setup()
{
    extern struct videoconfig config;

    COUNT set_mode();

    if (!set_mode())
            {
            printf("This video mode not supported.\n");
            exit(0);
            }
    _getvideoconfig(&config);
    _setlogorg(config.numxpixels / 2 - 1,
            config.numypixels / 2 - 1);


}
COUNT set_mode()
{
        if(_setvideomode(_ERESCOLOR))
            return(_ERESCOLOR);
        if (_setvideomode(_HRES16COLOR))
            return(_HRES16COLOR);
        if (_setvideomode(_HRESBW))
```

continued

```
                return(_HRESBW);
        else
                return(0);
}
/* RESTORE VIDEO MODE */
void cleanup()
{
        extern struct videoconfig config;

        _clearscreen(0);
        _setvideomode(_DEFAULTMODE);
}


/* DISPLAY A FORM ON THE SCREEN */
void display_form(form, color)
struct data_frame form[];
COUNT color;
{
        extern struct videoconfig config;

        COUNT index;
        COUNT z, maxlen=1;
        COUNT leftcol=80;
        COUNT lastrow=0;
        COUNT xorigin, yorigin, width, height;

        _setcolor(color);
        /* find the longest message line & leftmost point */
        for (index=0; form[index].msg != NULL; ++index)
                {
                z = strlen(form[index].msg);
                if (z>maxlen)
                        maxlen = z;
                if (form[index].col<leftcol)
                        leftcol=form[index].col;
                 if (form[index].row>lastrow)
                        lastrow = form[index].row;
                }
        /* set origin of display from first row and column */
        yorigin = (form[0].row-2) * config.numypixels / config.numtextrows;
        xorigin = (COUNT) (((long) (leftcol-2)) * (long) config.numxpixels /
            (long) config.numtextcols);
        _setlogorg(xorigin,yorigin);
        /* convert frame to pixel size and output */          continued
```

```
            width = (COUNT) (((long) (maxlen+2)) * (long) config.numxpixels /
                 (long) config.numtextcols);
            height = (lastrow+2-form[0].row) * config.numypixels /
                 config.numtextrows;
            _rectangle(_GFILLINTERIOR,0,0,width,height);
            /* output all text lines */
            for (index=0; form[index].msg != NULL; ++index)
                 displayline(&form[index]);
}
/* DISPLAY A LINE IN THE FORM */
void displayline(ptr_form)
struct data_frame *ptr_form;
{
            _settextposition(ptr_form->row,ptr_form->col);
            _outtext(ptr_form->msg);
}

/* DISPLAY TITLE */
void display_title_frame(title, color)
char title[];
COUNT color;
{
            extern struct videoconfig config;
            extern char address_file[];

            char buffer[80];
            COUNT h, h1, w, w1, height, width, xorigin, yorigin;

            h = ((config.numtextcols - strlen(title))/2);
            h1 = h;
            if (h>MENULEFT)
                 h1 = MENULEFT;
            xorigin = (h1-2) * config.numxpixels / config.numtextcols;
            yorigin =  2 * config.numypixels / config. numtextrows;
            _setlogorg(xorigin,yorigin);
            w = strlen(title);
            w1 = w;
            if (w < MENULEFT-10)
                 w1 = MENULEFT-10;
            width = (COUNT) (((long) (w1+2)) * (long) config.numxpixels /
                 (long) config.numtextcols);
            height = 5 * config.numypixels / config.numtextrows;
            _setcolor(color);
            _rectangle(_GFILLINTERIOR,0,0,width,height);
```

continued

```
    _settextposition(4,h);
    _outtext(title);
    _settextposition(5,MENULEFT);
    _outtext("MAILING LIST PROGRAM");
    _settextposition(6,MENULEFT+1);
    sprintf(buffer,"%s%s","FILE: ",address_file);
    _outtext(buffer);
}

/* EXTRACT A FIELD FROM A RECORD */
recfield(dest_string,sourc_string,field)
char dest_string[];
char sourc_string[];
COUNT field;

{

    COUNT dest,source;

    /* get to start of field */
    for (source = 0; --field && sourc_string[source] != '\0';)
        {
        while (sourc_string[source] != '\0' &&
            sourc_string[source] != DELIM)
            ++source;
        if (sourc_string[source] == DELIM)
            ++source;
        }

    /* copy from source to destination */
    for (dest = 0; sourc_string[source] !='\0' &&
        sourc_string[source] != DELIM;
        ++source, ++dest)
        dest_string[dest] = sourc_string[source];
    dest_string[dest] = '\0';
    return;
}
```

Designing Submenus

The design of any submenus called from the main menu follows the same rules of the main menu. Then two submenus are used: *mailrpt( )* for reports and *mailmisc()* for miscellaneous functions. The program for *mailrpt()* is shown in Listing 18.4. The program for *mailmisc()* is shown in Listing 18.5.

Listing 18.4
The MAILRPT Program

```
/* report menu */
/* 11.18.87 */
#include <stdio.h>
#include <graph.h>
#include <conio.h>
#include <ctype.h>
#include "mail.h"
mailrpt()
{
        extern struct videoconfig config;
        extern char ctitle[];

        COUNT option;
        static struct data_frame misc_menu[]=
                {
                MENUSTART, MENULEFT-1, "REPORT MENU",
                MENUSTART+3, MENULEFT, "L)abel Print",
                MENUSTART+4, MENULEFT, "D)irectory Print",
                MENUSTART+5, MENULEFT, "E)xit",
                0,  0,    NULL
                };
    /* display menu & get option */
    while (TRUE) {
            _clearscreen(0);
            /* display screen */
            display_title_frame(ctitle, GREEN);
            display_form(misc_menu, BLUE);
            /* get input option */
            _settextposition(20,10);
            _displaycursor(_GCURSORON);
            _outtext("Option: ");
            option=getche();
            _displaycursor(_GCURSOROFF);
            if (islower(option))
                    option = _toupper(option);
            switch(option)
            {
                case 'L' :
```

continued

```
                           maillbl();
                           break;
                    case 'D' :
                           maillst();
                           break;
                    case 'E' :
                           return;
                           break;
                    default :
                           _settextposition(config.numtextrows,1);
                           _outtext("Illegal input - press <CR> to
continue");

                           getche();
              }
       }
}
```

Listing 18.5
The MAILMISC Program

```
/* miscellaneous menu */
#include <stdio.h>
#include <graph.h>
#include <conio.h>
#include <ctype.h>
#include "mail.h"
mailmisc()
{
     extern struct videoconfig config;
     extern char ctitle[];

     COUNT option;
     static struct data_frame misc_menu[]=
          {
           MENUSTART, MENULEFT-1, "MISCELLANEOUS MENU",
           MENUSTART+3, MENULEFT, "P)arameter Edit",
           MENUSTART+4, MENULEFT, "S)tatus Report",
           MENUSTART+5, MENULEFT, "E)xit",
           0,  0,    NULL
          };

     while (TRUE) {
          _clearscreen(0);
```

continued

```
      /* display screen */
      display_title_frame(ctitle, GREEN);
      display_form(misc_menu, BLUE);
      /* get input option */
      _settextposition(20,10);
      _displaycursor(_GCURSORON);
      _outtext("Option: ");
      option=getche();
      _displaycursor(_GCURSOROFF);
      if (islower(option))
            option = _toupper(option);
      switch(option)
      {
            case 'P' :
                  mailpara();
                  break;
            case 'S' :
                  mailstat();
                  break;
            case 'E' :
                  return;
                  break;
            default :
                  _settextposition(config.numtextrows,1);
                  _outtext("Illegal input - press <CR> to
continue");
                  getche();
      }
   }
}
```

19

Adding Database Records

One of the first programs you would want to write after the menu is the program to add addresses to the database. This permits you to create the address file. This program is particularly important, as many of the design features you incorporate in this program will eventually be a part of other programs. In fact, you may find it takes you as long to write this first program as to write all the others in the system.

Basic Design Concepts

The basic design questions involve questions about the screen display concept, the file design, and the pseudocode and functional definitions.

The Screen Displays

The program flow is a sequence of two screen displays, with each screen display limited to a single objective or goal. Each screen display that will be used by the program is defined by one or more *data_frame* structures, the same structure used for the menus of the previous chapter. The structure is an array of one or more structures of the form *row, col,* and *text*.

```
struct data_frame
    {
    short row,col;
    char *msg;
    } ;
```

The File Design

The database record is defined by a structure (see Chapter 13). The record field lengths are defined using *#define* directives:

```
#define MAXLAST 25
#define MAXFIRST 25
#define MAXSTREET 40
#define MAXCITY 20
#define MAXSTATE 2
#define MAXZIP 5
#define PAD 2
struct address_rec
    {
    char aflag[5];
    char last[MAXLAST+PAD];
    char first[MAXFIRST+PAD];
    char street[MAXSTREET+PAD];
    char city[MAXCITY+PAD];
    char state[MAXSTATE+PAD];
    char zip[MAXZIP+PAD];
    };
struct address_rec address,new_address;
```

The actual record contains two additional bytes for each field to store the null character. There is no delimiter, as each field is a fixed length. All fields are character arrays, as that limitation is required of the file read and write functions that will be used. If you have numeric values, they should be converted to ASCII for disk storage using the *ltoa( )* or *itoa( )* functions. Notice that a flag is used to control the deleting. Then, *aflag* is set to the ASCII value of ASCII 3 to indicate a valid record. Any other value suggests there is no record in that file location.

This *address_rec* structure is the template for the record that will be written to the disk, which is identified by the data variable name *address*:

```
struct address_rec address;
```

It is also a good idea to create a dummy record with the same structure for editing and control purposes, which we will call *new_address*:

```
struct address_rec address, new_address;
```

The basic idea is to create the address using *new_address*. This is edited until it is correct. This record is then copied to *address*, which is written to the disk.

The structure for the two database record images can be processed in either one of two ways:

1. The structure can be global, with the records defined in the program using the structure. The addresses of the records are passed to the functions using them.

2. The entire record images can be kept global, making them available to any function.

For our purposes, as we have only two record variables, we can simplify the number of arguments used with the functions by keeping the records global. This will make the functions less portable to other programs we may wish to use them with, but does simplify the programming.

Another important design decision is when to open and close files. A basic rule is to keep the files closed as much as possible, keeping files open only as necessary to keep up with the user. This is particularly true of indexed files, as the indexes may be corrupted if the system crashes during an address update.

There is, therefore, a trade-off decision that must be made. If you have several index files with the data file, it will take a long time to open all the files each time you use them, making the program unable to keep up with the user. The temptation here is to open all files on starting the program and keep them open, making the program vulnerable to crashes. It is those very times, however, when you need to keep everything closed until the last minute.

In our example the answer is simple, as there is only one file. Keep it closed until you really need it, open it and do what is necessary, then close it again.

The Pseudocode and Function Definitions

As before, you should start with pseudocode, defining in English narrative exactly what you wish the program to do. Try to use functional descriptions that match what will be a part of other programs later.

The general program flow becomes:

1. Input the value of the key field.
2. Open the file and try to locate the desired record. Be sure no address is already using this location (membership number).
3. Close the file.
4. Display the edit buffer (*new_address*), which initially is empty.
5. Enter and edit the values for the address.
6. After the new address is valid, copy it to the record buffer (*address*).
7. Query to write the record to disk. If it is to be written, open the file, locate the correct position, and write the new record to the file.
8. Close the file.

At the highest level, the pseudocode becomes:

```
DO WHILE (TRUE))
    <clear edit buffer>
    <get address number>        /* screen 1 */
    IF (no address number)
        <return>
    ELSE
        <display forms>
        DO WHILE (invalid address)
            <display edit buffer>
            <get address data>  /* screen 2 */
        ENDDO
        <save it>
```

This actually defines the functions for the next level that this program will use. The next question is quite logical: how do I know what to break off as a function and what to keep in the main program? The basic rule is quite simple. Keep one idea and objective to a code module. If you think you might use the idea or objective in another program or function, break the module off as a function. If not, keep it in the main program but identify it with comments as a functional block.

The edit buffer is the temporary holding area for the new record we are entering (*new_record*).

You will also wish to stay in the functional block until the objective for that block is completed. Here, there are two "loop" functions, or functions that contain a loop that will continue until a condition is satisfied:

1. *get address number*—this gets the address number. The program stays in this loop until either a valid address number is entered or the user wishes to exit. If the user enters a number that is already on file, a message must be displayed and the looping continued. This routine could be expanded to include other error traps, such as a negative number entry. In a more generic situation where an index is used, this function gets the key value from the user and verifies it.

2. *get address data*—this gets the actual address data. The key value (the address number) is fixed at this point. The key value is displayed, but cannot be changed. The data is entered and checked for validation (fields correct length, numbers within range, and so forth).

There are two functions that execute and return:

1. The *display forms* function clears the screen and displays two forms: the title block at the top of the page and the basic form for the input data.

2. The *write_data( )* function verifies that the user wishes to save the record, then copies the input data from the *new_address* record to the *address record* and saves it. If an index file is used, it is also updated at this time.

Writing the Program

The actual program for writing the records is shown in Listing 19.1. The entire program is written as an eternal loop, with an exit when a blank address number is entered in *get_address_no()*. The two program screens are shown in Figures 19.1 and 19.2.

Figure 19.1
The First Program Screen

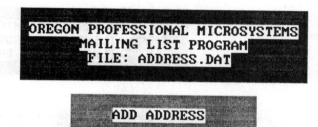

Enter a blank number to exit

The program calls the following new functions:

get_address_no(mode)
Displays the first screen and gets the address number for the record to be added. The value of mode determines whether adding, editing, displaying or deleting is being done. A return value of 0 suggests no address was entered.

display_current_data(address_no_ptr)
Displays the current data in the record defined by address_no_ptr.

get_form_data()
Get in the input data for the record from the user.

`write_data(address_no_ptr)`	Write the record to the address defined by address__no__ptr.
`err_msg1(msg)`	Process for error and display msg at line 23 of the screen.

Both the *get__address__no()* and *write__data()* functions open the file, do their work, and then close the file again.

Figure 19.2
The Second Program Screen

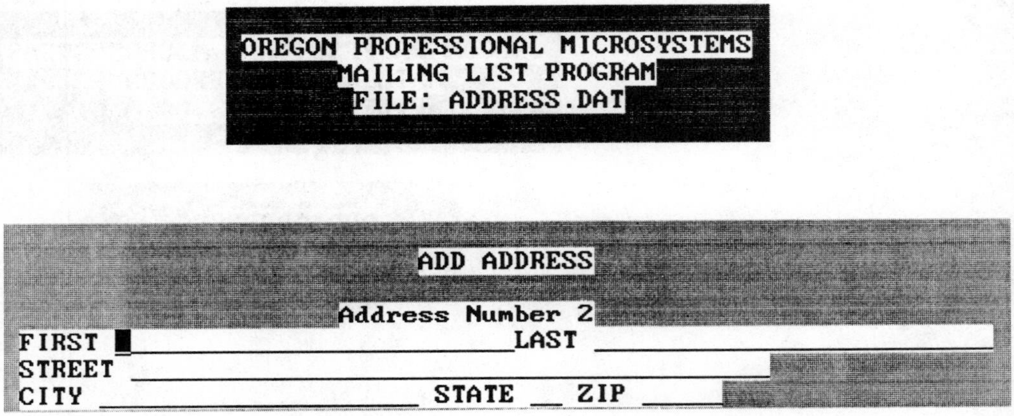

The Input Function

Most of the C input functions are not adequate for programs you will wish to write, and you should write your own input functions to support your needs. These can then be used in any programs you write. You will need at least two for general applications: one for text input, the other for numeric input. Here, only the text input version is needed, and is called *get__reply()*. The routine is called from *get__form__data()*. The *get__reply()* function displays the current data and then reads an input character at a time, checking it before reading the next input character. The general form for the function is:

```
get_reply(row,col,text,len)
```

where:

row,col =	coordinates for beginning the character echo
text =	current contents of buffer

$len =$ maximum length of input text

The cursor is turned on before reading each character and turned off immediately after. The current version has limited capabilities, permitting a ⟨Control-E⟩ to clear the field. The Backspace will also work. You may wish to expand this with additional features.

General Design Rules

The general design rules for an add program are as follows:

1. Use the first screen to enter only the primary key value. Check for a duplicate before continuing. (Primary keys should not have duplicates in the file.)

2. Use the second screen to enter all values except the primary key.

3. On all screens, be sure the function name is displayed so that the user will know where he or she is.

4. On all screens, hold the screen in a loop until all input values are verified.

5. Use the methods of the previous chapter for screen design. Use simple, clear words and keep the screen balanced.

6. Use the last line of the screen for error messages. Trap all potential errors and give the user a simple, clear message. For example, don't use:

```
Illegal input
```

Instead, you might use:

```
Address already on file - press any key to continue.
```

7. Never leave the user hanging about what to do next. For example, on the screen for enter the address number, you should also display a message about what to do if the user wishes to quit. On error messages, hold the error message but tell the user what to do next (such as "press any key to continue").

8. Use a temporary record structure to hold the data while verifying. Isolate the data input from the disk updating as much as possible.

9. Be sure the data processing keeps up with the user.

10. You may also wish to create a separate audit file that contains a copy of the new records that are added at the same time you are adding to the address file. This can be proofed for errors later.

Adding from a Batch File

Another alternative, which is useful particularly for slow and complex processing, is to enter the records to a separate batch file. There is no validation at this time. Later this batch file is processed, and the records added to the main file. Invalid records (duplications) are not added, but noted in a separate error log. The batch file becomes the audit file. This is the general approach for adding records in job costing systems, general ledgers, and a wide variety of similar programs.

The advantage is that the add process keeps up with the user, as the processing is done at a later time. Later, during the actual processing, timing to open and close files as well as that to update indexes is not as critical.

Listing 19.1
The MAILADD Program

```
/* add to mailing list */
#include <stdio.h>
#include <graph.h>
#include "mail.h"

mailadd()
{
    extern struct videoconfig config;
    extern struct address_rec new_address;
    extern char ctitle[];

    COUNT  ch;
    long address_no;
    long no_on_file;
    COUNT exitflg, mode, iflag, address_flag;
    static struct data_frame input_form[]=
        {
        STARTROW, 35, "ADD ADDRESS",
        STARTROW+2, 30, "Address Number ",
        STARTROW+3, 10,
"FIRST _____ LAST _____",
        STARTROW+4, 10, "STREET _____",
        STARTROW+5, 10, "CITY _____ STATE __ ZIP _____",
        0,  0,   NULL
        };

    /* eternal loop */
    while (TRUE)
```

continued

```
{
mode = ADD;
/* get address no */
exitflg = get_address_no(mode,&address_no, &no_on_file);
/* initialize */
new_address.first[0] = '\0';
new_address.last[0] = '\0';
new_address.street[0] = '\0';
new_address.city[0]='\0';
new_address.state[0] = '\0';
new_address.zip[0] = '\0';
/* check for exit */
if (exitflg == 2)
    return;
/* add an address */
_clearscreen(0);
display_title_frame(ctitle, GREEN);
display_form(input_form, BLUE);
address_flag = TRUE;
while (address_flag)
    {
    display_current_data(&address_no);
    get_form_data();
    _settextposition(20,15);
    _outtext("Accept address? ");
    _displaycursor(_GCURSORON);
    ch=getche();
    _displaycursor(_GCURSOROFF);
    if (ch == 'y'|| ch == 'Y')
        address_flag=FALSE;
    };
_settextposition(20,15);
_displaycursor(_GCURSORON);
_outtext("Write address to disk? ");
ch=getche();
_displaycursor(_GCURSOROFF);
if (ch == 'y'|| ch == 'Y')
    {
    iflag = FLAG;
    itoa(iflag,address.aflag,10);
    write_data(&address_no, &no_on_file);
    }
};
}
```

continued

```
/* ERROR MESSAGE ROUTINE #1 */
void err_msg(msg,err_num)
char msg[];
int err_num;
{
    puts(msg);
    puts("Press any key to continue");
    getche();
    exit(err_num);
}


/* ERROR MESSAGE ROUTINE #2 */
COUNT err_msg1(msg)
char msg[];
{
    extern struct videoconfig config;

    _settextposition(config.numtextrows,1);
    _outtext(msg);
    getche();
    return(1);
}

/* GET ADDRESS NUMBER */
COUNT get_address_no(mode, address_no_ptr, no_on_file_ptr)
long *address_no_ptr;
long *no_on_file_ptr;
COUNT mode;
{
    extern struct videoconfig config;
    extern struct address_rec address,header;
    extern char address_file[];

    COUNT exitflg, iflag;
    char address_no_string[5];
    char title2[40];

    /* open the file to read in binary mode */
    if ( (in = fopen(address_file,"rb")) == NULL)
        {
        err_msg1("No file: address.dat - press any key to continue");
        return(1);
        }
```

continued

```
/* get header record */
fseek(in,(long) 0,0);
fread(&header, sizeof header, 1, in);
*no_on_file_ptr = atol(header.aflag);
/* outer loop, to eternal loop */
/* display first screen and loop until valid */
do
    {
    iflag = 0;
    exitflg=0;
    _clearscreen(0);
    display_title_frame(ctitle, GREEN);
    if (mode == ADD);
        strcpy(title2,"ADD ADDRESS");
    if (mode == EDIT)
        strcpy(title2,"EDIT ADDRESS");
    if (mode == DISPLAY)
        strcpy(title2,"DISPLAY ADDRESS");
    if (mode == DELETE)
        strcpy(title2,"DELETE ADDRESS");
    display_address_no(title2, BLUE);
    _settextposition(config.numtextrows-1,15);
    _outtext("Enter a blank number to exit");
    _settextposition(12,45);
    _displaycursor(_GCURSORON);
    gets(address_no_string);
    _displaycursor(_GCURSOROFF);
    if (strlen(address_no_string) == 0)
        {
        exitflg=2;
        break;
        }
    *address_no_ptr = atol(address_no_string);
    if (*no_on_file_ptr >= *address_no_ptr)
        {
        fseek(in, (long) *address_no_ptr * sizeof address,0);
        fread(&address, sizeof address, 1, in);
        iflag = atoi(address.aflag);
        }
    if (mode == ADD && iflag == FLAG)
        {
        exitflg = err_msg1("Address already on file - press any key to
            continue");
        }
```

continued

315

```
        if (mode != ADD && iflag != FLAG)
            {
            exitflg = err_msg1("Address not on file - press any key to
                continue");
            }
        } while (exitflg != 0);
    fclose(in);
    return(exitflg);
}


/* DISPLAY CURRENT DATA */
void display_current_data(address_no_ptr)
long *address_no_ptr;
{
        extern struct address_rec new_address;

        char address_no_string[5];

        ltoa(*address_no_ptr,address_no_string,10);
        _settextposition(STARTROW+3,16);
        puts(new_address.first);
        _settextposition(STARTROW+3,46);
        puts(new_address.last);
        _settextposition(STARTROW+4,17);
        puts(new_address.street);
        _settextposition(STARTROW+5,15);
        puts(new_address.city);
        _settextposition(STARTROW+5,42);
        puts(new_address.state);
        _settextposition(STARTROW+5,49);
        puts(new_address.zip);
        _settextposition(STARTROW+2,45);
        _outtext(address_no_string);
}
/* GET DATA IN FORM */
void get_form_data()
{
    extern struct address_rec new_address;

    get_reply(STARTROW+3,16,new_address.first,MAXFIRST);
    get_reply(STARTROW+3,46,new_address.last,MAXLAST);
    get_reply(STARTROW+4,17,new_address.street,MAXSTREET);
    get_reply(STARTROW+5,15,new_address.city,MAXCITY);
    get_reply(STARTROW+5,42,new_address.state,MAXSTATE);
```

continued

```
        get_reply(STARTROW+5,49,new_address.zip,MAXZIP);
}


/* WRITE ADDRESS TO DISK */
void write_data(address_no_ptr,no_on_file_ptr)
long *address_no_ptr;
long *no_on_file_ptr;
{
    extern struct address_rec address, new_address, header;
    extern char address_file[];

    /* copy record to disk image record */
    strcpy(address.first,new_address.first);
    strcpy(address.last,new_address.last);
    strcpy(address.street,new_address.street);
    strcpy(address.city,new_address.city);
    strcpy(address.state,new_address.state);
    strcpy(address.zip,new_address.zip);
    /* open the file to write in binary mode */
    if ( (out = fopen(address_file,"rb+")) == NULL)
        {
        err_msg1("No file: address.dat - press any key to continue");
        return;
        }
    if (*no_on_file_ptr<*address_no_ptr)
        {
        ltoa(*address_no_ptr,header.aflag,10);
        fseek(out, (long) 0 ,0);
        fwrite(&header,sizeof header, 1, out);
        }
    fseek(out, (long) *address_no_ptr * sizeof address,0);
    fwrite(&address,sizeof address, 1, out);
    fclose(out);
}


/* DISPLAY REQUEST FOR ADDRESS NUMBER */
void display_address_no(title, color)
char title[];
COUNT color;
{
    extern struct videoconfig config;

    COUNT h, h1, w, w1, height, width, xorigin, yorigin;
    h = ((80 - strlen(title))/2);
```

continued

```
    h1 = h;
    if (h>30)
        h1 = 30;
    xorigin = (COUNT) (((long) (h1-2)) * (long) config.numxpixels /
        (long) config.numtextcols);
    yorigin =  8 * config.numypixels / config. numtextrows;
    _setlogorg(xorigin,yorigin);
    w = strlen(title);
    w1 = w;
    if (w < 20)
        w1 = 20;
    width = (w1+2) * config.numxpixels / config.numtextcols;
    height = 4 * config.numypixels / config.numtextrows;
    _setcolor(color);
    _rectangle(_GFILLINTERIOR,0,0,width,height);
    _settextposition(10,h);
    _outtext(title);
    _settextposition(12,30);
    _outtext("ADDRESS NUMBER ____");
}

/* GET REPLY - MAIN INPUT ROUTINE */
void get_reply(row,col,text,len)
COUNT row,col,len;
char *text;
{
    char buffer[80];
    COUNT ich, cont;

    /* copy to buffer & display current value */
    strcpy(buffer,text);
    for (ich = strlen(buffer); ich < len; ++ich)
        buffer[ich] = '_';
    buffer[ich] = '\0';
    _settextposition(row,col);
    _outtext(buffer);
    _settextposition(row,col);
    strcpy(buffer,text);
    for (ich=0, cont=TRUE; ich<len && cont;)
        {
        _displaycursor(_GCURSORON);
        buffer[ich] = getch();
        _displaycursor(_GCURSOROFF);
        buffer[ich+1] = '\0';
```

continued

```
switch(buffer[ich])
    {
    case '\x05':  /* ^E, restart */
        strcpy(buffer,text);
        for (ich = 0; ich < len; ++ich)
          buffer[ich] = '_';
        _settextposition(row,col);
        _outtext(buffer);
        ich = 0;
        buffer[ich] = text[ich] = '\0';
        _settextposition(row,col);
        break;
    case '\r' :        /* carriage return */
    case '\n' :
        /* send default value back */
        if (ich == 0 && text[0] != '\0')
            {
            strcpy(buffer,text);
            cont = FALSE;
            }
        else
            {
            buffer[ich] = '\0';
            cont = FALSE;
            }
        break;
    case '\b':    /* backspace */
        buffer[ich] = '\0';
        if (ich > 0)
            {
            buffer[--ich] = '\0';
            _settextposition(row,col+ich);
            _outtext("_");
            _settextposition(row,col+ich);
            }
        break;
    default :
            /* legal character */
            buffer[ich+1] ='\0';
            _outtext(&buffer[ich]);
            ich++;
            if (ich>len)
                cont = FALSE;
            break;
```

continued

```
            }
        }
    strcpy(text,buffer);
    ich = strlen(text);
    _settextposition(row,ich+col);
    for (; ich<len; ++ich)
        _outtext("_");
    return;
}
```

20

Editing and Deleting Records

The editing and deleting process is quite similar to the add process in many respects. The functions are the same. The primary difference is that with the editing, the primary key number must be verified as a valid address before continuing. Second, the address data currently on file must be loaded to the edit buffer for editing.

Editing

First, let's look at the process of editing records.

The Design Rules

The basic design rules of the previous chapter are the same for here, except that the pseudocode is slightly different. The screen design and record structure is, of course, the same.

The pseudocode becomes:

```
DO WHILE (TRUE)
    <clear edit buffer>
    <get address number>      /* screen 1 */
    IF (no address number)
    <return>
ELSE
    <display forms>
    <copy data from record buffer to edit buffer>
    DO WHILE (Invalid Address)
        <display edit buffer>
        <get address data>  /* screen 2 */
```

```
        ENDDO
        <save it>
    ENDDO
```

There is one difference here: a function is added to copy data from the record buffer to the edit buffer. This means we need to add one function:

get_current_data()   Copy data from the record buffer to the edit buffer.

Essentially, this will copy the data from record to *new_record*.

Writing the Program

The general program flow becomes:

1. Input the value of the primary key field value.
2. Open the file and locate the desired record. Be sure the record is found.
3. Copy the current file record values to the edit buffer (*new_address*).
4. Close the file.
5. Display and edit the variables.
6. After the new address is valid, copy it to the record buffer (*address*).
7. Query to write the record to disk. If it is to be written, open the file, locate the correct position, and write the new record to the file.
8. Close the file if it was opened.

The program listing is shown in Listing 20.1. The *mail.h* file is identical to that of the MAILADD program. Except for the function to copy the record buffer to the edit buffer, there are no new functions.

Listing 20.1
The MAILEDIT Program

```
/* edits mailing list */
#include <stdio.h>
#include <graph.h>
#include "mail.h"

mailedit()
{
    extern struct videoconfig config;
    extern struct address_rec new_address;
    extern char ctitle[];

    long address_no;
```

continued

```
     long no_on_file;
     COUNT exitflg, mode, iflag, address_flag, ch;
     static struct data_frame input_form[]=
          {
          STARTROW, 35, "EDIT ADDRESS",
          STARTROW+2, 30, "Address Number ",
          STARTROW+3, 10,
"FIRST _____ LAST _____",
          STARTROW+4, 10, "STREET _____",
          STARTROW+5, 10, "CITY _____ STATE __ ZIP _____",
          0,  0,   NULL
          };

/* eternal loop */
while (TRUE)
     {
     mode = EDIT;
     /* get address no */
     exitflg = get_address_no(mode,&address_no, &no_on_file);
     if (exitflg == 2)
          return;
     /* get current record */
     read_data(&address_no);
     /* edit an address */
     _clearscreen(0);
     display_title_frame(ctitle, GREEN);
     display_form(input_form, BLUE);
     address_flag=TRUE;
     while (address_flag)
          {
          display_current_data(&address_no);
          get_form_data();
          _settextposition(20,15);
          _displaycursor(_GCURSORON);
          _outtext("Accept address?");
          ch=getche();
          _displaycursor(_GCURSOROFF);
          if (ch == 'y'|| ch == 'Y')
               address_flag=FALSE;
          };
     _settextposition(20,15);
     _outtext("Write address to disk?");
     _displaycursor(_GCURSORON);
     ch=getche();
```

continued

```
        _displaycursor(_GCURSOROFF);
        if (ch == 'y'|| ch == 'Y')
            {
            iflag = FLAG;
            itoa(iflag,address.aflag,10);
            write_data(&address_no, &no_on_file);
            }
    };
}


/* READ DATA FROM FILE */
void read_data(address_no_ptr)
long *address_no_ptr;
{
    extern struct address_rec address, new_address;
    extern char address_file[];

    /* open the file to read in binary mode */
    if ( (in = fopen(address_file,"rb")) == NULL)
        {
        err_msg1("No file: address.dat - press any key to continue");
        return;
        }
    /* read record */
    fseek( in, (long) *address_no_ptr * sizeof address,0);
    fread(&address,sizeof address, 1, in);
    /* copy record to disk image record */
    strcpy(new_address.first,address.first);
    strcpy(new_address.last,address.last);
    strcpy(new_address.street,address.street);
    strcpy(new_address.city,address.city);
    strcpy(new_address.state,address.state);
    strcpy(new_address.zip,address.zip);
    fclose(in);
}
```

General Rules for Edit Programs

The general design rules for an edit program are as follows:

1. Use the first screen to enter only the key value. Check to be sure the record exists before continuing.

2. Copy the record values to the edit buffer, then use the second screen to edit all values except the key.

3. On all screens, be sure the function name is displayed so that the user will know where he or she is.

4. On all screens, hold the screen in a loop until all input values are verified.

5. Use the methods of Chapter 18 for screen design: use simple, clear words and keep the screen balanced.

6. Use the last line of the screen for error messages. Trap all potential errors and give the user a simple, clear message. For example, don't use:

```
Illegal input
```

Instead, you might use:

```
Address not on file - press any key to continue.
```

7. Never leave the user hanging wondering what to do next. For example, on the screen to enter the address number, display a message about what to do if the user wishes to quit. On error messages, hold the error message but tell the user what to do next (such as "press any key to continue").

8. Use a temporary record structure to hold the data while verifying. Isolate the data input from the disk updating as much as possible.

9. Be sure the data processing keeps up with the user.

10. You may also wish to create a separate audit file that contains a copy of the new data for the records that are edited while editing the master address file. The audit file can be proofed for errors later.

Updating from a Transaction File

As with the program to add records, with editing it is necessary for the program to keep up with the user. If a lot of processing is involved for each record, you should use a transaction file. Proposed edit information is entered quickly to the transaction file, which is then used at a later time to update the master file.

The transaction file has a special record structure, which should be:

File Name	Description
transaction_code	Code to indicate type of transaction (add, edit, delete)
field_name	Name of the field to change
old_value	The old value of the field
new_value	The new value of the field

If several fields of a record are to be changed, there should be one record in the transaction file for each field to change.

Editing the Parameter File

There is one other editing program in the system, the program to edit the parameter file. This program displays the current data in a form, permits editing, and then writes it to the parameter file. Password control variables in the file cannot be changed from this program (Listing 20.2). There are no new functions used.

Listing 20.2
The MAILPARA Program

```
/* edit parameter file edit */
#include <stdio.h>
#include <graph.h>
#include <conio.h>
#include <ctype.h>
#include <string.h>
#include "mail.h"

void mailpara()
{
     extern char ctitle[], address_file[], label_string[];
     extern char passwrd[];
     extern char pass[];
     extern char address_filex[];

     COUNT param_file;
     char param_record[80];
     COUNT z, len_record, ch;
     static struct data_frame param_form[]=
         { 10, 29, "PARAMETER EDIT",
           13, 15, "COMPANY NAME _____",
           14, 15, "ADDRESS FILE _____",
           15, 15, "NUMBER OF LINES PER LABEL __",
           0,  0,    NULL
           };
         FILE *fparam;

     /* display form & get input */
     while (TRUE)
```

continued

```
{
_clearscreen(0);
/* display screen */
display_title_frame(ctitle, GREEN);
display_form(param_form, BLUE);
/* display current data */
_settextposition(13,28);
_outtext(ctitle);
_settextposition(14,28);
_outtext(address_filex);
_settextposition(15,41);
_outtext(label_string);
get_reply(13,28,ctitle,35);
get_reply(14,28,address_filex,8);
get_reply(15,41,label_string,2);
_settextposition(20,15);
_displaycursor(_GCURSORON);
_outtext("Accept Parameters? ");
ch = getche();
_displaycursor(_GCURSOROFF);
if (ch == 'y' || ch == 'Y')
    {
    len_record = sprintf(param_record,"%s%c%s%c%s%c%s%c%s",
        ctitle,DELIM,pass,DELIM,passwrd,DELIM,
        address_filex,DELIM,label_string);
    if( (fparam = fopen("PARAM.DAT","rb+")) == NULL)
        {
        err_msg1("Error on opening file - press any key");
        return;
        }
    if (( z = fwrite(param_record, 180, 1, fparam)) != 1)
        {
        err_msg1("Error in writing to file - press any key to
            continue");
        return;
        }
    fclose(fparam);
    strcpy(address_file,address_filex);
    strcat(address_file,".DAT");
    return;
    }
}
}
```

Deleting Records

The deletion of records in the address file of this program is a simple process of setting the flag in the record to any value other than 3. The flag is used to indicate the record is valid. By turning the flag off, this essentially invalidates any of the data in the record.

The Pseudocode

As before, we begin by writing the pseudocode:

```
DO WHILE (TRUE)
    <clear edit buffer>
    <get address number>       /* screen 1 */
    IF (no address number)
        <return>
    ELSE
        <display forms>
        <display record >    /* screen 2 */
        <query to set delete flag>
        IF (DELETE)
        <turn off flag>
        <save record>
ENDDO
```

The difference here is that there is no loop for receiving the input data from the user. The record is displayed, and the user is given a chance to delete it. If deleted, the delete flag is set to 0 and the record is written to the disk again.

Programming for Deletion

At a more detailed level, the program outline would be:

1. Input the value of the key field.
2. Open the file and locate the desired record. Be sure the record is found.
3. Close the file.
4. Copy the record buffer to the edit buffer and display the edit buffer.
5. Query for deletion.
6. Query to write the record to disk.
7. If it is to be written, open the file, locate the correct position, and write the record to the file with the new flag.
8. Close the file if it was opened.

A listing of the program is given in Listing 20.3.

Listing 20.3
The MAILDEL Program

```c
/* deletes from  mailing list */
#include <stdio.h>
#include <graph.h>
#include "mail.h"

maildel()
{
    extern struct videoconfig config;
    extern struct address_rec new_address;
    extern char ctitle[];

    long address_no;
    long no_on_file;
    COUNT exitflg, mode, iflag, address_flag, ch;
    static struct data_frame input_form[]=
        {
        STARTROW, 35, "DELETE ADDRESS",
        STARTROW+2, 30, "Address Number ",
        STARTROW+3, 10,
"FIRST _____ LAST _____",
        STARTROW+4, 10, "STREET _____",
        STARTROW+5, 10, "CITY _____ STATE __ ZIP _____",
        0, 0,   NULL
        };

    /* eternal loop */
    while (TRUE)
        {
        mode = DELETE;
        /* get address no */
        exitflg = get_address_no(mode,&address_no, &no_on_file);
        if (exitflg == 2)
            return;
        /* get current record */
        read_data(&address_no);
        /* edit an address */
        _clearscreen(0);
        display_title_frame(ctitle, GREEN);
        display_form(input_form, BLUE);
```

continued

```
        address_flag=TRUE;
        display_current_data(&address_no);
        _settextposition(20,15);
        _outtext("Delete address?");
        _displaycursor(_GCURSORON);
        ch=getche();
        _displaycursor(_GCURSOROFF);
        if (ch == 'y'|| ch == 'Y')
                {
                iflag = 0;
                itoa(iflag,address.aflag,10);
                write_data(&address_no, &no_on_file);
                }
    };
}
```

General Rules for Delete Programs

The general design rules for a delete program are as follows:

1. Use the first screen to enter only the key value. Check to be sure the record exists before continuing.

2. The second screen should display the current values and query for deletion.

3. On all screens, be sure the function name is displayed so that the user will know where he or she is.

4. On all screens, hold the screen in a loop until all input values are verified.

5. Use the methods of Chapter 18 for screen design. Use simple, clear words and keep the screen balanced.

6. Use the last line of the screen for error messages. Trap all potential errors and give the user a simple, clear message. For example, don't use:

```
Illegal input
```

Instead, you might use:

```
Address not on file - press any key to continue.
```

7. Never leave the user hanging wondering what to do next. On the screen to enter the address number, display a message about what to do if the user

wishes to quit. On error messages, hold the error message but tell the user what to do next (such as "press any key to continue").

8. Use a temporary record structure to hold the data while verifying. Isolate the data input from the disk updating as much as possible.

9. Be sure the data processing keeps up with the user.

10. You may also wish to create a separate audit file that contains a copy of the new data for the record deleted.

Deleting with Indexed Files

The general procedure is the same for indexed files as with other programs. A flag is used to control the deletion process. If a record is to be deleted, the record delete flag is set to zero; but the physical record remains in the file. A separate program should be written to pack the file. This program copies the file to another temporary file. Deleted records are not copied. If the copy is successful, the old file is then deleted. The new file is renamed to the proper name and reindexed.

The delete method of this chapter (and described here for indexed files) has an advantage over other methods in that the deleted record still remains in the file, at least until repacking. If necessary, the record can be recovered and used again by simply setting the delete flag in the record to 3 if you have not repacked the file.

21

Reporting and Processing Programs

The purpose of a computer program is generally to process input data to produce conclusions or to control a device. The conclusions or control is the "output" (Figure 21.1). Some of the output, in turn, becomes new input that is used to make even better conclusions.

Figure 21.1
A System Diagram

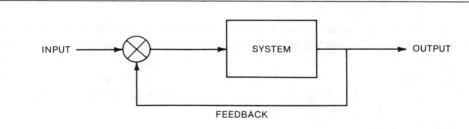

The output, as the end product, is very important. With a spreadsheet, the output is used to make financial decisions that can determine the success or failure of the company. With a desktop publishing program, the output is sent out to a printer for printing. With a database manager, the output may be a set of mailing labels, an inventory report, or a list of prospects to call for the day.

We live in an information-overloaded society. Once the computer is reporting its output, we also want it in a form in which the conclusions are easy to read. We don't want a lot of extra information that is irrelevant, and also don't want important information missing from the report.

This chapter will explore the design of reporting programs, and will also discuss processing programs. Processing programs create new data from current data in the file or put current data in a different form.

Initial Report Program Design

Let's look at some basic questions about designing a report program.

1. In starting to design the report program, the first decision is what should be in it. Too much information is as bad as too little. The report should contain only what is necessary. What does the user need for decisions? Are multiple reports needed for different users?

2. What should the basic form of the report be (list, graph, and so forth)?

3. How should the form be ordered (what columns if a list, how many on a row for labels, type of graph for a graph, and so forth)?

4. If a list, what should be the order of the list (alphabetical, zip, and so forth)?

A good place to start is to get current output reports and examine these. In what ways are they good? How can they be improved? Create forms with dummy data and work with these until the reports are correct. Explore how to make conclusions stand out (bold print, italics, and so forth).

Basic Flow Diagram

The program uses basically multiple screens, similar to the other programs in our system. On entering the program, query the user to see if a report is actually desired. If the program is called from a menu in which a carriage return is not entered with the option, it's easy to get to a report program by mistake. The program should check with the user before beginning the print.

Here's the basic flow:

1. Check with the user that a report is really desired.

2. Get any control information (file name, starting point, ending point, order of printout, and so forth).

3. Open the files for reading.

4. Index on the order for printout if necessary.

5. Print the report lines from a WHILE loop, checking for paging on each iteration. Skip records that do not need to be in the report. Display a screen message about the status of the report (if possible, display a message that shows how far the printing is in the report).

6. Print any conclusions: totals, text, and so forth.
The pseudocode becomes:

```
<Check for valid entry>
<Get control information>
```

```
<Open files>
<Index for printing order>
DO WHILE (not EOF or end)
    if (heading needed)
        <print heading>
    <Print line>
    <increment line counter>
ENDDO
<print totals>
```

Controlling Paging

To control paging, first initialize two variables: a page counter and a line counter. Initialize the line counter to a high value so you can test this variable and block ejection on the first page:

```
pagectr = 0;
linectr = 90;
```

Before printing each line, check for the line counter overflow and, if necessary, eject to the next page and print a heading from a subroutine. Then increment the pagecounter and reset the line counter:

```
if (linectr>60)
    {
    if (linectr != 90)
        printf("\v");
    header(pagectr++);
    linectr = 0;
    }
linectr++;
```

Indexing

You may often wish to print records in a different order than their order in the file. Professional programmers generally purchase indexing routines commercially that do the indexing. For the mailing list program, we'll create an array with two components. The first component is the record number of the record, the second is the key field (or fields) to control the order of the printout. The array is loaded from the file, then sorted by the key field. The sorted array is then used to drive the loop that prints the records using the record number in the sorted array to access the record to print.

Report Design Techniques

Here is a summary of some basic report design techniques:

1. Give a user a chance to exit on entry.

2. During printing, display a message on the screen about what the printer is doing and how much of the printing is completed.

3. Indexes can be created for data files and be continuously maintained, or you can create an index "on-the-fly" for a particular report. Keeping the number of indexes maintained continuously small will help add and edit programs run faster.

4. Keep the program to print the header as a separate program, as it will often be used with several reports.

5. Be sure to trap all possible errors.

6. Keep screen designs simple and uncluttered.

The Programs

The report menu calls either of the two report programs *maillbl( )* or *maillst( )*. Both programs contain functions that load the array and then sort it. The *maillbl( )* program sorts by zip+lastname+firstname and the *maillst( )* program sorts by lastname+firstname. Reporting programs should open files for read only.

The *maillbl( )* program prints labels in a one-up continuous form. The number of lines for each label can be set from the parameter file and changed with the MAILPARA program. Listing 21.1 shows the listing.

Listing 21.1
The MAILLBL Program

```
/*  mailing list  labels */
#include <stdio.h>
#include <graph.h>
#include "mail.h"

struct sort_structure
    {
    COUNT rec_no;
    char zip[MAXZIP+MAXLAST+MAXFIRST];
    };
struct sort_structure sort_array[MAXADDRESSES];
```
continued

```
void maillbl()
{
     extern char ctitle[];
     extern struct sort_structure sort_array[];
     extern char label_string[];
     extern char address_file[];

     FILE *in;
     COUNT  ch, sample, max, k, no_lines;
     char maxa[5],ia[5];
     COUNT i;
     char buffer[80];
     static struct data_frame input_form[]=
          {
          12, 35, "PRINT LABELS",
          14, 35, "Continue? ",
          0,  0,   NULL
          };

     _clearscreen(0);
     display_title_frame(ctitle, GREEN);
     display_form(input_form, BLUE);
     _settextposition(14,46);
     _displaycursor(_GCURSORON);
     ch = getche();
     _displaycursor(_GCURSOROFF);
     if (ch=='n' || ch == 'N')
          return;
     do  {
          _settextposition(20,15);
          _outtext("Print sample label? ");
          _settextposition(20,35);
          _displaycursor(_GCURSORON);
          sample = getche();
          _displaycursor(_GCURSOROFF);
          if (sample=='y' || sample =='Y')
               {
               fputs("John Doe\r",stdprn);
               fputs("Box 3\r",stdprn);
               fputs("Portland, OR  97211\r\r\r\r\r\r",stdprn);
               _settextposition(20,15);
               _outtext("Print sample label? ");
               _displaycursor(_GCURSORON);
```

continued

337

```
                    _settextposition(20,35);
                    sample = getche();
                    _displaycursor(_GCURSOROFF);
                    }
            }
    while (sample == 'y' || sample == 'Y');
    max = load_sortz();
    _settextposition(20,15);
    _outtext("Sorting...                          ");
    sorterz(max);
    /* open the file in binary mode */
    if ( (in = fopen(address_file,"rb")) == NULL)
            {
            err_msg1("No address file - press any key to continue");
            return;
            }
    for (i=0;i<max;i++)
            {
            if (i % 10 == 0)
                    {
                    buffer[0] = '\0';
                    itoa(i+1,ia,10);
                    itoa(max,maxa,10);
                    strcat(buffer," addresses.                          ");
                    sprintf(buffer,"%s%s%s%s%s","Printing ",ia," of ",maxa,
                        " addresses.                    ");
                    _settextposition(20,10);
                    _outtext(buffer);
                    }
            fseek(in, (long) sort_array[i].rec_no * sizeof address,0);
            fread(&address, sizeof (address), 1,  in);
            sprintf(buffer,"%s%s%s%s",address.first," ",address.last,CRLF);
            fputs(buffer,stdprn);
            sprintf(buffer,"%s%s",address.street,CRLF);
            fputs(buffer,stdprn);
            sprintf(buffer,"%s%s%s%s%s%s",address.city,", ",address.state," ",
                    address.zip,CRLF);
            fputs(buffer,stdprn);
            no_lines = atoi(label_string);
            for (k=3;k<no_lines;k++)
                    fputs(CRLF,stdprn);
            }
}
```

continued

```
COUNT load_sortz()
{
    extern struct address_rec address,header;
    extern char ctitle[];
    extern struct sort_structure sort_array[];
    extern char address_file[];

    COUNT iflag;
    char ja[5], total[5];
    char buffer[80];
    COUNT i=0, j=0;

    /* open the file in binary mode */
    if ( (in = fopen(address_file,"rb")) == NULL)
        {
        err_msg1("No address file - press any key to continue");
        return;
        }
    fseek(in, (long) 0 * sizeof (header), 0);
    fread(&header, sizeof (header), 1, in);
    strcpy(total,header.aflag);
    fseek(in, (long) 1 * sizeof (address), 0);
    while (fread(&address, sizeof (address), 1, in) != 0)
        {
        iflag = atoi(address.aflag);
        if ((j % 10) ==0)
            {
            itoa(j+1,ja,10);
            sprintf(buffer,"%s%s%s%s%s","Reading record ",ja,
                " in a file of ",total," records.            ");
            _settextposition(20,10);
            _outtext(buffer);
            }
        if (iflag == 3)
            {
            sort_array[i].rec_no = j+1;
            strcpy(sort_array[i].zip,address.zip);
            strcat(sort_array[i].zip,address.last);
            strcat(sort_array[i].zip,address.first);
            i++;
            }
        j++;
        }
    fclose(in);
```

continued

```
        return(i);
}


void sorterz(size)
COUNT size;
{
        extern struct sort_structure sort_array[];
        COUNT i, j;
        COUNT tempn;
        char buffer[MAXZIP+MAXLAST+MAXFIRST];

        for (i=0;i<size-1;i++)
             for (j=i+1;j<size;j++)
             if (strcmp(sort_array[i].zip,sort_array[j].zip)>0)
                 {
                 tempn = sort_array[i].rec_no;
                 sort_array[i].rec_no = sort_array[j].rec_no;
                 sort_array[j].rec_no = tempn;
                 strcpy(buffer,sort_array[i].zip);
                 strcpy(sort_array[i].zip,sort_array[jr k].zip);
                 strcpy(sort_array[j].zip,buffer);
                 }
        return;
}
```

The *maillst()* program prints a directory in a one-up form. It has paging control and uses a *page_header()* function to print a heading on each page. It also tabs each line of the address over by one tab on the printout. Listing 21.2 shows the listing. Each address is printed with the membership number (record number).

Listing 21.2
The MAILLST Program

```
/* list mailing list */
#include <stdio.h>
#include <graph.h>
#include "mail.h"

struct sort_structure
    {
    COUNT rec_no;
    char name[MAXLAST+MAXFIRST];
```
continued

```
        };
struct sort_structure sort_array[MAXADDRESSES];

void maillst()
{
        extern char ctitle[];
        extern struct sort_structure sort_array[];
        extern char label_string[];
        extern char address_file[];
        extern struct address_rec address;

        COUNT max, k, no_lines;
        char maxa[5],ia[5];
        COUNT i, ch, sample;
        char buffer[80];
        COUNT pagectr=1,linectr;
        char linectra[5];
        static struct data_frame input_form[]=
            {
            12, 35, "PRINT DIRECTORY",
            14, 35, "Continue? ",
            0,  0,   NULL
            };
        char recnoa[5];

        _clearscreen(0);
        display_title_frame(ctitle, GREEN);
        display_form(input_form, BLUE);
        _settextposition(14,46);
        _displaycursor(_GCURSORON);
        ch = getche();
        _displaycursor(_GCURSOROFF);
        if (ch=='n' || ch == 'N')
            return;
        max = load_sorta();
        _settextposition(20,15);
        _outtext("Sorting...                         ");
        sortera(max);
        linectr = 90;
        /* open the file in binary mode */
        if ( (in = fopen(address_file,"rb")) == NULL)
            {
            err_msg1("No address file - press any key to continue");
            return;
```

continued

```
            }
    for (i=0;i<max;i++)
        {
        if (i % 10 == 0)
            {
            buffer[0] = '\0';
            itoa(i+1,ia,10);
            itoa(max,maxa,10);
            sprintf(buffer,"%s%s%s%s%s","Printing ",ia," of ",maxa,
                " addresses.                              ");
            _settextposition(20,10);
            _outtext(buffer);
            }
        /* check for paging */
        if (linectr>(58-atoi(label_string)))
            {
            if (linectr != 90)
                fputs("\x0c",stdprn);
            page_header(pagectr++);
            linectr = 0;
            }
        /* get & print the record */
        fseek(in, (long) sort_array[i].rec_no * sizeof (address), 0);
        fread(&address, sizeof (address), 1, in);
        itoa(sort_array[i].rec_no,recnoa,10);
        sprintf(buffer,"%s%s%s","\t",recnoa,CRLF);
        fputs(buffer,stdprn);
        linectr++;
        sprintf(buffer,"%s%s%s%s%s","\t",address.first," ",
            address.last,CRLF);
        fputs(buffer,stdprn);
        linectr++;
        sprintf(buffer,"%s%s%s","\t",address.street,CRLF);
        fputs(buffer,stdprn);
        linectr++;
        sprintf(buffer,"%s%s%s%s%s%s%s","\t",address.city," , ",
            address.state,"  ",address.zip,CRLF);
        fputs(buffer,stdprn);
        linectr++;
        no_lines = atoi(label_string);
        for (k=4;k<no_lines;k++)
            {
            fputs(CRLF,stdprn);
            linectr++;
```

continued

```
            }
        }
        /* final eject */
        fputs("\x0c",stdprn);
}

COUNT load_sorta()
{
        extern struct address_rec address,header;
        extern char ctitle[];
        extern char address_file[];
        extern struct sort_structure sort_array[];

        COUNT iflag;
        char ja[5], total[5];
        char buffer[80];
        COUNT i=0, j=0;

        /* open the file in binary mode */
        if ( (in =fopen(address_file,"rb")) == NULL)
            {
            err_msg1("No address file- press any key to continue");
            return;
            }
        fseek(in, (long) 0 * sizeof (header), 0);
        fread(&header, sizeof (header), 1, in);
        strcpy(total,header.aflag);
        fseek(in, (long) 1 * sizeof (address), 0);
        while (fread(&address, sizeof (address), 1, in) != 0)
            {
            iflag = atoi(address.aflag);
            if ((j % 10) ==0)
                {
                itoa(j+1,ja,10);
                sprintf(buffer,"%s%s%s%s%s","Reading record ",ja,
                    " in a file of ",
                    total," records.                    ");
                _settextposition(20,10);
                _outtext(buffer);
                }
            if (iflag == 3)
                {
                sort_array[i].rec_no = j+1;
                strcpy(sort_array[i].name,address.last);
```

continued

343

```
                strcat(sort_array[i].name,address.first);
                i++;
                }
          j++;
          }
     fclose(in);
     return(i);
}

void sortera(size)
COUNT size;
{
     extern struct sort_structure sort_array[];
     COUNT i, j;
     COUNT tempn;
     char buffer[MAXLAST+MAXFIRST];

     for (i=0;i<size-1;i++)
          for (j=i+1;j<size;j++)
          if (strcmp(sort_array[i].name,sort_array[j].name)>0)
               {
               tempn = sort_array[i].rec_no;
               sort_array[i].rec_no = sort_array[j].rec_no;
               sort_array[j].rec_no = tempn;
               strcpy(buffer,sort_array[i].name);
               strcpy(sort_array[i].name,sort_array[j rk].name);
               strcpy(sort_array[j].name,buffer);
               }
     return;
}
void page_header(page)
COUNT page;
{
     extern char ctitle[];

     char pagea[5];
     COUNT i,x,y;

     x = (80 - strlen(ctitle))/2;
     fputs(CRLF,stdprn);
     fputs(CRLF,stdprn);
     for (i=0;i<x; i++)
          fputs(" ",stdprn);
     fputs(ctitle,stdprn);
```

continued

```
    y = 70 - x - strlen(ctitle);
    for (i=0;i<y;i++)
        fputs(" ",stdprn);
    fputs("PAGE ",stdprn);
    itoa(page,pagea,10);
    fputs(pagea,stdprn);
    fputs(CRLF,stdprn);
    fputs(CRLF,stdprn);
}
```

There is also one other reporting program that can be found on the miscellaneous menu—the status program. This program uses the header record to find the number of records in the file, then scans the entire file to count the number of nondeleted records. The output is displayed on the screen (Listing 21.3).

Listing 21.3
The MAILSTAT Program

```
/* mailing list status */
#include <stdio.h>
#include <graph.h>
#include "mail.h"

void mailstat()
{
    extern struct videoconfig config;
    extern struct address_rec address;
    extern char ctitle[];

    COUNT max;
    COUNT  ch;
    char maxa[5];
    char buffer[80];
    char total[5];
    static struct data_frame input_form[]=
        {
        12, 27, "ADDRESS FILE STATUS REPORT",
        14, 27, "Continue? ",
        0,  0,   NULL
        };

    _clearscreen(0);
    display_title_frame(ctitle, GREEN);
```

continued

```
        display_form(input_form, BLUE);
        _settextposition(14,38);
        _displaycursor(_GCURSORON);
        ch=getche();
        _displaycursor(_GCURSOROFF);
        if (ch == 'y'|| ch == 'Y')
            {
            max = count_file(total);
            itoa(max,maxa,10);
            sprintf(buffer,"%s%s%s%s%s","There are ",maxa,"
                addresses in a file of ",
                total," records.               ");
            _settextposition(20,10);
            _outtext(buffer);
            _settextposition(config.numtextrows,1);
            _outtext("Press any key to continue");
            getche();
            }
}

COUNT count_file(total)
char total[];
{
        extern struct address_rec address, header;
        extern char address_file[];

        FILE *in;
        COUNT  iflag;
        COUNT i=0, j=0;
        char ja[5], buffer[80];

        /* open the file to read in binary mode */
        if ( (in = fopen(address_file,"rb")) == NULL)
            {
            err_msg1("No address file - press any key to continue");
            return;
            }
        fseek(in, (long) 0 * sizeof (header), 0);
        fread(&header,sizeof (header), 1, in);
        strcpy(total,header.aflag);
        fseek(in, (long) 1 * sizeof address,0);
        while (fread(&address, sizeof address, 1, in) != 0)
            {
            iflag = atoi(address.aflag);
```

continued

```
        itoa(j,ja,10);
        sprintf(buffer,"%s%s%s%s%s","Reading record ",ja," in a file of ",
            total," records.              ");
        _settextposition(20,10);
        _outtext(buffer);
        if (iflag == FLAG)
            i++;
        j++;
        }
    fclose(in);
    return(i);
}
```

All three of these programs use moving variables on the screen to keep the user informed about the status of the printing or processing. The total number is displayed with a variable indicating the current record being processed. By "moving," the implication is that the variable is constantly changing. Usually, since C executes so fast, you will want to use the modulo operator to change the variable every certain number of records instead of on each record. In this example, the display is changed every tenth record.

Processing Programs

Processing programs process existing data, creating new data or reordering the current data. One common example is the posting program in a general ledger system or a reindexing program that recreates the index files for a system.

More frequently, processing is a part of other programs. Common examples include sorting for printing, scanning for a status report, or building an array in memory that will be used for an output. In each case, the design rules are similar for other programs. In these programs, however, it is particularly important to suggest to the user what is happening and, if possible, use a moving variable to keep the user informed about the status of the processing.

Although there are no programs in this system that are processing programs, the report and status programs all have processing functions.

Appendices

A

Installation and Setup

Before you can develop programs using QuickC, you must install it to your hard disk. Before starting, be sure you have everything you need:

- IBM compatible computer
- 448K of memory
- two floppy-disk drives or a floppy-disk drive and one hard disk

The following are optional, but are suggested:

- Mouse (Microsoft-compatible)
- Hard disk
- EGA or VGA-compatible monitor

This appendix assumes you use a system with a hard disk. If you are using a system without a hard disk, refer to your user manual for alternative procedures. Installation involves the following seven steps:

1. Organizing the hard disk.
2. Backing up your program disks.
3. Reading README.DOC files on the disks.
4. Running the QuickC SETUP program to install the software to the proper directories. This step also creates five directories for the QuickC product: INCLUDE, LIB, TMP, BIN, and a working directory.
5. Modifying the CONFIG.SYS file to expand the environment to include the new SET commands.
6. Modifying the AUTOEXEC.BAT file to define the new system variables and include the new path.
7. Optionally, creating your QuickC library.

A review of these steps follows.

Organizing the Hard Disk

If necessary, clear enough disk space to install QuickC. You will also need space to store your own development program.

Basic Disk Organization

QuickC utilizes five directories:

Program Directory: This is used to store the executables for all the QuickC development tools. It is normally called \BIN, \C5, or \QC.

Library Directory: This is used to store the libraries (LIB files) for QuickC. It is normally called \LIB.

Include Directory: This is used to store the include files (H files) used in the C programs. It is normally called \INCLUDE.

Source Code Directory: This is used to store the source (C), object (OBJ), executables (EXE), and make files (MAKE) of the programs that you develop with QuickC. You may name this directory whatever you wish.

Temporary Directory: This is a directory used by the compiler for temporary or scratch files. This is normally called \TMP.

These directories can be set up under the root directory or under a directory you specify.

Organizing the Disk

For maximum efficiency, you should organize your hard disk before you start using certain general rules:

1. Consider using at least two logical directories (C and D). Use one (C) for application programs that seldom change. Use the second (D) for application program data.

2. Keep directory sizes small. MS-DOS slows down dramatically if there are too many files in a directory. The limit for maximum efficiency varies with the number of buffers open and other factors, but a good limit should be a maximum of about 100 files. For maximum speed, use several directories and limit the number of files in a directory.

3. The root directory should only contain the AUTOEXEC.BAT, COMMAND.COM, CONFIG.SYS and other files needed for startup (other SYS files).

4. All the DOS programs should be in a \DOS directory.

5. Create a \BAT directory for batch files. Create a batch file for starting each application program. The batch file should switch the system to the appropriate directory and do any other necessary startup chores (setting path, turning off resident programs as necessary, and so forth). After terminating the application program, the same batch file should restore the system, resetting anything that was changed. Keep all the program startup batch files in the \BAT directory.

6. Create a utility directory (or directories) for utility programs that are used (Norton utilities, PC TOOLS, and so forth).

7. Keep each application program in a separate directory. Isolate each set of data used with the programs in another directory. In some cases you may want to put the application data in a directory off the application program directory. If you have a second logical drive for the data (D), it could be off the root directory of that drive. Design so that you can back up by directory. Program directories, which very seldom change, should very seldom be backed up. Data directories should be backed up at least every day they are changed.

8. Add a path command to the AUTOEXEC file to permit access to all the directories that are used frequently, as:

```
PATH C:\;C\DOS;C:\BAT;C:\MW
```

> **Note**
>
> The sequence of directories in the path command shows the sequence in which the directories will be searched for a file. The most frequently used directories should be first. If you are using Retail Windows (that is, C:\WIN or C:\WINDOWS directory), this should be near the beginning of the path, as window directories are used as a virtual memory as a Windows program is executing.

9. Create the five directories needed for QuickC: \BIN, \LIB, \INCLUDE, \TMP, and the working directory.

Backing Up the Program Disks

Create a copy of each QuickC disk. The original disks are not copy-protected. Use the copies, storing the masters in a separate and safe place.

Read All Disk Documentation

Locate any README and UPDATE text files on the disk. Print these and read them carefully. Any information in the disk files supersedes any instructions in the QuickC manual or this book.

Run the Setup Program

This program installs QuickC and creates the special combined libraries that are needed. Be sure you have defined the directories for QuickC. Put the setup disk in the floppy disk drive, change to this drive and start setup from Drive A. To read the current instructions, use:

```
A>SETUP HELP    ⟨Enter⟩
```

The generic form of the command is:

```
SETUP ⟨dest⟩ <mem> <em> <\bin> <\incl> <\lib>
```

where:

⟨dest⟩	is destination drive
⟨mem⟩	is memory model to use (you can use multiple models).
⟨em⟩	is the floating point option
⟨\bin⟩	is the directory for the QuickC executables
⟨\incl⟩	is the directory for the include files
⟨\lib⟩	is the directory for the library files

For example, to create a small and medium model:

```
A>SETUP D: M EM \BIN \INCLUDE \LIB   ⟨Enter⟩
```

Note

Always install QuickC for the medium model, and always use EM for the floating point option.

The setup program will then validate the parameters you used and then prompt for the necessary disks as it installs.

There are a few questions you will need to answer during the installation:

1. Which floating point libraries do you want to use?

You can choose from any of three libraries: the floating point emulator, the hardware processor, or the alternative library. You can make multiple selections here if you wish.

2. Should the graphic libraries be a part of the combined libraries?

The setup program creates combined libraries for QuickC to speed up linking. It creates a combined library for each model specified during setup. You can choose to make the graphics library a part of each model (which takes more space), or keep it separate and include it manually during linking. To simplify your work now, request to include it in the combined directory you create.

3. Do you want to delete files after creating the library?

After creating the combined library, the program requests if you wish to delete the library files that were used to make the combined library. As they are not used any more, it is generally best to delete them to save disk space.

Modifying the CONFIG.SYS File

The CONFIG.SYS file must be modified to take advantage of the new environment, the new path, and the extended number of buffers and files needed. Installing QuickC with SETUP modifies this file to include the changes suggested here. You should check it and make additional changes you may wish manually.

The Environment

The *environment* is a portion of the operating system area that is used as a table or common system memory. The table can be referenced by any program running under DOS. Any kind of information can be placed in this memory area and used by programs in any desirable way. As such, you could consider it a system common memory block with data for any executable program. The area in memory containing this table is called the Master Environment Block.

You can examine the current contents of the environment using the SET command as:

```
C>SET  <Enter>
```

Once the command is issued, you will see the current environment contents, such as:

```
PATH=C:\;C:WIN
```

```
COMSPEC=C:\COMMAND.COM
PROMPT=$c$g
```

The PATH variable reflects the current path as defined by your AUTOEXEC.BAT file. The COMSPEC variable defines where DOS expects to find COMMAND.COM, which is a part of DOS. The PROMPT command defines the prompt that DOS will use on the screen. The default prompt is the logical disk drive name and a right arrow as:

```
C>
```

The prompt defined here (cg) will display the current disk and directory path:

```
C:\QC>
```

All these commands are defined in your DOS manual if you need further help.

Notice the general form of this environment table. It consists of several lines of the type:

```
variable=phrase
```

Where *variable* is the name of a variable you wish to use system-wide, and *phrase* is the string value which the variable will represent.

You can set any variable you wish to use at any time from the system prompt with the SET command. For example:

```
SET COMSPEC=D:\COMMAND.COM
```

would enable you to retrieve COMMAND.COM from a RAMdisk set up as disk drive D. These can be a part of the AUTOEXEC.BAT file. Here, you would first use the AUTOEXEC.BAT to copy the COMMAND.COM to the RAMdisk, then use the SET COMSPEC command to switch access to the RAMdisk.

Many development tools, such as Microsoft's C, use the environment and system variables point to directories where certain files are located. This simplifies access control, as the normal PATH command can only control access for COM, BAT, and EXE files. To use it with QuickC, however, you must first expand the size for this environment area.

To expand the environment area, you will need to modify the CONFIG.SYS file by using the SHELL command. In DOS 3.2 or later you can expand the environment by adding the following line in the CONFIG.SYS file:

```
SHELL=COMMAND.COM /e:512 /p
```

The /e:512 tells DOS to open 512 bytes of environment space. The /p parameter tells DOS to read the AUTOEXEC.BAT file after reading CONFIG.SYS.

If you are using DOS 3.0 or 3.1, the SHELL command is still available, although undocumented. The parameters, however, work slightly differently. Here, the *e* parameter defines how many 16-byte memory paragraphs to reserve for the environment. For DOS 3.0 or 3.1, the last line becomes:

```
SHELL=COMMAND.COM /e:32 /p
```

to get a 512 byte environment. For DOS 3.1 or earlier, the environment is limited to 992 bytes, even if you specify a larger size.

Some manufacturers have customizations of DOS in which a SETENV or similar command can be used for the same purpose:

```
SETENV COMMAND.COM 512
```

This command can be used from an AUTOEXEC.BAT file.

Expanding the Number of Buffers and Files Available

If you have not already done so, expand the buffer and file allocations for DOS by adding the following lines to the CONFIG.SYS file:

```
FILES=20
BUFFERS=40
```

Note

The number of buffers needed can be set low (2) if you are using a disk cache.

Changing the PATH Command

The PATH command, as mentioned, defines the directories that are searched for COM, EXE, and BAT files and specifies the order in which directories will be searched. The search always starts from the current directory, then follows the directories of the path chain in the order given. As you will normally wish to use QuickC from your working directory (C:\C or whichever directory has the source files), the directory with the QuickC executables (C:\QC, C:\C5, or C:\BIN) should be added to the path chain.

```
PATH C:\;C:\WIN;C:\DOS;C:\BAT;C:\QC;C:\MW
```

357

Once you have edited the CONFIG.SYS file, reboot the system and be sure the bootup works properly.

Adding the ANSI Driver

As a final step, add the ANSI driver to the CONFIG.SYS file, as this will be needed in some of the programs of this text, including the example of the second chapter. This driver permits you to clear the screen by using such statements as:

```
puts("\033[2J")
```

To add the ANSI driver, add the following line to the CONFIG.SYS file:

```
device=ANSI.SYS
```

You must also be sure the ANSI.SYS file is on the root directory. This file is provided as a part of DOS.

Setting the New Environment Parameters

Your next task is to add the proper SET commands to a batch file or the AUTOEXEC.BAT file to define the system variables used by QuickC. Microsoft products use the INC variable to show the location of the *include* and *h* files and the LIB variable to show the location of the library files. To use QuickC, you need to add the following lines to your AUTOEXEC.BAT file:

```
SET LIB=C:\LIB
SET INCLUDE=C:\INCLUDE
SET TMP=C:\TMP
```

(This assumes you plan to use the C drive for the QuickC program, with the LIB directory for the library files and the INC directory for the include files.) Also, you will need to modify the PATH variable to include all the QuickC directories that are used in compiling.

Note
Do not use any spaces before or after the equal sign in the lines in the commands.

The SET commands can be executed in either of two ways. If this is the only environment setup you need, you can put it in the AUTOEXEC.BAT file for execution on startup. It does not interfere with any programs that do not use these variable names (such as application programs). If you are using other development tools (such as Turbo C, Microsoft C Version 4.0, and so forth) you will probably have environment setups for each of these. Then you will need a separate batch file for each tool with the appropriate SET and PATH commands, and this file will have to be executed before using the tool.

Once this is done, open the new environment by rebooting the system (if you used the AUTOEXEC.BAT file) or by initiating the batch file that you created.

Accessing QuickC Libraries

When using the QuickC programming environment, you must provide some means of making libraries available to programs you create. The libraries you created in setting up QuickC are available to the command line compiler (QCL), but not kept in memory when you are using the QuickC environment. There is not enough room in memory for all the library routines. You can have all the libraries available, however, in either of two ways. The first method is to create a new special library QCLIB.QLB that contains the library routines you expect to use. This is the method assumed for the text of this book. The second method is through the use of program lists. Both methods are described here.

Creating a Special Library

The first method is to create your own library with the QCL compiler that contains the functions that you use, then use this library with QuickC.

```
C\QC>QC  \lQCLIB    ⟨Enter⟩
```

Here is the general procedure for that method:

1. Create a source file QCLIB.C with a main program that consists only of dummy calls to each routine you will use. The easiest way to do this is to load QuickC using QC from the source file directory:

   ```
   C:\C>QC   ⟨Enter⟩
   ```

   Enter the program, then use the File menu and the Save As option to save it as QCLIB. Then use the File menu and exit. Do not compile the

program in the QuickC programming environment. A sample program
would be:

```
#include  <math.h>
#include  <graph.h>
main()
{
    clear_screen();
    pow();
}
```

Be sure to include the H files using the *#include* statement. The previous
program will work for all programs in this book.

2. Compile the program to an object file using:

```
C:\C>QCL /c /AM QCLIB.C  <Enter>
```

Note

The case is important here. The *c* is lowercase, the *AM* is uppercase.

There may be some error messages about the number of parameters, but
there should be no other error messages. Use the DIR command to be
sure the QCLIB.OBJ file now exists on the disk.

3. Link the program to a library file as:

```
C:\C>C:\QC\LINK C:\LIB\QUICKLIB.OBJ+QCLIB,QCLIB.QLB, , /Q;
<Enter>
```

After completion, there should be a QCLIB.QLB file on the disk. Use
DIR to check this.

4. You can now start QuickC using the library as:

```
C:\C>QC  \lQCLIB  <Enter>
```

Note

The L after the backslash must be a lowercase l.

When QuickC is installed with SETUP, the installation does create a
GRAPHICS.QLB library in the /LIB directory that can be used in starting QC
with the l option, as shown previously. This library contains only the graphic
functions, however, and not the math functions. For example, GRAPHICS.QLB

could not be used with the example of the first chapter, which requires the *pow( )* function.

Using Program Lists

The second method of accessing the full QuickC library is to use a program list, which is an option on the File menu. The source program, as with the method of the previous section, should have an include for the desired library. Before compiling your program, select Set Program List on the File menu. Enter the name of the MAKE file you wish to create to control the program compiling. Then, when prompted for the name of the programs for the list, add the name of your application program, such as MAIL.C.

Note

Only .C, .LIB, and .OBJ files can be a part of the list. Do not add any .H files to this list.

Now compile the program from the RUN menu. This time the compile will take longer, as the external linker will be used with the disk-based libraries. QuickC should, however, resolve all functions.

Creating a QC Batch File

You can use a batch file to start QuickC and load any library you have just created. This file can be kept in your \BAT directory and executed from any other directory. Assume this as QCX.BAT:

```
C:\cd\c
C:\qc \lqclib %1.c
```

This permits you to start QuickC from any directory, even specifying the name of the file to edit:

```
C:\>QCX FRAME  <Enter>
```

B

QuickC Library Summary††

The Microsoft C Compiler contains an extensive set of UNIX System V compatible library routines. This set includes most of the functions included in the emerging ANSI standard. (Functions new in this version are designated by a dagger [†] before the function name. Functions implemented as macros are designated by a double dagger [‡]. Routines with intrinsic inline code are followed by an asterisk [*]. Intrinsics with faster calls are followed by a double asterisk [**].)

Buffer Manipulation

memccpy	memcmp*	memicmp	memset*
memchr	memcpy*	†memmove	movedata

Character Classification and Conversion

‡isalnum	‡isgraph	‡isspace	‡tolower
‡isalpha	‡islower	‡isupper	‡_tolower
‡isascii	‡isprint	‡isxdigit	‡toupper
‡iscntrl	‡ispunct	‡toascii	‡_toupper
‡isdigit			

Data Conversion

atof	†dmsbintoieee	†fmsbintoieee	strtod
atoi	ecvt	gcvt	strtol
atol	fcvt	itoa	†strtoul
†dieeetomsbin	†fieeetomsbin	ltoa	ultoa

---

††©1987 by Microsoft Corporation

Directory Control

chdir	mkdir	rmdir
getcwd		

File Handling

access	fstat	mktemp	†_splitpath
chmod	isatty	remove	stat
chsize	locking	rename	umask
filelength	†_makepath	setmode	unlink

Graphics Functions

†_arc	†_getphyscoord	†_putimage	†_setlinestyle
†_clearscreen	†_getpixel	†_rectangle	†_setlogorg
†_ellipse	†_gettextcolor	†_remapallpalette	†_setpixel
†_floodfill	†_gettextposition	†_remappalette	†_settextcolor
†_getbkcolor	†_getvideoconfig	†_selectpalette	†_settextposition
†_getcolor	†_imagesize	†_setactivepage	†_settextwindow
†_getcurrentposition	†_lineto	†_setbkcolor	†_setvideomode
†_getfillmask	†_moveto	†_setcliprgn	†_setviewport
†_getimage	†_outtext	†_setcolor	†_setvisualpage
†_getlinestyle	†_pie	†_setfillmask	†_wrapon
†_getlogcoord			

I/O Stream Routines

clearerr	flushall	fwrite	scanf
fclose	fopen	‡getc	setbuf
fcloseall	fprintf	‡getchar	setvbuf
fdopen	fputc	gets	sprintf
‡feof	fputchar	getw	sscanf
‡ferror	fputs	printf	tempnam
fflush	fread	‡putc	tmpfile
fgetc	freopen	‡putchar	tmpnam
fgetchar	fscanf	puts	ungetc
†fgetpos	fseek	putw	vfprintf
fgets	‡fsetpos	rewind	vprintf
‡fileno	ftell	rmtmp	vsprintf

Low-Level I/O Routines

close	dup2	open	tell
creat	eof	read	write
dup	lseek	sopen	

Console and Port I/O Routines

cgets	getch	‡inpw	†outpw
cprintf	getche	kbhit	putch
cputs	inp*	outp†	ungetch
cscanf			

Math (Floating Point)

acos**	_control87	frexp	pow**
asin**	cos**	hypot	sin**
atan**	cosh**	ldexp	sinh**
atan2**	exp**	log**	sqrt**
bessel	fabs*	log10**	_status87
cabs	floor**	matherr	tan**
ceil**	fmod**	modf	tanh**
_clear87	_fpreset		

Memory Allocation

alloca	_fmsize	hfree	†_nheapset
calloc	free	malloc	†_nheapwalk
_expand	_freect	_memavl	_nmalloc
_ffree	halloc	†_memmax	_nmsize
†_fheapchk	†_heapchk	_msize	realloc
†_fheapset	†_heapset	_nfree	sbrk
†_fheapwalk	†_heapwalk	†_nheapchk	stackavail
_fmalloc			

MS-DOS Interface

bdos	†_dos_freemem	†_dos_read	FP_OFF
†_chain_intr	†_dos_getdate	†_dos_setblock	FP_SEG
†_disable	†_dos_getdiskfree	†_dos_setdate	†_harderr
dosexterr	†_dos_getdrive	†_dos_setdrive	†_hardresume
†_dos_allocmem	†_dos_getfileattr	†_dos_setfileattr	†_hardretn
†_dos_close	†_dos_getftime	†_dos_setftime	int86
†_dos_creat	†_dos_gettime	†_dos_settime	int86x
†_dos_creatnew	†_dos_getveet	†_dos_setveet	intdos
†_dos_findfirst	†_dos_keep	†_dos_write	intdosx
†_dos_findnext	†_dos_open	†_enable	segread

Process Control

abort	execle	execv	execvpe
atexit	execlp	execve	exit
execl	execlpe	execvp	_exit

getpid   spawnl   spawnlpe   spawnvp
onexit   spawnle   spawnv   spawnvpe
†raise   spawnlp   spawnve   system
signal

Searching and Sorting

bsearch   lsearch   qsort
lfind

String Manipulation

strcat*   strdup   strncmp   strrev
strchr   strerror   strncpy   strset*
strcmp*   stricmp   strnicmp   strspn
strcmpi   strlen*   strnset   strstr
strcpy*   strlwr   strpbrk   strtok
strcspn   strncat   strrchr   strupr

Time

asctime   ftime   †mktime   time
†clock   gmtime   †_strdate   tzset
ctime   localtime   †_strtime   utime
difftime

Variable-Length Argument Lists

‡va_alist   ‡va_dcl   ‡va_list   ‡va_start
‡va_arg   ‡va_end

Miscellaneous

‡abs*   labs*   perror   †_searchenv
‡assert   †ldiv   putenv   setjmp
†div   longjmp   rand   †_settime
getenv   †_lrotl*   †_rotl*   srand
†_gettime   †_lrotr*   †_rotr*   swab

C

ASCII Character Set

Nonprinting ASCII Characters

Decimal	Key	Hexadecimal	Octal	Escape Sequence	Name
0	^@	'\x00'	'\000'		NULL
1	^A	'\x01'	'\001'		SOTT
2	^B	'\x02'	'\002'		STX
3	^C	'\x03'	'\003'		ETY
4	^D	'\x04'	'\004'		EOT
5	^E	'\x05'	'\005'		ENQ
6	^F	'\x06'	'\006'		ACK
7	^G	'\x07'	'\007'		BELL
8	^H	'\x08'	'\010'	'\b'	BKSPC
9	^I	'\x09'	'\011'	'\t'	HZTAB
10	^J	'\x0a'	'\012'	'\n'	NEWLN
11	^K	'\x0b'	'\013'	'\v'	VTAB
12	^L	'\x0c'	'\014'	'\f'	FF
13	^M	'\x0d'	'\015'	'\r'	CR
14	^N	'\x0e'	'\016'		SO
15	^O	'\x0f'	'\017'		SI
16	^P	'\x10'	'\020'		DLE
17	^Q	'\x11'	'\021'		DC1
18	^R	'\x12'	'\022'		DC2
19	^S	'\x13'	'\023'		DC3
20	^T	'\x14'	'\024'		DC4
21	^U	'\x15'	'\025'		NAK
22	^V	'\x16'	'\026'		SYN

Appendices

Decimal	Key	Hexadecimal	Octal	Escape Sequence	Name
23	^W	'\x17'	'\027'		ETB
24	^X	'\x18'	'\030'		CAN
25	^Y	'\x19'	'\031'		EM
26	^Z	'\x1a'	'\032'		SUB
27	ESC	'\x1b'	'\033'		ES C
28		'\x1c'	'\034'		FS
29		'\x1d'	'\035'		GS
30		'\x1e'	'\036'		RS
31		'\x1f'	'\037'		US
127	DEL	'\x7f'	'\177'		DEL

Printing ASCII Characters

Decimal	Key	Hexadecimal	Octal
32		'\x20'	'\040'
33	!	'\x21'	'\041'
34	"	'\x22'	'\042'
35	#	'\x23'	'\043'
36	$	'\x24'	'\044'
37	%	'\x25'	'\045'
38	&	'\x26'	'\046'
39	'	'\x27'	'\047'
40	(	'\x28'	'\050'
41	)	'\x29'	'\051'
42	*	'\x2a'	'\052'
43	+	'\x2b'	'\053'
44	,	'\x2c'	'\054'
45	—	'\x2d'	'\055'
46	.	'\x2e'	'\056'
47	/	'\x2f'	'\057'
48	0	'\x30'	'\060'
49	1	'\x31'	'\061'
50	2	'\x32'	'\062'
51	3	'\x33'	'\063'
52	4	'\x34'	'\064'
53	5	'\x35'	'\065'
54	6	'\x36'	'\066'
55	7	'\x37'	'\067'
56	8	'\x38'	'\070'

Decimal	Key	Hexadecimal	Octal
57	9	'\x39'	'\071'
58	:	'\x3a'	'\072'
59	;	'\x3b'	'\073'
60	<	'\x3c'	'\074'
61	=	'\x3d'	'\075'
62	>	'\x3e'	'\076'
63	?	'\x3f'	'\077'
64	@	'\x40'	'\100'
65	A	'\x41'	'\101'
66	B	'\x42'	'\102'
67	C	'\x43'	'\103'
68	D	'\x44'	'\104'
69	E	'\x45'	'\105'
70	F	'\x46'	'\106'
71	G	'\x47'	'\107'
72	H	'\x48'	'\110'
73	I	'\x49'	'\111'
74	J	'\x4a'	'\112'
75	K	'\x4b'	'\113'
76	L	'\x4c'	'\114'
77	M	'\x4d'	'\115'
78	N	'\x4e'	'\116'
79	O	'\x4f'	'\117'
80	P	'\x50'	'\120'
81	Q	'\x51'	'\121'
82	R	'\x52'	'\122'
83	S	'\x53'	'\123'
84	T	'\x54'	'\124'
85	U	'\x55'	'\125'
86	V	'\x56'	'\126'
87	W	'\x57'	'\127'
88	X	'\x58'	'\130'
89	Y	'\x59'	'\131'
90	Z	'\x5a'	'\132'
91	[	'\x5b'	'\133'
92	\	'\x5c'	'\134'
93	]	'\x5d'	'\135'
94	^	'\x5e'	'\136'
95	—	'\x5f'	'\137'

Decimal	Key	Hexadecimal	Octal
96	`	'\x60'	'\140'
97	a	'\x61'	'\141'
98	b	'\x62'	'\142'
99	c	'\x63'	'\143'
100	d	'\x64'	'\144'
101	e	'\x65'	'\145'
102	f	'\x66'	'\146'
103	g	'\x67'	'\147'
104	h	'\x68'	'\150'
105	i	'\x69'	'\151'
106	j	'\x6a'	'\152'
107	k	'\x6b'	'\153'
108	l	'\x6c'	'\154'
109	m	'\x6d'	'\155'
110	n	'\x6e'	'\156'
111	o	'\x6f'	'\157'
112	p	'\x70'	'\160'
113	q	'\x71'	'\161'
114	r	'\x72'	'\162'
115	s	'\x73'	'\163'
116	t	'\x74'	'\164'
117	u	'\x75'	'\165'
118	v	'\x76'	'\166'
119	w	'\x77'	'\167'
120	x	'\x78'	'\170'
121	y	'\x79'	'\171'
122	z	'\x7a'	'\172'
123	{	'\x7b'	'\173'
124	—	'\x7c'	'\174'
125	}	'\x7d'	'\175'
126	~	'\x7e'	'\176'

Extended ASCII Set

IBM Graphic	Dec	Hex	IBM Graphic	Dec	Hex	IBM Graphic	Dec	Hex	IBM Graphic	Dec	Hex
Ç	128	80	á	160	A0	└	192	C0	α	224	E0
ü	129	81	í	161	A1	┴	193	C1	β	225	E1
é	130	82	ó	162	A2	┬	194	C2	Γ	226	E2
â	131	83	ú	163	A3	├	195	C3	π	227	E3
ä	132	84	ñ	164	A4	─	196	C4	Σ	228	E4
à	133	85	Ñ	165	A5	+	197	C5	σ	229	E5
å	134	86	ª	166	A6	╞	198	C6	μ	230	E6
ç	135	87	º	167	A7	╟	199	C7	τ	231	E7
ê	136	88	¿	168	A8	╚	200	C8	Φ	232	E8
ë	137	89	⌐	169	A9	╔	201	C9	Θ	233	E9
è	138	8A	¬	170	AA	╩	202	CA	Ω	234	EA
ï	139	8B	½	171	AB	╦	203	CB	δ	235	EB
î	140	8C	¼	172	AC	╠	204	CC	∞	236	EC
ì	141	8D	¡	173	AD	=	205	CD	φ	237	ED
Ä	142	8E	«	174	AE	╬	206	CE	ϵ	238	EE
Å	143	8F	»	175	AF	╧	207	CF	$\cap$	239	EF
É	144	90	░	176	B0	╨	208	D0	$\equiv$	240	F0
æ	145	91	▒	177	B1	╤	209	D1	$\pm$	241	F1
Æ	146	92	▓	178	B2	╥	210	D2	$\geq$	242	F2
ô	147	93	│	179	B3	╙	211	D3	$\leq$	243	F3
ö	148	94	┤	180	B4	╘	212	D4	⌠	244	F4
ò	149	95	╡	181	B5	╒	213	D5	⌡	245	F5
û	150	96	╢	182	B6	╓	214	D6	$\div$	246	F6
ù	151	97	╖	183	B7	╫	215	D7	$\approx$	247	F7
ÿ	152	98	╕	184	B8	╪	216	D8	°	248	F8
Ö	153	99	╣	185	B9	┘	217	D9	·	249	F9
Ü	154	9A	║	186	BA	┌	218	DA	·	250	FA
¢	155	9B	╗	187	BB	█	219	DB	$\sqrt{}$	251	FB
£	156	9C	╝	188	BC	▄	220	DC	η	252	FC
¥	157	9D	╜	189	BD	▌	221	DD	²	253	FD
P_t	158	9E	╛	190	BE	▐	222	DE	■	254	FE
f	159	9F	┐	191	BF	▀	223	DF		255	FF

D

QuickC Operators

These are C's operators, in descending order of precedence. The L (for left-to-right) or R (for right-to-left) after the precedence number indicates the grouping order of the operator.

Precedence	Type	Operator	Name
15L	Primary	( )	Parentheses
		[]	Subscript
		– >	Arrow
		.	Dot
14R	Unary	!	Logical not
		~	Bitwise NOT
		++	Increment
		– –	Decrement
		–	Negative
		(type)	Cast
		*	Indirection
		&	Address of
		sizeof	Size of
13L	Arithmetic	*	Multiplication
		/	Division
		%	Remainder (modules)
12L	Arithmetic	+	Addition
	–	Subtraction	
11L	Bitwise	< <	Left shift
		> >	Right shift
10L	Relational	>	Greater than

Precedence	Type	Operator	Name
		>=	Greater than or equal to
		<	Less than
		<=	Less than or equal to
9L	Relational	==	Equal to
		!=	Not equal to
8L	Bitwise	&	Bitwise AND
7L	Bitwise	^	Exclusive OR (XOR)
6L	Bitwise	—	Bitwise OR
5L	Logical	&&	Logical AND
4L	Logical	——	Logical OR
3R	Conditional	?:	Then, else
2R	Assignment	=	Assignment
2R	Assignment	+=, /= (see below)	Shorthand assignment
1L	Sequence	,	Comma

This is the complete list of assignment shorthand operators.

E

QuickC Data Types††

Fundamental Types and Type Specifiers

char	float	signed	unsigned
const	int	struct	void
double	long	typedef*name*	volatile
enum	short	union	

††©1987 by Microsoft Corporation

F

QuickC Keywords[††]

Keywords

auto	double	int	struct
break	else	long	switch
case	extern	register	typedef
char	float	return	union
continue	for	short	unsigned
default	goto	sizeof	while
do	if	static	

Implementation-Dependent Keywords

cdecl	fortran	near	pascal
far	huge		

ANSI Extension to K&R

const	signed	void	†volatile
enum			

---

† Semantics not yet implemented
††©1987 by Microsoft Corporation

G

Resources

A disk with the mailing list program of Part III is available as MAILOUT II. See the diskette order form in the back of the book.

The following resources are recommended for QuickC programmers:

Harbison, Samuel P. and Steele, Guy L., Jr. *C: A Reference Manual: Second Edition.* Englewood Cliffs, NJ: Prentice Hall, 1987.

Lafore, Robert. *Microsoft C Programming for the IBM.* Indianapolis, IN: Howard W. Sams & Company, 1987.

Schustack, Steve. *Variations in C.* Bellevue, WA: Microsoft Press, 1985.

Waite, Mitchell et al. *C Primer Plus.* Indianapolis, IN: Howard W. Sams & Company, 1987.

Note

The Harbison book is particularly recommended as a manual for style and technical referencing for C programmers.

H

Tips for QuickC Users

1. In declaring integer variables, the *int* type is preferred over the *short*. For most compilers, the *int* type is the most efficient. An even better alternative is to define your own type as:

```
typedef COUNT int;
```

and use this in your program. You can then switch all integer declarations by editing a single statement if necessary.

2. Use the *scanf( )* function only for machine-readable input. Do not use *scanf( )* for user input through the keyboard. With most compilers, the function has unusual and undefined side effects with certain types of input.

3. If possible, use *fgets( )* for user input. This is the preferred input function for user input. The QuickC *gets( )* function will not check for input buffer overflow. Loading a long string to a local variable can corrupt the local variable stack on overflow. The *fgets( )* does a check and avoids this overflow problem. You must allow, however, two extra buffer bytes for the carriage return and line feed characters.

4. Avoid the use of the *char* type to hold single characters or small numbers. The *int* type is considered more efficient with most compilers.

5. Don't confuse the equality operator (==) with the assignment operator (=). The assignment operator is used to change the value of the variable to the left of the operator.

6. Avoid floating point comparisons. Use integers when testing for equality.

7. Avoid confusing the backslash with the forward slash. The backslash is used for directory names and for writing escape characters. The forward slash is used for compiler options, comments, and division.

8. Pointers are one of the most confusing issues for beginning C

programmers, as they are not supported in most other languages. Initialize pointers to NULL. Don't assign a value to an address contained by a pointer without assigning an address to the pointer. For example:

```
/* Don't do this */
main()
{
    int *ptr;
    *ptr = 5;
    printf("%d",*ptr);
}
```

One particularly dangerous issue is that the program may work, as the value will be stored at an arbitrary and random address. If the random address is in the middle of your code, however, you could create a strange effect.

9. Always be sure to include the break statement at the end of each case block in your switch structures. If you fail to do this, all case statements after the matching case will be executed.

10. An array starts at 0, not one. The general form for the *for* statement is:

```
for(i=0; i < END_VALUE; i++)
    list[i]= 0;.
```

11. In naming variables, pick names that are significant within the context of your program. Don't start a name with an underscore, as names starting with an underscore are reserved for system use.

12. In declaring strings for input with the *scanf( )* function, use arrays instead of pointer variables.

13. Keep expressions simple. If necessary, use macros and multiple statements to simplify expressions.

14. Keep the scope of your variables as small as possible. Pass values and addresses with arguments and return values, not by using global variables. This keeps your functions portable and you can use them in other programs. It also simplifies debugging.

15. Don't use the same variable name for two different variables. If *square* is used as an auto variable in the main program, don't use the same name for an auto variable in a function.

16. Don't initialize a variable unless necessary. For example, it is not necessary to initialize a *for . . . else* loop counter, as the *for . . . else* construct initializes the counter.

```
int ctr = 0;
for (ctr = 1; ctr <=10; ++ctr)
```

17. Always use the *extern* keyword for external referencing, even when the function immediately follows the declaration. It improves the readability of the program.

18. In declaring a static or global array, you can omit the value for the array size if you initialize it:

```
static char msg[] = "Hello out there";
```

This saves you the need to count the characters.

19. If you are using register variables, use register variables for loop counters.

20. Avoid superseding a declaration. Do not redeclare a variable you have already declared.

Note

The *extern* keyword does not redeclare a variable, but only references a variable already declared.

---

21. Avoid overloading, or trying to minimize variables by using a variable name for multiple purposes.

22. Keep declarations at the beginning of the block in which they are used.

23. References to external variables in a function should be before local declarations.

24. Keep your variable scopes as small as possible. Pass values by addresses and return values, not by using global variables. This keeps functions portable and simplifies debugging.

25. When using large constants, parameterize the constant to improve portability when changing machines or compilers. For example, notice how MAXNEGINT is used here:

```
#define MAXSIZE 20
#define MAXNEGINT 0100000
main()
{
    static int values[MAXSIZE];
    int index = 0, size, max = MAXNEGINT;
    char inputa[10];

    do {
        printf("Please enter a number: ");
        fgets(inputa,10,stdin);
```

continued

383

```
            values[index] = atoi(inputa);
        }
    while (values[index++] != 0);
    size = index - 1;
    for (index=0; index < size; index++)
        if (values[index]>max)
            max = values[index];
      printf("The maximum value is %d\n", max);
}
```

The following for the same declaration would be poor style:

```
int index = 0, size, max = -32768;
```

26. Declare all globals in one place, and that should be in the include file. In this file, a comment statement should label them as globals. For example, suppose you wrote the previous example as:

```
{
short number, square, cube, quad;
main()
      extern int number, square, cube, quad;
/* Don't do it this way */
          .
          .
```

The variables are declared globally as *short*, and then accessed within the function using the extern keyword as *int*. The results are unpredictable and will vary with the compiler. Declaring all globals in one place minimizes this. An even better idea is illustrated in Chapter 16.

Arrays of class automatic are created out of stack space and are not cleared to zero on starting. For this reason, you should always initialize any automatic class arrays. Arrays that are declared static or external are cleared by the C run-time startup code.

27. Avoid using *long* type when *int* will do. Cast if necessary. For example:

```
width = (w1+2) * config.numxpixels / config.numtextcols;
```

in *mail.c* will not work. The value of (w1+2) could be as high as 80 and *config.numxpixels* as high as 640. The product exceeds the range for an *int* type. You could solve this by typing everything *long*, but a better method is to *cast*:

```
width = (int) (((long) (w1+2)) * (long) config.numxpixels /
(long) config.numtextcols);
```

28. Use high-level file I/O instead of low-level unless you have a specific need to use low-level file I/O.

Portability Issues

When porting code between C implementations, the following tips apply:

1. Keep macros to eight arguments or less.
2. Keep text strings to 512 characters or less.
3. You may get different error messages, depending upon how rigorously the compiler checks the code. For example, QuickC will compile:

```
#define FALSE 0
#define FALSE 0
```

without an error message about the variable defined twice. Another compiler may give an error message.

On Optimization

QuickC, unlike Microsoft C version 5.0 and Turbo C, is not an optimizing compiler. If the Optimization option is checked on compiling, QuickC generates 80286 code and does some constant folding, but that's about it.

Some programmers try clever tricks to hand optimize their code, such as using deeply nested expressions to eliminate lines of code. This may or may not provide any real optimization. The same number of code lines may be generated or, even worse, the compiler may not accept the complex statement.

Index

W

The Waite Group's
Advanced C Primer ++
Stephen Prata, The Waite Group

ogrammers, students, managers, and
ckers alike, will learn to master the
programming language. Anyone who
ows the basics of C will learn prac-
al C tips never before published. This
depth coverage gives you rare and
mplete examination of video access
rts, segmented memory, and registers.

lvanced C Primer + + takes the
ader further than most C books on
e market, showing how to manipulate
e hardware of the IBM PC family of
mputers directly from C. Readers
rn how to access routines in the
ad Only Memory (ROM) of an IBM
, how to use system calls in PC
)S from C and i/o ports, how to con-
l the video screen, and to integrate
sembly routines into C programs.

pics covered include:

Advanced C Programming
Register and Bit Level System
Control
Hardware Operation for Beginners
and Experienced Users
Advanced Use of Pointers,
Functions, Storage Classes, Arrays
and Structures
C Library Access
Use of Assembly Language Modules
Binary and Text File Input and
Output

ludes chapter questions and answers.

2 Pages, 7½ x 9¾, Softbound
N: 0-672-22486-0
22486, $23.95

The Waite Group's
C Primer Plus, Revised Edition
Mitchell Waite, Stephen Prata, and
Donald Martin, The Waite Group

This revised and expanded edition of a
best-seller presents everything you
should know to begin programming in
the exciting C language, now used by
over 80 percent of the software com-
munity. The book is organized for quick
learning and encourages problem solving through questions and exercises.

Topics covered include:

■ Structure of a Simple C Program
■ Variables, Constants, and Data Types
■ Character Strings, *#define, print( ),*
  and scanf( )
■ Operators, Expressions, and
  Statements
■ Input/Output Functions and
  Redirection
■ Choosing Alternatives: *if, else,*
  Relational and Conditional Operators
■ Loops and Other Control Aids
■ How to "Function" Properly
■ Storage Classes and Program
  Development
■ The C Preprocessor
■ Arrays and Pointers
■ Character Strings and String
  Functions
■ Structures and Other Data Delights
■ The C Library and File I/O
■ Bit Fiddling, Keywords, Binary
  Numbers, IBM® PC Music, and More

576 Pages, 7½ x 9¾, Softbound
ISBN: 0-672-22582-4
No. 22582, $24.95

The Waite Group's
Microsoft® C Programming
for the IBM®
Robert Lafore, The Waite Group

Programmers using the Microsoft C
compiler can learn to write useful and
marketable programs with this entry
level book on Microsoft C programming.

This title is a tutorial geared specifically
to the IBM PC family of computers.
Unlike other introductory C titles, it is
written for the Microsoft C compiler. It
provides special coverage of IBM
features such as sound, color graphics
including CGA and EGA, keyboard,
variable storage, and character graphics.

Topics covered include:

■ Getting Started
■ Building Blocks
■ Loops
■ Decisions
■ Functions
■ Arrays and Strings
■ Pointers
■ Keyboard and Cursor
■ Structures, Unions, and ROM Bios
■ Memory and the Monochrome
  Display
■ CGA and EGA Color Graphics
■ Files Preprocessor
■ Serial Ports and Telecommunications
■ Larger Programs
■ Advanced Variables
■ Appendices Include: Supplemental
  Programs, Hexadecimal Numbering,
  IBM Character Codes, and a
  Bibliography

640 Pages, 7½ x 9¾, Softbound
ISBN: 0-672-22515-8
No. 22515, $24.95

The Waite Group's
Turbo C® Programming for
the IBM®
Robert Lafore, The Waite Group

This entry-level text teaches readers the
C language while also helping them
write useful and marketable programs
for the IBM PC, XT, AT, and PC/2.

This tutorial is based on Borland's new
Turbo C compiler with its powerful integrated environment that makes it easy
to edit, compile, and run C programs.
The author's proven hands-on intensive
approach includes example programs,
exercises, and questions and answers
and covers CGA and EGA graphic
modes.

Topics covered include:

■ C Building Blocks
■ Loops
■ Decisions
■ Functions
■ Arrays and Strings
■ Pointers
■ Keyboard and Cursor
■ Structures, Unions, and ROM BIOS
■ Memory and the Character Display
■ CGA and EGA Color Graphics
■ Files
■ Larger Programs
■ Advanced Variables
■ Appendices Include: References,
  Hexadecimal Numbering,
  Bibliography, ASCII Chart, and
  Answers to Questions and Exercises

608 Pages, 7½ x 9¾, Softbound
ISBN: 0-672-22614-6
No. 22614, $22.95

Visit your local book retailer, use the order form provided, or call 800-428-SAMS.

Programming in C, Revised Edition
Stephen G. Kochan

This timely revision provides complete coverage of the C language, including all language features and over 90 program examples. The comprehensive tutorial approach teaches the beginner how to write, compile, and execute programs and teaches the experienced programmer how to write applications using features unique to C. It is written in a clear instructive style and is ideally suited for classroom use or as a self-study guide.

Topics covered include:

- Introduction and Fundamentals
- Writing a Program in C
- Variables, Constants, Data Types, and Arithmetic Expressions
- Program Looping
- Making Decisions
- Arrays
- Functions
- Structures
- Character Strings
- Pointers
- Operations on Bits
- The Preprocessor
- Working with Larger Programs
- Input and Output
- Miscellaneous and Advanced Features
- Appendices: Language Summary, ANSI Standard C, Common Programming Mistakes, the UNIX C Library, Compiling Programs under UNIX, the Program LINT, the ASCII Character Set

476 Pages, 7½ x 9¾, Softbound
ISBN: 0-672-48420-X
No. 48420, $24.95

Programming in ANSI C
Stephen G. Kochan

This comprehensive programming guide is the newest title in the Hayden Books C Library, written by the series editor Stephen G. Kochan. A tutorial in nature, the book teaches the beginner how to write, compile and execute programs even with no previous experience with C.

The book details such C essentials as program looping, decision making, arrays, functions, structures, character strings, bit operations, and enumerated data types. Examples are complete with step-by-step explanations of each procedure and routine involved as well as end-of-chapter exercises, making it ideally suited for classroom use.

Topics covered include:

- Introduction and Fundamentals
- Writing a Program in ANSI C
- Variables, Data Types, and Arithmetic Expressions
- Program Looping
- Making Decisions
- Arrays, Functions, Structures
- Character Strings, Pointers
- Operations on Bits
- The Preprocessor
- More on Data Types
- Working with Larger Programs
- Input and Output
- Miscellaneous Features and Topics
- Appendices: ANSI C Language Summary, The UNIX C Library, Compiling Programs Under UNIX, The Program LINT, The ASCII Character Set

450 Pages, 7½ x 9¾, Softbound
ISBN: 0-672-48408-0
No. 48408, $24.95

Advanced C: Tips and Techniques
Paul L. Anderson and Gail C. Anderson

If you have a working knowledge of the C language and want to enhance your programming skills, the examples and techniques found in this new book are just what you need. It is an in-depth look at the C programming language with special emphasis on portability, execution efficiency, and application techniques.

With entire chapters devoted to special areas of C such as debugging techniques, C's run-time environment, and a memory object allocator, the book contains detailed explanations and examples that will show you how to speed up your C programs. Techniques for creating and deciphering expressions, moving data, and coding expressions that execute predictably are included as well as end-of-chapter exercises that help you learn what has been explained.

Topics covered include:

- C Refresher
- The Run-Time Environment
- Bits of C
- There's No Such Thing as an Array
- A Closer Look at C
- C Debugging Techniques
- A Memory Object Allocator
- Appendices: Portable C Under UNIX System V, Microsoft C Under XENIX, Microsoft C Under DOS, Turbo C Under DOS

325 Pages, 7½ x 9¾, Softbound
ISBN: 0-672-48417-X
No. 48417, $24.95

Topics in C Programming
Stephen G. Kochan and Patrick H. Wood

Here is the most advanced and comprehensive coverage of the maturing market. This sequel to *Programming C* describes in detail some of the most difficult concepts in the C language—structures and pointers. It also explores the standard C library and standard I library, dynamic memory allocation, linked lists, tree structures, and dispatables.

Experienced C programmers can examine the UNIX System Interface through discussions on controlling processes, pipes, and terminal I/O. *Topics in C Programming* also explains how to write terminal-independent programs, how to debug C programs and analyze their performance, and how to use "make" for automatic generation of a programming system.

Topics covered include:

- Structures and Pointers
- The Standard C Library
- The Standard I/O Library
- UNIX System Interface
- Writing Terminal-Independent Programs with the "curses" Library
- Debug and Performance Analysis C Programs
- Generating Program Systems with "make"

400 Pages, 7½ x 9¾, Softbound
ISBN: 0-672-46290-7
No. 46290, $24.95

Visit your local book retailer, use the order form provided, or call 800-428-SAMS.

C Programmer's Guide to Serial Communications
Joe Campbell

~itten for those with an understanding
assembly language and C program-
ng, this sequel to the best-selling *The
-232 Solution* offers comprehensive
verage of C programming and serial
d asynchronous communications. It
esses the generality of program
sign and the portability of C code
·oss operating environments such as
DOS™ and CP/M.®

pics covered include:

ASCII
Fundamentals of
Asynchronous Technology
Flow Control and Transfer
Protocols
RS-232 and Modems
The UART—A Conceptual Model
Designing an SIO Library
Portability Considerations
Timer Functions
Functions for Baud Rate and
Data Format
Functions for RS-232 Input
and Output
Miscellaneous I/O Functions
Formatted Output and Input
Smartmodem Programming
Xmodem File Transfer
Interrupts

Pages, 7½ x 9¾, Softbound
N: 0-672-22584-0
22584, $26.95

C with Excellence: Programming Proverbs
Henry Ledgard with John Tauer

C programmers will learn how to increase their programming skills and to
write carefully constructed and readable
programs with this handbook on C programming. Its clear and concise style
provides both the novice and the expert
programmer with guidelines or "proverbs" for writing high-quality, error-free
software.

The reader familiar with the fundamentals of C, BASIC, or Pascal will be able
to apply these principles to develop
systems and application software as
well as write C programs that can be
easily ported from one microcomputer
to another.

After introducing the 24 "proverbs" and
their applications, this handbook focuses
on the entire development process from
conceptualizing to coding, documenting,
testing, debugging, and maintaining and
modifying programs.

Topics covered include:

■ Programming Proverbs
■ Structure Is Logic
■ Coding the Program
■ Global Variables, Selecting Names,
  Recursion, and Efficiency
■ Top-down Programming
■ Appendices Include: Summary of
  Program Standards and a Program
  for Kriegspiel Checkers

288 Pages, 7½ x 9¾, Softbound
ISBN: 0-672-46294-X
No. 46294, $18.95

UNIX® Shell Programming
Kochan and Wood

Here's a complete, easy-to-understand
introduction to UNIX shell programming. The book covers all the features
of the standard shell, including the
System V, Release 2 shell and the
newer Korn shell. Many complete, practical programs are included, and the exercises provide reinforcement for each
new shell application.

Topics covered include:

■ A Review of the UNIX System
■ What the Shell Is and What It Does
■ Shell Programming Tools
■ Writing Your Own Commands
  and Shell Variables
■ Writing Shell Programs
■ How to Set Up Program Loops
■ Reading Data
■ Your Environment
■ Parameters
■ The Rolo Program
■ The Korn Shell
■ The C Shell

432 Pages, 7 x 9¾, Softbound
ISBN: 0-8104-6309-1
No. 46309, $24.95

The Waite Group's UNIX® System V Primer, Revised Edition
Waite, Martin, and Prata,
The Waite Group

This primer provides a comprehensive
overview and introduction to the UNIX
System V operating system for the
beginning UNIX user. It gives the reader
review questions and exercises at the
terminal, for an applied, hands-on approach to learning not found in other
books on the subject.

New material has been added to the second edition. It includes a new chapter
on the extended electronic mail programs and new information detailing
the use of the new shell layer manager
for multiprocessing and the enhanced
screen display page. The previously
strong coverage of the editors has been
enhanced considerably with additional
information on the *ex* and *vi* editors.

End-of-chapter exercises and questions
have been added to enhance this strong
teaching apparatus.

Topics covered include:

■ Introduction to UNIX
■ Getting Started
■ Electronic Mail and On-Line Help
■ Files and Directories
■ Using Editors
■ The *vi* Screen Editor
■ Manipulating Files and Directories
■ Using Programming Languages
■ The UNIX Shell
■ File Management Command
■ More Text Processing
■ Information Processing
■ Extended Electronic Mail Program

450 Pages, 7½ x 9¾, Softbound
ISBN: 0-672-22570-0
No. 22570, $22.95

Visit your local book retailer, use the order form provided, or call 800-428-SAMS.

A disk with the mailing list program of Part III is available as MAILOUT II. The diskette is a 5-1/4″ floppy prepared for IBM-compatible personal computers running under DOS 2.0 or higher.

The diskette sells for $19.95 (U.S.), including shipping and handling, and may be purchased with a check or money order made out to "Oregon Professional Microsystems." (No cash, please.)

Send this form with your payment to:

Oregon Professional Microsystems
c/o Howard W. Sams & Company
Public Relations Department
4300 West 62nd Street
Indianapolis, In 46268

Howard W. Sams & Company assumes no liability with respect to the use or accuracy of the information contained on this diskette.

- -

Diskette Order Form

Townsend, *QuickC Programming for the IBM,* #22622

Name _____ Company _____

Address _____

City _____ State _____

Phone _(___)_____ Date _____

Place of book purchase _____

Number of disks ordered_____ @ $19.95 Amount enclosed $ _____

☐ Check number _____ ☐ Money order number _____